WILLIAM WORDSWORTH

William Wordsworth:

Interviews and Recollections

edited by

Harold Orel

University Professor Emeritus
English Department
University of Kansas
Lawrence, Kansas 66045-2115
USA

palgrave
macmillan

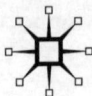

First published 2005 by
PALGRAVE MACMILLAN
Houndmills, Basingstoke, Hampshire RG21 6XS and
175 Fifth Avenue, New York, N.Y. 10010
Companies and representatives throughout the world

PALGRAVE MACMILLAN is the global academic imprint of the Palgrave Macmillan division of St. Martin's Press, LLC and of Palgrave Macmillan Ltd. Macmillan® is a registered trademark in the United States, United Kingdom and other countries. Palgrave is a registered trademark in the European Union and other countries.

ISBN-13: 978–1–4039–3962–3 hardback
ISBN-10: 1–4039–3962–4   hardback

This book is printed on paper suitable for recycling and made from fully managed and sustained forest sources.

A catalogue record for this book is available from the British Library.

Library of Congress Cataloging-in-Publication Data

William Wordsworth : interviews and recollections / edited by Harold Orel.
    p. cm.
    Includes bibliographical references and index.
    ISBN 1-4039-3962-4
    1. Wordsworth, William, 1770–1850. 2. Wordsworth, William, 1770–1850–Friends and associates. 3. Wordsworth, William, 1770–1850–Contemporaries. 4. Poets, English–19th century–Biography. I. Orel, Harold, 1926–

PR5881.W4725 2005
821'.7–dc22   2005048759

10   9   8   7   6   5   4   3   2   1
13 12 11 10 09 08 07 06 05 04

Printed and bound in Great Britain by
Antony Rowe Ltd, Chippenham and Eastbourne

To Tim Farmiloe, editor, friend, and inspiration

Contents

Preface

This anthology deals largely with opinions evaluating Wordsworth the man, and the selections for the most part represent the views of well-known men of letters. The major exception, Sir Humphry Davy, known primarily for his scientific work, was in fact deeply interested in literature, and greatly admired Wordsworth's poetry. Only a few selections (e.g., by Ralph Waldo Emerson and Matthew Arnold) were recorded after Wordsworth's death in 1850.

The texts, always readable and possessing, I believe, a high entertainment quotient, may occasionally be anecdotal or digressive, but their main value resides in the fact that their authors are rendering judgments that have a special authority: these writers had met and conversed with the living poet. The lone exception to this generalization about the value bestowed by a first-hand witnessing of Wordsworth's appearance and behavior is Shelley, who never met Wordsworth; even so, his high praise of Wordsworth's poetry – dinned into Lord Byron's ear until the latter modified his harsher views of Wordsworth's talent – entitles him to be heard.

The selections demonstrate how and why Wordsworth became an inescapable presence for both Romantic and Victorian writers, and indeed for all readers of poetry during the nineteenth century. Taken as a whole, the testimony presents a humanized portrait of a poet who early in his career had become a sage, somewhat forbidding in demeanor, and whose changing reputation even before 1850 was closely related to that stern image, often at the expense of a nuanced judgment of his poetry. And, almost needless to add, Wordsworth's opinions of most of these writers, sometimes pungently expressed, are worth recording too, if only to make more clear why some friendships flourished over a long period of years and others withered on the vine.

The selections are not intended to deliver a collective verdict on the quality of Wordsworth's art, or to recapitulate the arguments about the nature and objectives of poetry in which Wordsworth engaged. Nevertheless, the running story of Wordsworth's relations to his contemporaries frequently includes evidence of an assumption by an individual author that the time had come (well before 1850) to summarize Wordsworth's total career. Most such assessments, we now know, were made prematurely, since Wordsworth continued to write serious poetry, and to undertake massive poetical projects, till the very end.

viii

Sir Walter Scott in his unsigned review, 'The Living Poets of Great Britain' (*The Edinburgh Annual: Register for 1808* [1810]), made a strong point of linking Wordsworth's 'secluded study' to the limited popularity of his poems. Wordsworth, he argued, would have benefitted if he had compared his own feelings with those of others; if he had depended less on theory and observed more closely the impulses that moved the mass of humanity. Wordsworth, Scott believed, needed more observation and knowledge of the world.

This line of argument, perhaps more ubiquitous during Wordsworth's lifetime than afterwards, has colored much that has been written about the greatest of the Lake poets.

But it remains an open question whether Wordsworth could or would have strengthened his 'moral poetry' by entering more wholeheartedly on the social rounds urged upon him by Scott. Any student of Wordsworth's life is inevitably impressed by the number of visitors who made a pilgrimage to the poet in his seclusion, and who came away from a meeting, however brief, with a sense that they had met a man who was secure in several convictions: that he was loved by wife and sister, that his opinions on all kinds of subjects were generally irrefutable, and that the work he was producing possessed high merit. There was, in brief, more *busyness* in the comings and goings of Wordsworth's life than Scott appreciated.

Several matters affecting the development of Wordsworth's reputation are treated in the letters, diary entries, essays, and reminiscences from which these excerpts have been drawn: Wordsworth's opinions of his rivals in the production of poetry, his generosity (or perceived lack of it), his handling of money matters, his steadfast loyalty to those who believed in him, his sense of obligation to patrons and various literary influences, and – in both general and particular instances – his wit and wisdom. Often those opinions changed over time, and occasionally Wordsworth regretted something he had said or written. Even so, Wordsworth is remarkably consistent in both the substance of his beliefs and the reasons he provided for having reached a particular point of view, and this consistency was noted, and respected, by all who knew him.

The specifics of a particular relationship are treated in the brief essays that precede each author's selections, and annotations have been added to provide additional details for the reprinted texts. In the pages that follow a reader may be informed or reminded of the great value placed by Wordsworth's contemporaries on the new direction in poetical statement and subject matter that his life provided. More than a century and a half later his writings still inspire faith in that value.

Abbreviations

Coleridge, Samuel Taylor

STC, CL   *Collected Letters of Samuel Taylor Coleridge*, I–VI, edited
               by Earl Leslie Griggs (New Haven, Conn.: Yale University
               Press, 1956–71)

STC, N   *The Notebooks of Samuel Taylor Coleridge*, III, 1794–1826,
               edited by Kathleen Coburn; IV, co-edited by Kathleen
               Coburn and Merten Christenson; Bollingen Series L
               (Princeton, N.J.: Princeton University Press, 1973)

STC, UL   *Unpublished Letters of Samuel Taylor Coleridge*, I–II, edited
               by Earl Leslie Griggs (New Haven, Conn.: Yale
               University Press, 1933)

De Quincey, Thomas

DeQ, W   *The Works of Thomas De Quincey*, I–XXI; Vol. XIX,
               Autobiographical Sketches, edited by Daniel Sanjiv
               Roberts (London: Pickering & Chatto, 2003)

Emerson, Ralph Waldo

RWE, CW   *The Collected Works of Ralph Waldo Emerson*, I–VI: V,
               English Traits, edited by Douglas Emory Wilson
               (Cambridge, Mass.: Harvard University Press, 1994)

Haydon, Benjamin Robert

BRH, D   *The Diary of Benjamin Robert Haydon*, I–V, edited by
               Willard Bissell Pope (Cambridge, Mass.: Harvard
               University Press, 1960–63)

Hazlitt, William

WH, CW   *Collected Works, Centenary Edition*, I–XXI, edited by P. P.
               Howe ('After the Edition of A. R. Waller and Arnold
               Glover') (London: J. M. Dent, 1930)

WH, SW   *Selected Writings of William Hazlitt*, I–IX, edited by
               Duncan Wu (London: Pickering & Chatto, 1998)

Keats, John

JK, L   *The Letters of John Keats*, I–II, edited by Maurice Buxton
               Forman (Oxford: Oxford University Press, 1931)

Lamb, Charles and Mary

CL, L   *The Letters of Charles and Mary Anne Lamb*, I–III, edited
               by Edwin W. Marrs, Jr. (Ithaca, N.Y.: Cornell University
               Press, 1975–78)

Landor, Walter Savage

WSL, W, V   *The Complete Works of Walter Savage Landor*, edited by
                   T. Earle Welby (London: Chapman and Hall, 1927)

WSL, L   *Letters and Other Unpublished Writings of Walter Savage
                   Landor*, edited by Stephen Wheeler (London: Richard
                   Bentley and Son, 1897)

Mill, John Stuart

JSM, A   *Autobiography and Literary Essays*, edited by John M.
                   Robson and Jack Stillinger (Toronto, Ontario: University
                   of Toronto Press, 1981)(Vol. I in *Collected Works*,
                   I–XXXIII, 1963–)

JSM, EL   *The Earlier Letters of John Stuart Mill, 1812–1848*, XII,
                   edited by Francis E. Mineka (Toronto, Ontario:
                   University of Toronto Press, 1963)

Reynolds, John Hamilton

JHR, L   *The Letters of John Hamilton Reynolds*, edited by Leonidas
                   M. Jones (Lincoln, Nebr.: University of Nebraska Press,
                   1973)

JHR, SP   *Selected Prose of John Hamilton Reynolds*, edited by
                   Leonidas M. Jones (Cambridge, Mass.: Harvard
                   University Press, 1966)

Robinson, Henry Crabb

HCR, C   *The Correspondence of Henry Crabb Robinson with the
                   Wordsworth Circle (1808–1866)*, I–II: I, *1808–1843*; II,
                   1844–1866, edited by Edith J. Morley (Oxford:
                   Clarendon Press, 1927)

Scott, Sir Walter

WS, J   *The Journal of Sir Walter Scott*, edited by
                   W. E. K. Anderson (Oxford: Clarendon Press,
                   1972)

Southey, Robert

RS, NL   *New Letters of Robert Southey*, I–II, edited by Kenneth
                   Curry (New York: Columbia University Press,
                   1965)

RS, SL   *Selections from the Letters of Robert Southey/ &c. &c. &c.*,
                   I–IV, edited by John Wood Warter (London: Longman,
                   Brown, Green, and Longmans, 1856)

Tennyson, Alfred Lord

AT, L   *Letters*, II *(1851–1870)*, edited by Cecil Y. Lang and
                   Edgar F. Shannon, Jr. (Cambridge, Mass.: Belknap Press
                   of Harvard University Press, 1987)

Wordsworth, William and Dorothy

WW, L	*Letters*, I–IX, 2nd edn, edited by Ernest De Selincourt et al. (Oxford: Clarendon Press, 1967–93). [Specific volume editors are named below.]
WW, L, I	*Letters, the Early Years 1787–1808*, revised by Chester L. Shaver (1967)
WW, L, II	*Letters, the Middle Years 1806–1811*, revised by Mary Moorman (1969)
WW, L, III	*Letters, the Middle Years 1812–1820*, revised by Mary Moorman and Alan G. Hill (1970)
WW, L, V	*Letters, the Later Years, Part II, 1820–1834*, revised by Alan G. Hill (1970)
WW, L, VII	*Letters, the Later Years, Part IV, 1840–1853*, revised by Alan G. Hill (1988)
WW, PrW, III	*The Prose Works of William Wordsworth*, III: *Critical and Ethical*, edited by Alexander B. Grosart (London: Edward Moxon, Son, 1876)

Samuel Taylor Coleridge (1772–1834)

Wordsworth's awareness of Coleridge's literary ability probably ante-dated 1 September 1795, when, so the story goes, the two men met at 7 Great George Street, Bristol, the home of John Pinney, who had made his fortune in the West Indies as a merchant trading in sugar. By that year Coleridge was an author with a growing reputation. Words-worth, a self-proclaimed poet, had not published much in the way of significant work up to that point. (The date and place have been chal-lenged by some biographers.)

Both men were much impressed by each other. Wordsworth wrote to William Mathews (26 October) that Coleridge's talent seemed to him to be 'very great', and Coleridge used similar language in conversations and correspondence for years afterwards.

Racedown, where Wordsworth was living with his sister at the time, was an isolated community, then and now. The Wordsworths moved to Alfoxden less than two years later. Still, during this period, probably one to be measured in months rather than years, Wordsworth defined for himself more clearly the significance of Nature, and grew to appreci-ate Dorothy's humanity and loving affection for himself. He describes it glowingly in *The Prelude*, Books X–XI.

Major shifts in his emotional reading of the universe, his political radicalism (tempered by events in France, which had declared war on England in 1793), and what he now perceived was his unfitness for a possible career in either law or the Church coincided with his growing affection for Coleridge. The propinquity of the relationship accounted for much; Coleridge, living in Nether Stowey, offered hospitality when Wordsworth traveled to and from Bristol, and often joined William and Dorothy at their home, taking every opportunity to enjoy long walks with one or both of them. They debated topics of common inter-est, read aloud their own poems (each listened patiently to the other's creative work), and joined their talents to assemble the contents of *Lyrical Ballads*. The project demanded continual consultation. Dorothy, whose opinions echoed and often shaped those of her brother, wrote Mary Hutchinson (June 1797) that the conversation of Coleridge 'teems with soul, mind, and spirit', and Coleridge reciprocated: Words-worth was 'the best poet of the age' and 'a very dear friend'. And, of course, the trip to Germany, taking more than a half-year, allowed them ample opportunity to explore their mutual likes and dislikes on a vast variety of subject-matter.

The publication of the first edition of *Lyrical Ballads* in 1798 did not identify the authors, and rapidly became a landmark in literary history. Among the *Ballads* were Coleridge's 'The Ancient Mariner', as well as 'The Nightingale' and two poems taken from his tragedy *Osorio*; and, equally as important, 19 poems by Wordsworth; while the second, much expanded Second Edition (1800, in two volumes) adds only one poem by Coleridge, 'Love'; the 'Ancient Mariner' is moved to the back of Volume 1. The *Advertisement*, which sought to 'ascertain how far the language of conversation in the middle and lower classes of society is adapted to the purposes of poetic pleasure', remained substantially the same in all subsequent editions. Wordsworth wrote a *Preface* for the 1800 edition that, in essence, explained and defended his aesthetics.

Coleridge, in two letters written in 1802, claimed that separating his contributions from those of Wordsworth was impossible, and that the *Preface* was 'half a child' of his own brain. Disentangling Coleridge's contribution from that of Wordsworth has attracted numerous critics and scholars over the past two centuries, but a consensus of which poet was responsible for which sections of the *Preface* has yet to be universally accepted. Because Coleridge changed his mind on some key issues that he had endorsed at the turn of the century, he eventually disapproved of parts of the *Preface* that Wordsworth had written. (His subsequent analysis of the *Preface* in *Biographia Literaria*, published in 1817, made clear that he had traveled a long way from sympathetic identification with many of Wordsworth's views.)

Wordsworth rewrote some of the *Preface* in reprints of the Second Edition. He also tinkered with the text of the *Appendix*, which he had affixed to the 1802 edition as a commentary on 'Poetic Diction'.

Useful annotations for the *Advertisement*, *Preface*, and *Appendix* to *Lyrical Ballads* may be studied in *The Prose Works of William Wordsworth*, edited by W. J. B. Owen and Jane Worthington Smyser (Oxford: Clarendon Press, 1974), vol. I, pp. 166–89.

Wordsworth's *Preface* and *Appendix*, and Coleridge's rebuttal to Wordsworth's critical points, constitute a significant chapter in the history of the Romantic Movement. Wordsworth reacted unhappily to several of Coleridge's literary arguments, and his friends observed him trying to avoid Coleridge on at least two social occasions during the next half-year. The discursive letter-writing habits of the members of the Wordsworth Circle (and those who, like Henry Crabb Robinson, did not belong to the center of the circle) have enlarged the opportunities for writing more accurate biographies, and for improving our understanding of the shock experienced by Coleridge in 1810, when he learned that Wordsworth entertained 'no hope' for him; indeed, that he had become 'an Absolute Nuisance' to the Wordsworth family.

The tactlessness of Basil Montagu, a mutual friend who felt called upon to inform Coleridge of some of Wordsworth's damning remarks, may have been more responsible than any other single factor for ending Coleridge's whole-hearted affection and veneration for Wordsworth. Robinson, years later, while recapitulating his own peace-making efforts, may have embroidered the language used by Wordsworth, and it is possible that Wordsworth did not actually make these specific comments, though he believed he had accumulated enough information about Coleridge's personality and habits to prepare something that amounted to a veritable bill of indictment. For example: Wordsworth and his sister were increasingly appalled by Coleridge's addiction to opium, bouts of heavy drinking, neglect of the welfare and education of his children, failure to meet printing deadlines, endless excuses for bad behavior, and long stretches of inactivity that alternated with feverishly intense periods of writing and editing. Wordsworth's disapproval of Coleridge's reluctant marriage to Sara Fricker (Coleridge confessed that he did not love her, but acted out of a sense of duty), and later of Coleridge's excessive attentions to Sara Hutchinson, Mary's sister, deepened Wordsworth's suspicion that Coleridge's behavior was, taken as a whole, unacceptable.

Some of the charges made on both sides are reprinted here. They trace a pattern of changing emotions and attitudes. Their importance in Wordsworth's life is very great, though our concern is primarily with how Coleridge regarded Wordsworth.

Coleridge was convinced, from the beginning, that Wordsworth's genius as poet surpassed his own more humble gifts. Despite the quarrel – a reconciliation, achieved after lengthy negotiations, explanations of what was 'meant', and well-meaning interventions by friends – never wholly patched up before Coleridge's death in 1834, his tributes to Wordsworth's poetry continued in conversation and were committed to print many times. Both men, assessing each other's literary productions, were candid but judicious; more serious was their failure to overcome disenchantment about each other's human limitations. Their correspondence indicates that Wordsworth tired of Coleridge's failings much earlier than the moment at which Coleridge gave up all efforts to ingratiate himself with Wordsworth. He did so at the end of a decade of serving Wordsworth's interests with little regard for his own: proofreading and seeing several of Wordsworth's productions through the press, cheering him on (his attitude toward Wordsworth's slow progress in writing *The Recluse* may be cited, and other examples abound), and modestly standing back as Wordsworth down-played the significance of his contributions to *Lyrical Ballads*. When Wordsworth explained that he had rejected 'Christabel' as a poem unsuitable for inclusion in the 1800 edition, he made no effort to soften the blow: the style of 'Christabel' was 'so discordant' from his own that 'it could not be printed' along with his poems 'with any propriety'.

This sad story concludes with the letter Wordsworth wrote to Henry Nelson Coleridge, a nephew, on 29 July 1834. The tie which had bound him to Coleridge for fully forty years is here described as 'frail'. Wordsworth, in formal language that hardly begins to measure the full dimensions of the role Coleridge played in his development as a poet, artist, and political propagandist, concludes with a melancholy observation that 'most of those who are nearest and dearest' to himself must now 'prepare and endeavour to follow him'.

STC, CL, I, 334: letter from Samuel Taylor Coleridge to Robert Southey, *circa* 17 July 1797

I had been on a visit to Wordsworth's at Racedown near Crewkherne— and I brought him & his Sister back with me & here I have *settled them*—.[1] By a combination of curious circumstances a gentleman's seat, with a park & woods, elegantly & completely *furnished*—with 9 *lodging rooms*, three parlours & a Hall—in a most beautiful & romantic situation by the sea side—4 miles from Stowey—this we have got for Wordsworth at the rent of 28£ *a year, taxes included*!!—The park and woods are *his* for all purpose *he* wants them—i.e. he may walk, ride, & keep a horse in them & the large gardens are altogether & entirely his.—Wordsworth is a very great man—the only man, to whom *at all times* & in *all modes of excellence* I feel myself inferior—the only one, I mean whom I *have yet met with*—for the London Literati appear to me to be very much like little Potatoes—i.e. *no great Things*—a compost of Nullity & Dullity.—

WW, L, I, 153: letter from William Wordsworth to William Mathews [20 and] 24 October [1795]

I have been indebted to you for sometime, not that I feel myself able to say anything which is likely to be particularly interesting; but it was my duty to assure you of the liveliness of my regard and of the strength of my esteem for you. I stayed at Bristol at least five weeks with a family whom I found amiable in all its branches; the weather was delightful, and my time slipped insensibly away.[2] I heard much of Mr Clone and his wife your Lisbon friends. They were both spoken highly of. I think I have heard you mention the latter in terms not the most respectful. I had not the pleasure of seeing either the one or the other. Coleridge was at Bristol part of the time I was there. I saw but little of him. I wished indeed to have seen more—his talent appears to me very great.

WW, *L*, I, 188–9: letter from Dorothy Wordsworth to Mary Hutchinson [June 1797]

You had a great loss in not seeing Coleridge. He is a wonderful man. His conversation teems with soul, mind, and spirit. Then he is so benevolent, so good tempered and cheerful, and, like William, interests himself so much about every little trifle. At first I thought him very plain, that is, for about three minutes: he is pale and thin, has a wide mouth, thick lips, and not very good teeth, longish loose-growing half-curling rough black hair. But if you hear him speak for five minutes you think no more of them. His eye is large and full, not dark but grey; such an eye as would receive from a heavy soul the dullest expression; but it speaks every emotion of his animated mind; it has more of the 'poet's eye in a fine frenzy rolling' than I ever witnessed. He has fine dark eyebrows, and an overhanging forehead.

The first thing that was read after he came was William's new poem *The Ruined Cottage*[3] with which he was much delighted; and after tea he repeated to us two acts and a half of his tragedy *Osorio*. The next morning William read his tragedy *The Borderers*.

WW, *L*, I, 190: letter from Dorothy Wordsworth to Mary Hutchinson, 14 August 1797

Here we are in a large mansion, in a large park, with seventy head of deer around us. But I must begin with the day of leaving Racedown to pay Coleridge a visit. You know how much we were delighted with the neighbourhood of Stowey.... The evening that I wrote to you, William and I had rambled as far as this house, and pryed into the recesses of our little brook, but without any more fixed thoughts upon it than some dreams of happiness in a little cottage, and passing wishes that such a place might be found out. We spent a fortnight at Coleridge's; in the course of that time we heard that this house was to let, applied for it, and took it. Our principal inducement was Coleridge's society. It was a month yesterday since we came to Alfoxden.

STC, CL, I, 403: letter from Samuel Taylor Coleridge to Joseph Cottle [early April 1798]

Wordsworth has been caballed against *so long and so loudly*, that he has found it impossible to prevail on the tenant of the Allfoxden estate, to let him the house, after their first agreement is expired, so he must quit it at Midsummer; whether we shall be able to procure him a house and furniture near Stowey, we know not, and yet we must: for the hills, and the woods, and the streams, and the sea, and the shores would break forth into reproaches against us, if we did not strain every nerve, to keep their Poet among them. Without joking, and in serious sadness, Poole and I cannot endure to think of losing him.

STC, CL, I, 410: letter from Samuel Taylor Coleridge to John Prior Estlin [18] May [1798]

I have now known [Wordsworth] a year & some months, and my admiration, I might say, my awe of his intellectual powers has increased even to this hour—& (what is of more importance) he is a tried good man.—On one subject we are habitually silent—we found our data dissimiliar, & never renewed the subject / It is his practice & almost his nature to convey all the truth he knows without any attack on what he supposes falsehood, if that falsehood be interwoven with virtues or happiness—he loves & venerates Christ & Christianity—I wish, he did more—but it were wrong indeed, if an incoincidence with one of our wishes altered our respect & affection to a man, whom we are as it were instructed by our great master to say that not being against us he is for us.—His genins is most *apparent* in poetry—and rarely, except to me in tete a tete breaks forth in conversational eloquence.—

STC, CL, I, 453: letter from Samuel Taylor Coleridge to William Wordsworth [December 1798]

I am sure I need not say how you are incorporated into the better part of my being; how, whenever I spring forward into the future with noble affections, I always alight by your side.

STC, CL, I, 527: letter from Samuel Taylor Coleridge to William Wordsworth [*circa* 10 September 1799]

I am anxiously eager to have you steadily employed on 'The Recluse.'
. . . My dear friend, I do entreat you go on with 'The Recluse;' and I
wish you would write a poem, in blank verse, addressed to those, who,
in consequence of the complete failure of the French Revolution, have
thrown up all hopes of the amelioration of mankind, and are sinking
into an almost epicurean selfishness, disguising the same under the
soft titles of domestic attachment and contempt for visionary *philo-
sophes*. It would do great good, and might form a part of 'The Recluse,'
for in my present mood I am wholly against the publication of any
small poems.

STC, CL, I, 538: letter from Samuel Taylor Coleridge to William Wordsworth, 12 October 1799

I long to see what you have been doing. O let it be the tail-piece of
'The Recluse!' for of nothing but 'The Recluse' can I hear patiently.
That it is to be addressed to me makes me more desirous that it should
not be a poem of itself. To be addressed, as a beloved man, by a
thinker, at the close of such a poem as 'The Recluse,' a poem *non unius
populi*, is the only event, I believe, capable of inciting in me an hour's
vanity—vanity, nay, it is too good a feeling to be so called; it would
indeed be a self-elevation produced *ab extra*.

STC, CL, I, 584: letter from Samuel Taylor Coleridge to Thomas Poole, 31 March 1800

You charge me with prostration in regard to Wordsworth. Have I
affirmed anything miraculous of W.? Is it impossible that a greater
poet than any since Milton may appear in our days? Have there any
great poets appeared since him? . . . Future greatness! Is it not an awful
thing, my dearest Poole? What if you had known Milton at the age of
thirty, and believed all you now know of him?—What if you should
meet in the letters of any then living man, expressions concerning the
young Milton *totidem verbis* the same as mine of Wordsworth, would it
not convey to you a most delicious sensation? Would it not be an
assurance to you that your admiration of the *Paradise Lost* was no
superstition, no shadow of flesh and bloodless abstraction, but that the

Man was even so, that the greatness was incarnate and personal? Wherein blame I you, my best friend? Only in being borne down by other men's rash opinions concerning W. You yourself, for yourself, judged wisely. . . .

WW, L, I, 324: letter from William Wordsworth to Thomas Poole, 9 April [1801]

We shall be highly delighted to see you in this country. I hope you will be able to stay some time with us. Coleridge was over at Grasmere a few days ago: he was both in better health and in better spirits than I have seen him for some time. He is a great man, and if God grant him life will do great things. My sister desires to be affectionately remembered to you and your Mother, not forgetting Wards.

STC, UL, I, 266: letter from Samuel Taylor Coleridge to William Wordsworth [6 August 1803]

You would be as much astonished at Hazlitt's coming, as I at his going. Sir G. and Lady B. are half-mad to see you—(Lady B. told me, that the night before last as she was reading your Poem on *Cape Rash Judgment*, had you entered the room, she believes she should have fallen at your feet).[4] Sir G. B. and his wife both say, that the Picture [a portrait by Hazlitt] gives them an idea of you as a profound strong-minded Philosopher, not as a Poet. I answered (and I believe, truly—) that so it must needs do, if it were a good Portrait—for that you were a great Poet by inspirations, and in the moments of revelation, but that you were a thinking feeling Philosopher habitually—that your Poetry was your Philosophy under the action of strong winds of Feeling—a sea rolling high.

WW, L, I, 530: letter from William Wordsworth to Walter Scott, 16 January [1805]

I ought to have told you above that it is near three months since we heard from Coleridge we are now very anxious about him, but we suppose that the reason of our not hearing from him is, the difficulty thrown in the way of Letters by the pestilential disease which Heaven grant may be kept out of Malta. He was benefited by the Climate when we last heard. Adieu.[5]

WW, *L*, II, 331–2: letter from William Wordsworth to Samuel Taylor Coleridge [5 May 1809]

I am very sorry to hear of your being taken ill again, were it only on account of the effect these seizures may have upon the work in which you are engaged. They prove that it is *absolutely necessary* that you should always be *beforehand* with your work. On the general question of your health, one thing is obvious, that health of mind, that is, resolution, self-denial, and well-regulated conditions of feeling, are what you must depend upon; and that Doctors can do you little or no good, and that Doctors' stuff has been one of your greatest curses; and of course, of ours through you.—I should not speak now upon this subject were it not on account of what you say about Mr. Harrison. You must know better than Mr. Harrison, Mr. King, or any Surgeon what is to do you good; what you are to do, and what to leave undone. Do not look out of yourself for that stay which can only be found within.

WW, *L*, II, 390–1: letter from Dorothy Wordsworth to Lady Beaumont, 28 February 1810

Coleridge's spirits have been irregular of late. He was damped after the 20th Number by the slow arrival of payments, and half persuaded himself that he ought not to go on. We laboured hard against such a resolve, and he seems determined to fight onwards; and indeed I do not think he had ever much reason to be discouraged, or *would have been* discouraged if his spirits had not before been damped; for there have been many untoward circumstances and much mismanagement to hinder the regular remittance of the money and many people have not yet paid, merely from thoughtlessness, who, no doubt, will pay ere long; and the work cannot but answer in a pecuniary point of view, if there is not in the end a very great failure in the payments. By the great quantity of labour that he has performed since the commencement of the Friend you will judge that he has upon the whole been very industrious; and you will hardly believe me when I tell you that there have been weeks and weeks when he has not composed a line. The fact is that he either does a great deal or nothing at all; and that he composes with a rapidity truly astonishing, if one did not reflect upon the large stores of thought which he has laid up, and the quantity of knowledge which he is continually gaining from books—add to this his habit of expressing his ideas in conversation in elegant language. He has written a whole Friend more than once in two days. They are never re-transcribed, and he generally has dictated to Miss Hutchinson, who takes the words down from his mouth. We truly rejoice in the satisfaction which the Friend has spread around your fireside, and there are many solitary individuals who have been proud to express their thankfulness to the Author. How have you liked the *Epitaphs from Chiabrera*?[6] The Essay of this week No 25 is by my Brother. He did not intend it to be published now; but Coleridge was in such bad spirits that when the time came he was utterly unprovided, and besides, had been put out of his regular course by waiting for books to consult respecting Duty; so my Brother's Essay, being ready was sent off. William requested Coleridge to proffer an apology for the breach of his promise; but he was, I believe, too languid even to make this exertion, and I fear that people would be disappointed, having framed their expectations for the conclusions of Sir Alexander's history; and here I must observe that we have often cautioned Coleridge against making promises, which even if performed are of no service, and if broken must be of great disservice.

WW, L, II, 398–400: letter from Dorothy Wordsworth to Catherine Clarkson [*circa* 12 April 1810]

We had a letter from dear Sara last night. She is very comfortable; and happy that she has been taken this journey, but her side for a few days was weak and painful, and she had thought proper to abstain from animal food which had relieved her. She is comfortable, but poor thing! she evidently feels a great want. There is not that life by the fireside that we have—they [Tom Hulchinson and his cousin John Monkhouse] are sleepy before supper time, being little interested for anything else than their own domestic or farming concerns, and people must needs languish with no other thoughts from morning till night. She gives a very pleasant description of the country, but it would be as bad to me as uninhab[ited] desart, the roads are so miserable. I need not tell you how sadly we miss Sara—but I must add the truth that we are all glad she is gone. True it is she was the cause of the continuance of The Friend so long; but I am far from believing that it would have gone on if she had stayed. He [Coleridge] was tired, and she had at last no power to drive him on; and now I really believe that *he* also is glad that she is not here, because he has nobody to teize him. His spirits have certainly been more equable, and much better. *Our* gladness proceeds from a different cause. He harassed and agitated her mind continually, and we saw that he was doing her health perpetual injury. I tell you this, that you may no longer lament her departure. As to Coleridge, if I thought I should distress you, I would say nothing about him; but I hope that you are sufficiently prepared for the worst. We have no hope of him—none that he will ever do anything more than he has already done. If he were not under our Roof, he would be just as much the slave of stimulants as ever; and his whole time and thoughts, (except when he is reading and he reads a great deal), are employed in deceiving himself, and seeking to deceive others. He will tell me that he has been writing, that he *has* written half a Friend; when I *know* that he has not written a single line. This Habit pervades all his words and actions, and you feel perpetually new hollowness and emptiness. I am loth to say this, and burn this letter, I entreat you. I am loth to say it, but it is the truth. He lies in bed, always till after 12 o'clock, sometimes much later; and never walks out—Even the finest spring day does not tempt him to seek the fresh air; and this beautiful valley seems a blank to him. He never leaves his own parlour except at dinner and tea, and sometimes supper, and then he always seems impatient to get back to his solitude—he goes the moment his food is swallowed. Sometimes he does not speak a word, and when he does talk it is always very much and upon subjects as far aloof from himself or his friends as possible. The Boys come every week and he talks to them, especially to Hartley, but he never examines them in their books. He speaks of *The Friend* always as if it were going on, and would go on; therefore, of course, you will drop no hint of my opinion. I heartily wish I may be mistaken. — I hope in about 3 weeks to inform you of the Birth of our 5th little one. Mary is now better than she was before Catharine was taken ill, being free from the Heartburn. Her spirits are very good, being now full of hope. William goes on writing industriously. God bless you my dear Friend—Do write again very soon and tell us all you do and see. Pray tell us all things. I am very much distressed about your headaches. God bless you for ever.

If from your medical Friends you can hear of anything that may be of use to Catharine pray tell us.

Friday morning: Coleridge is just come down stairs, $\frac{1}{2}$ past 12 o'clock. He is in great spirits and says to me that he is going to set to work in good earnest. I replied it *cannot* be out this week. 'No' said he, 'but we will get it out as fast as possible'. What will come of this resolution

I know not, I only venture to wish or entertain the smallest hope for the 40 numbers, and I *do* wish that he may go on *so* far.

With respect to Coleridge, do not think that it is his love for Sara which has stopped him in his work—do not believe it: his love for her is no more than a fanciful dream—otherwise he would prove it by a desire to make her happy. No! He likes to have her about him as his own, as one devoted to him, but when she stood in the way of other gratifications it was all over. I speak this very unwillingly, and again I beg, *burn* this letter. I need not add, keep its contents to yourself alone.

STC, *N*, III [not paginated]: # 3991, # 3992, # 3997

[October 1810] 3991   Not *Loved* but one whose Love is what has given pleasure/O this is a sad mistake! How perceptibly has—'s love for poor C lessened since he has procured other enthusiastic admirers!—As long as C. almost all dissenting, was the *sole* Admirer & Lover, *so long* he was loved.—But poor C. *loved*, truly loved!—

Of this accursed analysis or rather anatomy of a friend's Character, as if a human Soul were made like a watch, or loved for this & that tangible & verbally expressible quality!—

W. authorized M.[7] to tell me, he had no Hope of me—God! what good reason for saying this? The very belief takes away all excuse, because all kind purpose for the declaration.

W. once—was unhappy, dissatisfied, full of craving, then what Love & Friendship, now all calm & attached—and what contempt for the moral comforts of others—

3992   O merciful God! and was Hume right in making the agreeable & disagreeable the sole principle of Love or Dislike, Esteem or Disapprobation?

3997   Sunday Night. No Hope of me! absol. Nuisance! God's mercy is it a Dream!

STC, *CL*, III, 380: letter from Samuel Taylor Coleridge to J. J. Morgan [24 March 1812]

[24 March 1812] ... the Grasmere Business has kept me in a fever of agitation—and will end in compleat alienation—I have refused to go over, & Wordsworth has refused to apologize and has thus made his choice between me and Basil Montagu, Esqre—and to omit less matters, lastly, Brown, the Printer of the Friend, who had the Friends, & 20 or 30£ worth of Paper of mine, and 36£ worth of Types, about 14 days ago run off and has absconded.—Every day I meant to write to you—but partly, I was in hopes that by delaying it I might be able to say definitely when I should set off, but chiefly, I have been in such a state of fever and irritation about the Wordsworths, my reason deciding one way, and my heart pulling me the contrary—scarcely daring to set off without seeing them, especially Miss Hutchinson who has done nothing to offend me—& yet—in short, I am unfit to bear these things —and make bad worse in consequence.—I have suffered so much that I wish I had not left London.

WW, L, III, 16–17: letter from William Wordsworth to Catherine Clarkson, 6 May [1812]

I came to Town with a *determination* to confront Coleridge and Montagu upon this vile business. But Coleridge is most averse to it; and from the difficulty of procuring a fit person to act as referee in such a case, and from the hostility which M. and C. feel towards each other, I have yielded to C.'s wish, being persuaded that much more harm than good would accrue from the interview. I have not seen C., nor written to him. Lamb has been the medium of communication between us. C. intimated to me by a letter addressed to Lamb that he would transmit to me a statement, begun some time ago, in order to be sent to Miss Hutchinson, but discontinued on account of his having heard that she had 'already *decided* against him.' A very delicate proposal! Upon this I told Lamb that I should feel somewhat degraded by consenting to read a paper, begun with such an intention and discontinued upon such a consideration. Why talk about '*deciding*' in the case? Why, if in this decision she had judged amiss, not send the paper to rectify her error? or why draw out a paper at all whose object it was to win from the sister of my wife an opinion in his favour, and therefore to my prejudice, upon a charge of *injuries*, grievous injuries, done by me to him; before he had openly preferred his complaint to myself, the supposed author of these injuries? All this is unmanly, to say the least of it.

Upon coming home yesterday I found, however, a letter from him, a long one, written apparently and sent before he could learn my mind from Lamb upon this proposal. The letter I have not opened; but I have just written to Lamb that if Coleridge will assure me that this letter contains nothing but a naked statement of what he believes Montagu said to him, I will read it and transmit it to Montagu, to see how their reports accord. And I will then give my own, stating what I believe myself to have said, under what circumstances I spoke, with what motive, and in what spirit. And there, I believe, the matter must end; only I shall admonish Coleridge to be more careful how he makes written and public mention of injuries done by me to him.

There is some dreadful foul play, and there are most atrocious false-hoods, in this business; the bottom of which, I believe, I shall never find, nor do I much care about it. All I want is to bring the parties for once to a naked and deliberate statement upon the subject, in order that documents may exist, to be referred to as the best authority which the case will admit.[. . .]

WW, L, III, 238: letter from William Wordsworth to Samuel Taylor Coleridge, 22 May 1815

24 Edward Street
Cavendish Sq^{re}
Monday Morn: 22nd May 1815

My dear Coleridge,

Let me beg out of kindness to me that you would relinquish the intention of publishing the Poem addressed to me after hearing *mine* to you.[8] The commendation would be injurious to us both, and my work when it appears, would labour under a great disadvantage in consequence of such a precursorship of Praise.

I shall be thankful for your remarks on the Poems, and also upon the Excursion, only begging that whenever it is possible references may be made to some passages which have given rise to the opinion whether favourable or otherwise; in consequence of this not having been done (when indeed it would have been out of Place) in your Letter to Lady B—[9] I have rather been perplexed than enlightened by your *comparative* censure. One of my principal aims in the Ex^n: has been to put the com-monplace truths, of the human affections especially, in an interesting point of view; and rather to remind men of their knowledge, as it lurks inoperative and unvalued in their own minds, than to attempt to convey recondite or refined truths. Pray point out to me the most strik-ing instances where I have failed, in producing poetic effect by an over-fondness for this practice, or through inability to realize my wishes.

I am happy to hear that you are going to press.[10]

And believe me my dear Coleridge in spite of your silence

Most affectionately yours
W. Wordsworth

WW, L, I, 727–9: letter from William Wordsworth to Henry Nelson Coleridge, 29 July [1834]

Though the account which Miss Hutchinson had given of the State of our Friend's health had prepared us for the sad Tidings of your Letter the announcement of his dissolution was not the less a great shock to my self and all this family.[11] We are much obliged to you for entering so far into the particulars of our ever-to-be-lamented Friend's Decease, and we sincerely congratulate you and his dear Daughter upon the calmness of mind and the firm faith in his Redeemer which supported him through his painful bodily and mental trials, and which we hope and trust have enrolled his Spirit among those of the blessed.—

Your letter was received on Sunday Morning, and would have been answered by return of Post, but I wished to see poor Hartley first, thinking it would be comfortable to yourself and his Sister to learn from a third Person how he appeared to bear his loss. Mrs Wordsworth called on him yesterday morning, he promised to go over to Rydal, but did not appear till after Post-time. He was calm; but much dejected; expressed strongly his regret that he had not seen his Father before his departure from this world, and also seemed to lament that he had been so little with him during the course of their lives. Mrs Wordsworth advised him to go over to Keswick, and there provide himself with fit mourning under the guidance of Miss Crosthwaite,[12] Ambleside being a bad place for procuring any kind of clothes. I mention this that you may name it to his Mother.—

I cannot give way to the expression of my feelings upon this mournful occasion; I have not strength of mind to do so—The last year has thinned off so many of my Friends, young and old, and brought with it so much anxiety, private and public, that it would be no kindness to you were I to yield to the solemn and sad thoughts and remembrances which press upon me. It is nearly 40 years since I first became acquainted with him whom we have just lost; and though with the exception of six weeks when we were on the continent together,[13] along with my Daughter, I have seen little of him for the last 20 years, his mind has been habitually present with me, with an accompanying feeling that he was still in the flesh. That frail tie is broken and I, and most of those who are nearest and dearest to me must prepare and endeavour to follow him. Give my affectionate love to Sara, and remember me tenderly to Mrs Coleridge; in these requests Mrs Wordsworth, my poor Sister, Miss H—, and Dora unite, and also in very kind regards to yourself; and believe me, my dear sir,

Gratefully yours,
W. Wordsworth

Pray remember us kindly to Mr and Mrs Gillman when you see them. We shall be happy to hear from you again at your leisure.

Notes

1   Even this burbling letter to Robert Southey does less than full justice to Coleridge's eagerness to succeed in his attempt to persuade the Wordsworths to move from Racedown to Nether Stowey, or somewhere near enough for him to communicate daily with a man he considered his artistic superior. The new residence of the Wordsworths, a generously sized home called Alfoxden House, was about four miles from Stowey, enabling both poets to hammer out their ideas about a suitable subject-matter and language for a volume to be entitled *Lyrical Ballads*.

2   A successful businessman (Wordsworth called him 'a very rich merchant of Bristol'), John Pretor Pinney learned that his sons, Azariah and John Frederick, had negotiated an agreement with Wordsworth to watch out for the welfare of younger members of the family in exchange for the privilege of living in Racedown Lodge (John's property). He immediately offered Wordsworth an invitation to stay at his Bristol home while awaiting the arrival of Dorothy, prior to their move to the lodge. He was unaware at the time that his sons had waived any rental fee.

3   A poem that was later incorporated into *The Excursion*, I.

4   William Hazlitt, before turning full time to literary criticism, was preparing himself to become a painter. The time he spent in executing portraits of Wordsworth, Coleridge, and his son Hartley enabled him to enter into several serious conversations about poetry. Coleridge was offended by some of Hazlitt's remarks that seemed to him to question God's wisdom and beneficence.

   Sir George and Lady Margaret Beaumont were deeply involved in the arts, and indeed they and their friends were often referred to as 'the Beaumont Circle'. He was a skilled painter, and amassed an impressive collection of works by members of the circle, as well as other artists. He acted for several years as Wordsworth's major patron, supplying him with money and steady encouragement. He gave Wordsworth a copy of Sir Joshua Reynolds's *Discourses*, which received careful attention; some key tenets of the book were adapted to Wordsworth's needs when he wrote subsequent essays.

   'Cape Rash Judgment' alludes to 'Poems on the Naming of Places, IV', in *Poetical Works of William Wordsworth*.

5   Coleride's health was particularly shaky in November 1805, but 'greatly improved' in December. Nevertheless, colic pains and overindulgence in strong liquors overwhelmed him shortly before Christmas, when, in a drunken semi-stupor, he wrote to Robert Southey complaining about his marriage.

6   Wordsworth borrowed a number of epitaphs from the writings of the Italian poet Chiabrera, who had recently died. He imitated one and 'carefully translated' nine others; see his *Essay upon Epitaphs, I*, which he gave to Coleridge to fill space in what was turning into an overdue issue of *The*

Friend. Two other essays would have been printed, but Coleridge suspended publication of *The Friend* after the issue of 15 March 1810. By year's end William and Dorothy gave up hope that Coleridge would (or could) reform himself, and they became especially incensed at his treatment of Sara Fricker, his wife.

7 Basil Montagu. In September 1810, Wordsworth warned him that he ran high risks if he invited Coleridge to live with them in London, as he planned to do. Montagu, as a consequence, persuaded Coleridge to live near by in separate quarters; after a quarrel in London (28 October 1810), Montagu told Coleridge what Wordsworth had told him: 'WW has commissioned me to tell you — for years past you have been an Absolute Nuisance to the family.' (Crabb Robinson believed that Montagu had embellished Wordsworth's statement, and doubted that Montagu had ever received such a commission.) Relations between Wordsworth and Coleridge became – and remained – frost bound for years afterwards.

8 Wordsworth cited as his reason for not wanting Coleridge's poem, 'To William Wordsworth', written in December 1806, to be printed because it might affect the reception of the not-yet-published *The Prelude*. Other reasons having to do with their personal relationship may have been operant.

9 Lady Beaumont, to whom Coleridge had written asking for a copy of 'To William Wordsworth', did not send it to him, and informed Wordsworth of Coleridge's request.

10 The publication of *Biographia Literaria* and *Sibylline Leaves* in two volumes was delayed, because of printing problems, until July 1817.

11 Coleridge died on 25 July 1834.

12 A draper.

13 In July and August 1798.

Charles Lamb (1775–1834)

Charles Lamb met Wordsworth in London during the summer of 1797. His pleasant manners, as well as his serene acceptance of the short-comings of others, impressed Wordsworth, who soon found multiple occasions to praise Lamb's writings (both prose and poems) for having provided him with 'April weather of smiles & tears', his command of Latin, and his sensible critical judgments.

Once (the year was not specified) he asked Lamb whether 'some person of real taste' might effectively so abridge a number of no-longer-read Elizabethan plays that they might gain a wider audience; when Lamb said that he thought 'it would not', Wordsworth respected his opinion though he could not share it: 'I, however, am inclined to think it would' (letter to Alexander Dyce, *c.* 19 April 1830). He thus left room for further debate of the issue, which he was not always inclined to do (a trait often remarked on by others). And it is worth noting that Lamb was so intrigued by Wordsworth's question that he set out to demonstrate that it *could* be done. He abridged and paraphrased Elizabethan plays in what proved to be a popular undertaking (com-missioned by Longmans), *Specimens of English Dramatic Poets contemporary with Shakespeare* (1808), followed by a similar *Specimens* of plays set upon the stage by David Garrick (in the late 1820s).

To be sure, Wordsworth objected to his amiable friend's expressing a few reservations about a very limited number of passages in the revised edition of *Lyrical Ballads*. Lamb had added, perhaps more imprudently than he realized at the time, that no single piece had moved him so forcibly as 'the Ancient *Marinere*, The Mad mother, and the Lines at Tintern Abbey'. The very sequence of the poems that he praised (Coler-idge's work had been named first) may have added to Wordsworth's desire to set Lamb right. On 15 February 1801, Lamb wrote to Thomas Manning, a mathematician and orientalist, 'The Post did not sleep a moment. I received almost instantaneously a long letter of four sweat-ing pages from my Reluctant Letter-Writer.' Despite his startled feeling that Wordsworth was unnecessarily creating mountains out of mole-hills, Lamb refused, in his customary good-humored way, to comment on Wordsworth's self-praise.

Not long afterward (August and September 1802), Lamb sought to convert Wordsworth to a heightened appreciation of the sights, sounds, and smells of London. It was a gallant but unsuccessful crusade, for Wordsworth had long since made up his mind about the excessive demands on one's mental alertness made by the cacophony of city life. Lamb even conceded, after paying a visit to the Lakes so well beloved by the Wordsworths, that the countryside might offer 'such a thing as that, which tourists call *romantic*'. In later years Wordsworth claimed that Lamb's 'declared detestation of [the country-side] was all affected; he enjoyed it and entered into its beauties; besides, Lamb was too kindly and sympathetic a nature to detest anything'.

Despite this camaraderie, Lamb demurred at the emphasis on theory in the 1800 edition, and told Wordsworth that he wished that the *Preface* had appeared in a separate treatise. Years later he complained to Manning (26 February 1808) that Wordsworth said (and believed) 'he does not see much difficulty in writing like Shakespeare, if he had a mind to try it. It is clear then nothing is wanting but the mind.' Lamb did not like *The White Doe of Rylstone*, a poem over which Wordsworth had labored mightily.

Although Wordsworth's reaction to Lamb's objection to the *Preface* may fairly be described as intemperate, the friendship never ruptured. Wordsworth greatly appreciated Lamb's praise of *The Excursion*. He dedicated *The Waggoner* (1819) 'in acknowledgement of the pleasure' he had derived from Lamb's writings.

It is worth recalling that, not long after Mary Lamb (Charles's sister) murdered their mother, Elizabeth, Charles wrote to Coleridge, request-ing, for the consolation that one of Wordsworth's poems might provide, a copy of *Lines left upon a Seat in a Yew-tree*: 'I have some scat-tered sentences ever floating on my memory, teasing me that I cannot remember more of it.'

(The full title is *Lines left upon a Seat in a Yew-tree, which stands near the lake of Esthwaite, as a desolate part of the Shore*.) Lamb may have taken to heart the poem's conclusion:

> True dignity abides with him alone
> Who in the silent hour of inward thought,
> Can still suspect and still revere himself
> In loneliness of heart.

Wordsworth outlived Lamb, among many others whose friendship he had cultivated and enjoyed. The *Epitaph* he composed and dedic-ated to the memory of a 'good Man' commemorated those aspects of Lamb's character that he had consistently admired. In this poem the warm affection which for many years had flowed in both directions pays an appropriate tribute to the way in which Lamb 'ranged the crowded streets/With a keen eye, and overflowing heart', and cherishes Lamb's 'Humour and wild instinctive wit, and all/The vivid flashes of his spoken words'.

CL, *L*, I, 265–8: letter from Charles Lamb to William Wordsworth, 30 January 1801

Thanks for your **Letter** and **Present.**—[1] I had already borrowed your second volume—. What most please me are, the Song of Lucy. . . . *Simon's sickly daughter* in the Sexton made me *cry*.—Next to these are the description of the continuous **Echoes** in the story of Joanna's laugh, where the mountains and all the scenery absolutely seem alive—and that fine Shakesperian character of the Happy Man, in the Brothers,

> that creeps about the fields,
> Following his fancies by the hour, to bring
> Tears down his cheek, or solitary smiles
> Into his face, **until the Setting Sun**
> **Write Fool upon his forehead.**—

I will mention one more: the delicate and curious feeling in the wish for the Cumberland Beggar, that he may ha[ve] about him the melody of Birds, altho' he hear them not.—Here the mind knowingly passes a fiction upon herself, first substituting her own feelings for the Beggar's, and, in the same breath detecting the fallacy, will not part with the wish.——The **Poets** Epitaph is disfigured, to my taste by the vulgar satire upon parsons and lawyers in the beginning, and the coarse epithet of pin point[2] in the 6th stanza.— All the rest is eminently good, and your own—. I will just add that it appears to me a fault in the Beggar, that the instructions conveyed in it are too direct and like a lecture: they dont slide into the mind of the reader, while he is imagining no such matter.— An intelligent reader finds a sort of insult in being told, I will teach you how to think upon this subject. This fault, if I am right, is in a ten thousandth worse degree to be found in **Sterne** and many many novelists & modern poets, who continually put a sign post up to shew **where you are to feel**. They set out with assuming their readers to be stupid. Very different from Robinson Crusoe, the

Vicar of Wakefie[l]d, Roderick Random, and other beautiful bare nar-
ratives.— There is implied an unwritten compact between Author and
reader; I will tell you a story, and I suppose you will understand it.—
Modern Novels 'St. Leons'[3] and the like are full of such flowers as these
'Let not my reader suppose'—'Imagine, **if you can**'—modest!—&c.—
I will here have done with praise and blame. I have written so much,
only that you may not think I have passed over your book without
observation. —— I am sorry that Coleridge has christened his Ancient
Marinere 'a poet's Reverie'—it is as bad as Bottom the Weaver's declaration that **he is** not a Lion but only the scenical representation of a
Lion.[4] What new idea is gained by this Title, but one subsersive of all
credit, which the Tale should force upon us, of its truth?— For me, I
was never so affected with any human Tale. After first reading it, I was
totally possessed with it for many days.— I dislike all the miraculous
part of it, but the feelings of the man under the operation of such
scenery dragged me along like Tom Piper's magic Whistle.— I totally
differ from your idea that the Marinere should have had a character
and profession.— This is a Beauty in Gulliver's Travels, where the mind
is kept in a placid state of little wonderments; but the **Ancient
Marinere** undergoes such **Trials**, as overwhelm and bury all individual-
ity or memory of what he was.— Like the state of a man in a **Bad
dream**, one terrible peculiarity of which is, that all consciousness of
personality is **gone**.— Your other observation is I think as well a little
unfounded: the **Marinere** from being conversant in supernatural
events *has* acquired a supernatural and strange **cast** of *phrase*, **eve**,
appearance &c. which frighten the wedding guest.— You will excuse
my remarks, because I am hurt and vexed that you should think it necessary, with a prose apology, to open [the] eyes of dead men that
cannot see ———. To sum up a general opinion of the second vol.—
I do not **feel** any one poem in it so forcibly as the Ancient Marinere,
the Mad mother, and the Lines at Tintern Abbey in the **first**. ——
I could, too, have wished that The Critical preface had appeared in a
separate treatise.— All its dogmas are true and just and most of them
new, *as* criticism.— But they associate a *diminishing* idea with the
Poems which follow, as having been written for **Experiments** on the
public taste, more than having sprung (as they must have done) from
living and daily circumstances.— — I am prolix, because I am gratified
in the opportunity of writing to you, and I dont well know when to
leave off.— I ought before this to have reply'd to your very kind invitation into Cumberland.— With you and your Sister I could gang any

where. But I am afraid whether I shall ever be able to afford **so** desperate a Journey.— Separate from the pleasure of your company, I dont mu[ch] care if I never see a mountain in my life.— I have passed all my days in London, until I have formed as many and intense local attachments, as any of you **Mountaineers** can have done with dead nature. The Lighted shops of the Strand and Fleet Street, the innumerable trades, tradesmen and customers, coaches, waggons, play houses, all the bustle and wickedness round about Covent Garden, the very women of the Town, the Watchmen, drunken scenes, rattles;—life awake, if you awake, at all hours of the night, the impossibility of being dull in Fleet Street, the crowds, the very dirt & mud, the Sun shining upon houses and pavements, the print shops, the **old Book** stalls, parsons cheap'ning books, coffee houses, steams of soups from kitchens, the pantomimes, London itself, a pantomime and a masquerade, all these things work themselves into my mind and feed me without a power of satiating me. The wonder of these sights impells me into night-walks about her crowded streets, and I often shed tears in the motley Strand from fullness of joy at so much **Life** — —. All these emotions must be strange to you. So are your rural emotions to me.— But consider, what must I have been doing all my life, not to have lent great portions of my heart with usury to such scenes?— —

My attachments are all local, purely local—. I have no passion (or have had none since I was in love, and then it was the spurious engendering of poetry & books) to groves and vallies.— The rooms where I was born, the furniture which has been before my eyes all my life, a book case which has followed me about, (like a faithful dog, only exceeding him in knowledge) wherever I have moved—old chairs, old tables, streets, squares, where I have sunned myself, my old school,— these are my mistresses—have I not enough, without your mountains? —I do not envy you. I should pity you, did I not know, that the Mind will make friends of any thing. Your sun & moon and skys and hills & lakes affect me no more, or scarcely come to me in more venerable characters, than as a gilded room with tapestry and tapers, where I might live with handsome visible objects.— I consider the clouds above me but as a **roof** beautifully painted, but unable to satisfy the mind, and at last, like the pictures of the apartment of a Connoisseur, unable to afford him any longer a pleasure. So **fading** upon me from disuse, have been the Beauties of Nature, as they have been confinedly called; so ever fresh & green and warm are all the inventions of men and assemblies of men in this great city—. I should certainly have laughed with dear Joanna.—[5]

CL, L, I, 272–4: letter from Charles Lamb to Thomas Manning [15 February 1801]

[February 15, 1801]

I had need be cautions henceforward what opinion I give of the Lyrical Balads.— All the north of England are in a turmoil. Cumberland and Westmorland have already declared a state of war.— I lately received from Wordsw. a copy of the second volume, accompanied by an acknowledgment of having received from me many months since a copy of a certain Tragedy, with excuses for not having made any acknowledgment sooner, it being owing to an 'almost insurmountable aversion from Letter writing.'— This letter I answered in due form and time, and enumerated several of the p[ass]ages which had most affected me, adding, unfortunately, that no single piece had moved me so forcibly as the Ancient Marinere, the Mad Mother, or the Lines at Tintern Abbey. The Post did not sleep a moment. I received almost instantaneously a long letter of four sweating pages from my **reluctant Letterwriter**, the purport of which was, that he was sorry his 2d vol. had not given me more pleasure (Devil a hint did I give that it had *not pleased me*) and 'was compelled to wish that my range of **Sensibility** was more extended, being obliged to believe that I should receive large influxes of happiness & happy Thoughts' (I suppose from the L.B.—) With a deal of stuff about a certain '**Union** of **Tenderness & Imagination**, which in the sense he used Imag, was not the characteristic of Shakesp. but which Milton possessed in a degree far exceeding other Poets: which **Union**, as the highest species of Poetry, and chiefly deserving that name, He was most proud to aspire to'—then illustrating the said Union by two quotations from his own 2d vol. (which I had been so unfortunate as to miss)—. Ist Specimen—A father addresses his Son—

> When thou
> First cams't into the world, as it befalls
> To new born Infants, thou didst sleep away
> Two days: *And Blessings from thy father's tongue*
> *Then fell upon thee*.

The lines were thus undermark'd & then followed 'This Passage as combining in an extraordinary degree that union of Imagination & Tenderness, which I am speaking of, I consider as one of the Best I ever wrote.'——

2d Specimen.— A Youth after years of absence revisits his native place, and thinks (as most people do) that there has been strange alteration in his absence——

> And that the rocks
> And Everlasting Hills themselves were chang'd——

You see both these are good Poetry: but after one has been reading Shaksp. twenty of the best years of one's life, to have a fellow start up, and prate about some unknown quality, which Shakspere possess'd in a degree inferior to Milton and somebody else! !—— This was not to be *all* my castigation.— Coleridge, who had not written to me some months before, starts up from his bed of sickness, to reprove me for my hardy presumption: four long pages, equally sweaty, and more tedious, came from him: assuring me, that, when the works of a man of true Genius, such as W. undoubtedly was, do not please me at first sight, I should suspect the fault to lie 'in me & not in them'—&c. &c. &c. &c. &c.—— What am I to do with such people?— I certainly shall write them a very merry Letter.—.—.——.

Writing to *you*, I [must] may say, that the 2d vol. has no such pieces as the 3 I enumerated.— It is full of original thinking and an observing mind, but it does not often make you laugh or cry.— It too artfully aims at simplicity of expression. And you sometimes doubt if simplicity be not a cover for Poverty. The best Piece in it I will send you, being *short*—I have grievously offended my friends in the North by declaring my undue preference. But I need not fear you—

> She dwelt among the untrodden ways
>   Beside the Springs of **Dove**,
> A maid whom there were few to praise,
>   And very few to love.—
>
> A Violet, by a mossy stone
>   Half hidden from the eye;
> Fair as a star, when only one
>   Is shining in the sky.—
>
> She lived unknown; & few could know,
>   When **Lucy** ceas'd to be.
> But she is in the grave, and Oh!
>   The difference to me.—

This is choice and genuine, and so are many many more. But one does not like to have 'em ramm'd down one's throat— 'Pray take it—its very good—let me help you—eat faster.'—.—.

CL, *L*, II, 151–3: letter from Charles Lamb to William Wordsworth [18 February 1805]

My dear Wordsworth,

[T]he subject of your letter[6] has never been out of our thoughts since the day we first heard of it, and many have been our impulses towards you, to write to you, or to write to enquire about you; but it never seemed the time. We felt all your situation, and how much you would want Coleridge at such a time, and we wanted somehow to make up to you his absence, for we loved & honoured your Brother, & his death always occurs to my mind with something like a feeling of reproach, as if we ought to have been nearer acquainted, & as if there had been some incivility shewn him by us, or something short of that respect which we now feel : but this is always a feeling, when people die, and I should not foolishly offer a piece of refinement, instead of sympathy, if I knew any other way of making you feel how little like indifferent his loss has been to us. I have been for some time wretchedly ill & low, and your letter this morning has affected me so with a pain in my inside & a confusion, that I hardly know what to write or how. I have this morning seen Stewart the 2d mate who was saved : but he can give me no satisfactory account, having been in quite another part of the ship when your brother went down. But I shall see Gilpin tomorrow, and will communicate your thanks, & learn from him all I can. All accounts agree that just before the vessel going down, your brother seemed like one overwhelmed with the situation, & careless of his own safety. Perhaps he might have saved himself; but a Captain who in such circumstances does all he can for his ship & nothing for himself, is the noblest idea. I can hardly express myself, I am so really ill. But the universal sentiment is, that your brother did all that duty required : and if he had been more alive to the feelings of those distant ones whom he loved, he would have been at that time a less admirable object ; less to be exulted in by them : for his character is high with all that I have heard speak of him, & no reproach can fix upon him. Tomorrow I shall see Gilpin, I hope, if I can get at him, for there is expected a complete investigation of the causes of the loss of the ship at the East India House, & all the Officers are to attend : but I could not put off writing to you a moment. It is most likely I shall have some thing to add tomorrow, in a second letter. If I do not write, you may suppose I have not seen G. but you shall hear from me in a day or two. We have done nothing but think of you, particularly of Dorothy. Mary is crying by me while I with difficulty write this: but as long as we remember any thing, we shall remember your Brother's noble person, & his sensible manly modest voice, & how safe & comfortable we all were together in our apartment, where I am now writing. When he returned, having been one of the triumphant China fleet, we thought of his pleasant exultation (which he exprest here one night) in the wish that he might meet a Frenchman in the seas; & it seem'd to be accomplished, all to his heart's desire.— I will conclude from utter inability to write any more, for I am seriously unwell: & because I mean to gather something like intelligence to send to you tomorrow: for as yet, I have but heard second hand, & seen one narrative, which is but a transcript of what was common to all the Papers. God bless you all, & reckon upon us as entering into all your griefs.

[C. Lamb]

CL, *L*, III, 95–6: letter from Charles Lamb to William Wordsworth, 9 August 1814

Dear Wordsworth,

I cannot tell you how pleased I was at the receit of the great Armful of Poetry[7] which you have sent me, and to get it before the rest of the world too! I have gone quite through with it, and was thinking to have accomplishd that pleasure a second time before I wrote to thank you, but M. Burney came in the night (while we were out) and made holy theft of it, but we expect restitution in a day or two. It is the noblest conversational poem I ever read. A day in heaven. The part (or rather main body) which has left the sweetest odour on my memory (a bad term for the remains of an impression so recent) is the Tales of the Church yard.[8] The only girl among seven brethren born out of due time and not duly taken away again—the deaf man and the blind man —the Jacobite and the Hanoverian whom antipathies reconcile—the **Scarron**-entry[9] of the rusticating parson upon his solitude—these were all new to me too. My having known the story of Margaret (at the beginning) a very old acquaintance even as long back as I saw you first at Stowey, did not make her reappearance less fresh—. I dont know what to pick out of this Best of Books upon the best subjects for partial naming—

that gorgeous Sunset is famous, I think it must have been the identical one we saw on Salisbury plain five years ago, that drew Phillips from the card table where he had sat from rise of that luminary to its unequall'd set, but neither he nor I had gifted eyes to see those symbols of common things glorified such as the prophets saw them, in that sunset—the wheel—the potters clay—the washpot—the winepress —the almond tree rod—the baskets of figs—the fourfold visaged foor— the throne & him that sat thereon

One (image) feeling I was particularly struck with as what I recognised so very lately at Harrow Church on entering in it after a hot & secular day's pleasure, the instantaneous coolness and calming almost transforming properties of a country church just entered—a certain fragrance which it has—either from its holiness, or being kept shut all the week, or the air that is let in being pure country—exactly what you have reduced into words but I am feeling I cannot.[10] The reading your lines about it fixed me for a time, a monument in Harrow Church, (do you know it?) with its fine long Spire white as washd marble, to be seen by vantage of its high scite as far as Salisbury spire itself almost——

I shall select a day or two very shortly when I am coolest in brain to have a steady second reading, which I feel will lead to many more, for it will be a stock book with me while **eyes** or spectacles shall be lent me.

There is a deal of noble matter about mountain scenery, yet not so much as to overpower & discountenance a poor **Londoner** or South-country man entirely, though Mary seems to have felt it occasionally a little too powerfully, for it was her remark during reading it that by your system it was doubtful whether a Liver in Towns had a Soul to be Saved. She almost trembled for that invisible part of us in her.

Notes

1 Marrs points out that the reference to a 'Present' may refer either to Vol. II of the second edition of *Lyrical Ballads* (1800) or to Vols. I and II.
2 'A Poet's Epitaph', l. 24.
3 A novel by William Godwin (1799).
4 *A Mid-summer Night's Dream*, III, i, 36–46.
5 'To Joanna', 11. 52–3.
6 John Wordsworth, William's brother and captain of the ship *Earl of Abergavenny*, which hit a reef fairly close to Portland Bill (5 February 1805), and sank. Only a quarter of those aboard survived; John did not. On 21 March his body was interred in Wyke Regis churchyard, Weymouth,

Dorset. William Wordsworth's letter to Lamb, though unrecovered, probably asked for more details on the tragedy, because, in the weeks that followed, Lamb went to great lengths to acquire and transmit such information to Wordsworth. He secured the testimony of Thomas Gilpin and Benjamin Yates, two survivors, and added, in several follow-up letters, news reports of what they and others had said and written.

7 *The Excursion*.
8 'The Churchyard among the Mountains', *The Excursion*, VI–VII.
9 Possibly Lamb's allusion to Charon, who ferried the shades of the dead across the river Styx. It may also refer to a difficult terrain, i.e., one that has the potential to injure or inflict scars on a traveler. Either interpretation can be documented by passages in *The Excursion*, VII.
10 *The Excursion*, V, 138–70.

Thomas de Quincey (1785–1859)

An unhappy pupil, Thomas de Quincey, still in his teens, dreamed of finding a happier environment for his literary ambitions than Manchester Grammar School. In 1802 he fled from it, and from the guardians who had taken over after his father, a prosperous but ailing merchant, died (1793). His mother (as her son described her) was a somewhat chilly presence, showing little sympathy for his imaginative interests. In partial compensation, the poetry of Wordsworth worked on him charm-like from the late 1790s on. De Quincey was confident that he had a talent for writing, and he believed it might flourish in the company of the Lake Poets, if only he could meet and be accepted by them.

The first draft of a letter to Wordsworth, begun on 14 May 1803, was very carefully phrased. (In a list of his favorite poets, Wordsworth's name was followed by three exclamation marks.) Its tone, a mixture of sincere humility and vaunting pride, caught Wordsworth's attention, and the answering letter of acknowledgment was both kind and encouraging, even going so far as to say that he would be 'very happy' to meet De Quincey personally.

The correspondence that blossomed as a consequence, and De Quincey's joy at the assurance that he would be made welcome whenever he visited Grasmere, led, after several delays (four whole years!), to his visiting Dove Cottage. (Earlier in that year of 1807, he had met Coleridge first, at Bridgewater. His relationship to Wordsworth, although increasingly troubled and ultimately impossible to sustain, proved more important, as he thought it might be.)

De Quincey, whose writings had not as yet resulted in significant publications, delighted in the opportunity to walk and converse with Wordsworth, and the interest that Wordsworth took in a new acolyte may have been paternalistic and more than a little patronizing, but it was generous withal. De Quincey's fitful education at Oxford – he did very well in the written examination, but never took his oral examination – seemed less vital to his happiness and development as a writer than the invitation, extended by Dorothy and William, to stay with them for several months. He strove to please by helping Coleridge establish his new publication, *The Friend*, playing with the children, suppressing or playing down his own conservative opinions so that Wordsworth might speak more freely, and acting as go-between to advance the editing and publication of Wordsworth's lengthy 'pamphlet' on the Convention of Cintra. This last yeoman effort required endless press negotiations, and involved misunderstandings and unwelcome delays, both in the delivery of Wordsworth's manuscript and in the corrections necessitated by misunderstandings of Wordsworth's instructions, which were not always clear or, for that matter, legible. Unfortunately, Wordsworth was stingy in his recognition of De Quincey's contribution to the pamphlet's slow progress through the press. Dorothy reproved her brother's habit of finding fault with almost everything De Quincey did. De Quincey himself was to brood for a lifetime over what he regarded, with some justification, as ingratitude.

De Quincey came to realize that Wordsworth never fully recognized his literary abilities, or confided in him, despite his efforts on behalf of Wordsworth and his family. He recognized and perhaps over-dramatized slights that were multiplying from year to year, and he did not appreciate Wordsworth's grave reserve for what it was, a habit of character that extended to practically all outsiders. De Quincey's falling in love with Margaret Simpson, a farmer's daughter whose lower social class bothered the Wordsworths, and their scornful remarks and attitudes underscored the estrangement. And, what was probably as aggravating to William and Dorothy as any other factor, De Quincey's addiction to opium reminded them all too vividly of similar problems created by Coleridge's dependence on drugs. De Quincey's financial problems, deteriorating health, smallish size (frequently commented on in a derogatory way), and a congenital inability to follow through on the promises he made, loomed larger with the passage of years.

When Coleridge died in 1834, De Quincey seized on his opportunity to write and publish a five-part essay for *Tait's Edinburgh Review*. His long-stored bitterness spilled over; he censured Coleridge for plagiarizing German texts, and he harped on Coleridge's unhappy marriage. He evaluated Coleridge's handling of *The Friend* as being very close to incompetent. The anger of the Wordsworths deepened. Sara Hutchinson called De Quincey 'the little Monster'; and Southey told Carlyle that Hartley Coleridge 'ought to take a strong cudgel, proceed straight to Edinburgh, and give De Quincey, publicly in the streets there, a sound beating — as a calumniator, cowardly spy, traitor, base betrayer of the hospitable social hearth . . .'

De Quincey's essays on Wordsworth (1839) help us to place in a larger context Wordsworth's decision to remain secluded, which had led many of Wordsworth's contemporaries to pontificate, on the basis of limited knowledge, about the Rydal poet's personality. They present a vivid, striking picture, perhaps the best such portrait printed during Wordsworth's lifetime. The details of Wordsworth's dress and manners, as described by De Quincey, are not flattering (as in his treatment of Coleridge, De Quincey was to repent of having written some especially impassioned remarks, and he deleted them before and after they were printed). Even so, De Quincey never faltered in his belief that Wordsworth was the greatest poet of the age, and his critique of *The Prelude* was an early recognition of its power and beauty. The series of essays offended the Wordsworths and their friends, but they remain an important statement by a permanently important figure in the Romantic Movement. To these articles De Quincey added, as his final treatment of Wordsworth, a fine essay entitled 'On Wordsworth's Poetry', published in *Tait's* (September 1845). It was a more generous tribute to Wordsworth's poetic genius than any printed tribute by Wordsworth to De Quincey's singular style.

For sympathetic and judicious summings-up of this complex, continually changing relationship, two scholarly books are recommended: John E. Jordan's *De Quincey to Wordsworth: a Biography of a Relationship*, which reprints De Quincey's letters to the Wordsworth family along with an extensive commentary (Berkeley and Los Angeles: University of California Press, 1962), and Grevel Lindop's *The Opium-Eater: a Life of Thomas De Quincey* (London: J. M. Dent, 1981).

De Q, W, XI, *Articles from Tait's Magazine and Blackwood's Magazine, 1838–1841*, edited by Julian North (London: Pickering & Chatto, 2003), 'Lake Reminiscences, No. I – William Wordsworth', 54–64

I was ushered up a little flight of stairs, fourteen in all, to a little dining-room, or whatever the reader chooses to call it. Wordsworth himself has described the fire-place of this as his

'Half-kitchen and half-parlour fire.'[1]

It was not fully seven feet six inches high, and, in other respects, pretty nearly of the same dimensions as the rustic hall below. There was, however, in a small recess, a library of perhaps 300 volumes, which seemed to consecrate the room as the poet's study and composing room; and so occasionally it was. But far oftener he both studied, as I found, and composed on the high road. I had not been two minutes at the fireside, when in came Wordsworth, returning from his friendly attentions to the travellers below, who, it seemed, had been over-persuaded by hospitable solicitations to stay for this night in Grasmere, and to make out the remaining thirteen miles of their road to Keswick on the following day. Wordsworth entered. And *'what-like'* – to use a Westmoreland, as well as a Scottish expression – *'what-like'* was

Wordsworth? A reviewer in *Tait's Magazine*, in noticing some recent collection of literary portraits, gives it as his opinion that Charles Lamb's head was the finest amongst them.[2] This remark may have been justified by the engraved portraits; but, certainly, the critic would have cancelled it had he seen the original heads – at least, had he seen them in youth or in maturity; for Charles Lamb bore age with less disadvantage to the intellectual expression of his appearance than Wordsworth, in whom a sanguine, or rather coarse complexion, (or rather not complexion, properly speaking, so much as texture of flesh,) has, of late years, usurped upon the original bronze-tint and finer skin; and this change of hue and change in the quality of skin, has been made fourfold more conspicuous, and more unfavourable in its general effect, by the harsh contrast of grizzled hair which has displaced the original brown. No change in personal appearance ever can have been so unfortunate; for, generally speaking, whatever other disadvantages old age may bring along with it, one effect, at least, in male subjects, has a compensating tendency – that it removes any tone of vigour too harsh, and mitigates the expression of power too unsubdued. But, in Wordsworth, the effect of the change has been to substitute an air of animal vigour, or, at least, hardiness, as if derived from constant exposure to the wind and weather, for the fine, sombre complexion which he once had, resembling that of a Venetian senator or a Spanish monk. Here, however, in describing the personal appearance of Wordsworth, I go back, of course, to the point of time at which I am speaking. To begin with his figure: – Wordsworth was, upon the whole, not a well-made man. His legs were pointedly condemned by all the female connoisseurs in legs that ever I heard lecture upon that topic; not that they were bad in any way which *would* force itself upon your notice – there was no absolute deformity about them; and undoubtedly they had been serviceable legs beyond the average standard of human requisition; for I calculate, upon good data, that with these identical legs Wordsworth must have traversed a distance of 175 to 180,000 English miles – a mode of exertion which, to him, stood in the stead of wine, spirits, and all other stimulants whatsoever to the animal spirits; to which he has been indebted for a life of unclouded happiness, and we for much of what is most excellent in his writings. But, useful, as they have proved themselves, the Wordsworthian legs were certainly not ornamental; and it was really a pity, as I agreed with a lady in thinking, that he had not another pair for evening dress parties – when no boots lend their friendly aid to masque our imperfections from the eyes of female rigourists – the *elegantes formarum spectatrices*.[3] A sculptor would certainly have disapproved of their contour. But the worst part of

Wordsworth's person was the bust: there was a narrowness and a droop about the shoulders which became striking, and had an effect of meanness when brought into close juxtaposition with a figure of a most statuesque order. Once on a summer morning, walking in the vale of Langdale with Wordsworth, his sister, and Mr J—, a native Westmoreland clergyman, I remember that Miss Wordsworth was positively mortified by the peculiar illustration which settled upon this defective conformation. Mr J—, a fine towering figure, six feet high, massy and columnar in his proportions, happened to be walking, a little in advance, with Wordsworth; Miss Wordsworth and myself being in the rear; and from the nature of the conversation which then prevailed in our front rank, something or other about money, devises, buying and selling, we of the rear-guard thought it requisite to preserve this arrangement for a space of three miles or more; during which time, at intervals, Miss W— would exclaim, in a tone of vexation, 'Is it possible? – can that be William? How very mean he looks!' and could not conceal a mortification that seemed really painful, until I, for my part, could not forbear laughing outright at the serious interest which she carried into this trifle. She was, however, right as regarded the mere visual judgment. Wordsworth's figure, with all its defects, was brought into powerful relief by one which had been cast in a more square and massy mould; and in such a case it impressed a spectator with a sense of absolute meanness, more especially when viewed from behind, and not counteracted by his countenance; and yet Wordsworth was of a good height, just five feet ten, and not a slender man; on the contrary, by the side of Southey his limbs looked thick, almost in a disproportionate degree. But the total effect of Wordsworth's person was always worst in a state of motion; for, according to the remark I have heard from many country people, 'he walked like a cade' – a cade being some sort of insect which advances by an oblique motion. This was not always perceptible, and in part depended (I believe) upon the position of his arms; when either of these happened (as was very customary) to be inserted into the unbuttoned waistcoat, his walk had a wry or twisted appearance; and not appearance only – for I have known it, by slow degrees, gradually to edge off his companion from the middle to the side of the highroad.* Meantime, his face – that was one which would have made amends for greater defects of figure; it was certainly the noblest for intellectual effects that, in actual life, I have seen, or at

---

* In our Westmoreland highroads, which are so fortunate as to have little breadth beyond that of lanes, there is no side-path, not even on approaching towns; consequently everybody walks at large upon the carriage track.

least have consciously been led to notice. Many such, or even finer, I have seen amongst the portraits of Titian, and, in a later period, amongst those of Vandyke, from the great era of Charles I., as also from the court of Elizabeth and of Charles II.; but none which has so much impressed me in my own time. Haydon, the eminent painter, in his great picture of *Christ's Entry into Jerusalem*, has introduced Wordsworth in the character of a disciple attending his Divine Master. This fact is well known; and, as the picture itself is tolerably well known to the public eye, there are multiudes now living who will have seen a very impressive likeness of Wordsworth – some consciously, some not suspecting it. There will, however, always be many who have *not* seen any portrait at all of Wordsworth; and therefore I will describe its general outline and effect. It was a face of the long order, often falsely classed as oval; but a greater mistake is made by many people in supposing the long face, which prevailed so remarkably in the Eliza-bethan and Carolinian periods, to have become extinct in our days. Miss Ferrier, in one of her brilliant novels, ('Marriage,' I think,) makes a Highland girl protest that 'no Englishman *with his round face*'[4] shall ever wean her heart from her own country; but England is not the land of round faces – and those have observed little indeed who think so . . . Wordsworth's forehead is also liable to caricature misrepresentations, in these days of phrenology, but, whatever it may appear to be in any man's fanciful portrait, the real living forehead, as I have been in the habit of seeing it for more than five-and-twenty years, is not remark-able for its height; but it *is* perhaps remarkable for its breadth and expansive development. Neither are the eyes of Wordsworth 'large,' as is erroneously stated somewhere in 'Peter's Letters;'[5] on the contrary, they are (I think) rather small; but *that* does not interfere with their effect, which at times is fine and suitable to his intellectual character. At times, I say, for the depth and subtlety of eyes varies exceedingly with the state of the stomach; and, if young ladies were aware of the magical transformations which can be wrought in the depth and sweetness of the eye by a few weeks' walking exercise, I fancy we should see their habits in this point altered greatly for the better. I have seen Wordsworth's eyes often times affected powerfully in this respect; his eyes are not, under any circumstances, bright, lustrous, or piercing; but, after a long day's toil in walking, I have seen them assume an appearance the most solemn and spiritual that it is possible for the human eye to wear. The light which resides in them is at no time a superficial light; but, under favourable accidents, it is a light which seems to come from depths below all depths; in fact, it is more truly entitled to be held 'The light that never was on land or sea,'[6] a light radiating from some far spiritual world, than any the most ideal-izing light that ever yet a painter's hand created. The nose, a little arched, and large, which, by the way, (according to a natural phreno-logy, existing centuries ago amongst some of the lowest amongst the human species,) has always been accounted an unequivocal expression of animal appetites organically strong. And that was in fact the basis of Wordsworth's intellectual power: his intellectual passions were fervent and strong; because they rested upon a basis of animal sensibility superior to that of most men, diffused through *all* the animal passions (or appetites); and something of that will be found to hold of all poets who have been great by original force and power, not (as Virgil) by means of fine management and exquisite artifice of composition applied to their conceptions. The mouth, and the region of the mouth, the whole circumjacencies of the mouth, were about the strongest feature in Wordsworth's face; there was nothing specially to be noticed that I know of, in the mere outline of the lips; but the swell and pro-trusion of the parts above and around the mouth, are both noticeable in themselves, and also because they remind me of a very interesting fact which I discovered about three years after this my first visit to Wordsworth. Being a great collector of everything relating to Milton, I had naturally possessed myself, whilst yet very young, of Richardson the painter's thick octavo volume of notes on the 'Paradise Lost.'[7] It happened, however, that my copy, in consequence of that mania for portrait collecting which has stripped so many English classics of their engraved portraits, had no picture of Milton. Subsequently I ascer-tained that it ought to have had a very good likeness of the great poet; and I never rested until I procured a copy of the book, which had not suffered in this respect by the fatal admiration of the amateur. The par-ticular copy offered to me was one which had been priced unusually high, on account of the unusually fine specimen which it contained of the engraved portrait. This, for a particular reason, I was exceedingly anxious to see; and the reason was – that, according to an anecdote reported by Richardson himself, this portrait, of all that was shewn to her, was the only one acknowledged, by Milton's last surviving daugh-ter, to be a strong likeness of her father. And her involuntary gestures concurred with her deliberate words: – for, on seeing all the rest, she was silent and inanimate; but the very instant she beheld this from a crayons drawing which embellishes the work of Richardson, she burst out into a rapture of passionate recognition; exclaiming – 'This is my father! this is my dear father!' Naturally, therefore, after such a testi-mony, so much stronger than any other person in the world could offer to the authentic value of this portrait, I was eager to see it.

Judge of my astonishment when, in this portrait of Milton, I saw a likeness nearly perfect of Wordsworth, better by much than any which I have since seen, of those expressly painted for himself. The likeness is tolerably preserved in that by Carruthers,[8] in which one of the little Rydal waterfalls, &c., composes a back-ground; yet this is much inferior, as a mere portrait of Wordsworth, to the Richardson head of Milton; and this, I believe, is the last which represents Wordsworth in the vigour of his power. The rest, which I have not seen, may be better as works of art, (for anything I know to the contrary,) but they must labour under the great disadvantage of presenting the features when 'defeatured,' in the degree and the way I have described, by the idio-syncrasies of old age, as it affects this family; for it is noticed of the Wordsworths, by those who are familiar with their peculiarities, that, in their very blood and constitutional differences, lie hidden causes, able, in some mysterious way –

'Those shocks of passion to prepare
   That kill the bloom before its time,
   And blanch, without the owner's crime,
      The most resplendent hair.'[9]

Some people, it is notorious, live faster than others; the oil is burned out sooner in one constitution than another – and the cause of this may be various; but, in the Wordsworths one part of the cause is, no doubt, the secret fire of a temperament too fervid; the self-consuming energies of the brain, that gnaw at the heart and life-strings for ever. In that account which 'The Excursion', presents to us of an imaginary Scotsman, who, to still the tumult of his heart, when visiting the 'forces' (*i.e.*, cataracts) of a mountainous region, obliges himself to study the laws of light and colour, as they affect the rainbow of the stormy waters; vainly attempting to mitigate the fever which con-sumed him, by entangling his mind in profound speculations; raising a cross-fire of artillery from the subtilizing intellect, under the vain conceit that in this way, he could silence the mighty battery of his impassioned brain – there we read a picture of Wordsworth and his own youth.[10] In Miss Wordsworth, every thoughtful observer might read the same self-consuming style of thought. And the effect upon each was so powerful for the promotion of a premature old age, and of a premature expression of old age, that strangers invariably supposed them fifteen to twenty years older than they were. And I remember Wordsworth once laughingly reporting to me, on returning from a

short journey in 1809, a little personal anecdote, which sufficiently
shewed what was the spontaneous impression upon that subject of
casual strangers, whose feelings were not confused by previous knowledge of the truth. He was travelling by a stage coach, and seated
outside, amongst a good half-dozen of fellow-passengers. One of these,
an elderly man, who confessed to having passed the grand climacterical year (9 multiplied into 7) of 63, though he did not say precisely by
how many years, said to Wordsworth, upon some anticipations which
they had been mutually discussing of changes likely to result from
enclosures, &c., then going on or projecting – 'Ay, ay, another dozen of
years will shew us strange sights; but you and I can hardly expect to see
them.' 'How so?' said W. 'Why, my friend, how old do you take me to
be?' 'Oh, I beg pardon,' said the other; 'I meant no offence – but what?'
looking at W. more attentively – 'you'll never see threescore, I'm of
opinion.' And, to shew that he was not singular in so thinking, he
appealed to all the other passengers; and the motion passed, *nem. con.*
that Wordsworth was rather over than under sixty. Upon this he told
them the literal truth – that he had not yet accomplished his thirty-
ninth year. 'God bless me!' said the climacterical man; 'so then, after
all, you'll have a chance to see your childer get up like, and get settled!
God bless me, to think of that!' And so closed the conversation, leaving
to W. a pointed expression of his own premature age, as revealing itself
by looks, in this unaffected astonishment, amongst a whole party of
plain men, that he should really belong to a generation of the forward-
looking, who live by hope; and might reasonably expect to see a child
of seven years old matured into a man.

Returning to the question of portraits, I would observe, that this
Richardson engraving of Milton has the advantage of presenting, not
only by far the best likeness of Wordsworth, but of Wordsworth in the
prime of his powers – a point so essential in the case of one so liable to
premature decay. It may be supposed that I took an early opportunity
of carrying the book down to Grasmere, and calling for the opinions of
Wordsworth's family upon this most remarkable coincidence. Not one
member of that family but was as much impressed as myself with the
accuracy of the likeness. All the peculiarities even were retained – a
drooping appearance of the eyelids, that remarkable swell which I have
noticed about the mouth, the way in which the hair lay upon the
forehead. In two points only there was a deviation from the rigorous
truth of Wordsworth's features – the face was a little too short and too
broad, and the eyes were too large. There was also a wreath of laurel
about the head, which (as Wordsworth remarked) disturbed the natural

expression of the whole picture; else, and with these few allowances, he also admitted that the resemblance was, *for that period of his life*, (but let not that restriction be forgotten,) perfect, or as nearly so as art could accomplish.

I have gone into so large and circumstantial a review of my recollections in a matter that would have been trifling and tedious in excess, had their recollection related to a less important man; but, with a certain knowledge that the least of them will possess a lasting and a growing interest in connexion with William Wordsworth – a man who is not simply destined to be had in everlasting remembrance by every generation of men, but (which is a modification of the kind worth any multiplication of the degree) to be had in that *sort* of remembrance which has for its shrine the heart of man – that world of fear and grief, of love and trembling hope, which constitutes the essential man; in *that* sort of remembrance, and not in such a remembrance as we grant to the ideas of a great philosopher, a great mathematician, or a great reformer. How different, how peculiar, is the interest which attends the great poets who have made themselves necessary to the human heart; who have first brought into consciousness, and next have clothed in words, those grand catholic feelings that belong to the grand catholic situations of life, through all its stages; who have clothed them in such words that human wit despairs of bettering them! How remote is that burning interest which settles upon men's living memories in our daily thoughts, from that which follows, in a disjointed and limping way, the mere nominal memories of those who have given a direction and movement to the currents of human thought, and who, by some leading impulse, have even quickened into life speculations appointed to terminate in positive revolutions of human power over physical agents! Mighty were the powers, solemn and serene is the memory, of Archimedes; and Apollonius shines like 'the starry Galileo,'[11] in the firmament of human genius; yet how frosty is the feeling associated with these names by comparison with that which, upon every sunny brae, by the side of every ancient forest, even in the farthest depths of Canada, many a young innocent girl, perhaps, at this very moment – looking now with fear to the dark recesses of the infinite forest, and now with love to the pages of the infinite poet, until the fear is absorbed and forgotten in the love – cherishes in her heart for the name and person of Shakspeare! The one is abstraction, and a shadow recurring only by distinct efforts of recollection, and even thus to none but the enlightened and the learned; the other is a household image, rising amongst household remembrances, never separated from the spirit of delight, and hallowed by a human love! Such a place in the affections of the young and the ingenuous, no less than of the old and philosophic, who happen to have any depth of feeling, will Words-worth occupy in every clime and in every land; for the language in which he writes, thanks be to Providence, which has beneficently opened the widest channels for the purest and most elevating liter-ature, is now ineradicably planted in all quarters of the earth; the echoes under every latitude of every longitude now reverberate English words; and all things seem tending to this result – that the English and the Spanish languages will finally share the earth between them. Wordsworth is peculiarly the poet for the solitary and the meditative and, throughout the countless myriads of future America and future Australia, no less than Polynesia and Southern Africa, there will be situ-ations without end fitted by their loneliness to favour his influence for centuries to come, by the end of which period it may be anticipated that education (of a more enlightened quality and more systematic than yet prevails) may have wrought such changes on the human species, as will uphold the growth of all philosophy, and, therefore, of all poetry which has its foundations laid in the heart of man. Commensurate with the interest in the poetry will be a secondary interest in the poet – in his personal appearance, and his habits of life, *so far as they can be supposed at all dependent upon his intellectual charac-teristics;*[12] for, with respect to differences that are purely casual, and which illustrate no principle of higher origin than accidents of educa-tion or chance position, it is a gossiping taste only that could seek for such information, and a gossiping taste that would choose to consult it. Meantime, it is under no such gossiping taste that volumes have been written upon the mere portraits and upon the possible portraits of Shakspeare; and how invaluable should we all feel any record to be, which should raise the curtain upon Shakspeare's daily life – his habits, personal and social, his intellectual tastes, and his opinions on con-temporary men, books, events, or national prospects! I cannot, there-fore, think it necessary to apologize for the most circumstantial notices past or to come of Wordsworth's person and habits of life. But one thing it is highly necessary that I should explain, and the more so because a grand confession which I shall make at this point, as in some measure necessary to protect myself from the appearance of a needless mystery and reserve, would, if unaccompanied by such an explanation, expose me to the suspicion of having, at times, yielded to a private prejudice, so far as to colour my account of Wordsworth with a spirit of pique or illiberality. I shall acknowledge then, on my own part – and

I feel that I might even make the same acknowledgement on the part of Professor Wilson, (though I have no authority for doing so) – that to neither of us, though, at all periods of our lives, treating him with the deep respect which is his due, and, in our earlier years, with a more than filial devotion – nay, with a blind loyalty of homage, which had in it, at that time, something of the spirit of martyrdom, which, for his sake, courted even reproach and contumely; yet to neither of us has Wordsworth made those returns of friendship and kindness which most firmly I maintain that we were entitled to have challenged. More by far in sorrow than in anger – sorrow that points to recollections too deep and too personal for a transient notice – I acknowledge myself to have been long alienated from Wordsworth; sometimes even I feel a rising emotion of hostility – nay, something, I fear, too nearly akin to vindictive hatred. Strange revolution of the human heart! strange example of the changes in human feeling that may be wrought by time and chance! to find myself carried by the great tide of affairs, and by error, more or less, on one side or the other, either on Wordsworth's in doing too little, or on mine in expecting too much – carried so far away from that early position which, for so long a course of years, I held in respect to him – that now, for that fountain of love towards Mr Wordsworth and all his household – fountain profound – fountain inexhaustible –

'Whose only business was to flow –
And flow it did, not taking heed
Of its own bounty or their need' –[13]

now, I find myself standing aloof, gloomily granting (because I cannot refuse) my intellectual homage, but no longer rendering my tribute as a willing service of the heart, or rejoicing in the prosperity of my idol! Could I have believed, twenty-five years ago, had a voice from Heaven revealed it, that, even then, with a view to what time should bring about, I might adopt the spirit of the old verses, and, apostrophizing Wordsworth, might say – Great Poet! when that day, so fervently desired, shall come, that men shall undo their wrongs, and when every tongue shall chant thy praises, and every heart

'Devote a wreath to thee –
That day (for come it will) that day
Shall I lament to see.'[14]

But no; not so. Lament I never did; nor suffered even 'the hectic of a moment' to sully or to trouble that purity of perfect pleasure with which I welcomed this great revolution in the public feeling. Let me render justice to Professor Wilson, as well as to myself: not for a moment, not by a solitary movement of reluctance or demur, did either of us hang back in giving that public acclamation which we, by so many years, had anticipated; yes, we singly – we with no sympathy to support us from any quarter. The public press remains, with its inexorable records, to vouch for us, that we paid an oriental homage, homage as to one who could have pleaded antique privilege, and the consecration of centuries, at a time when the finger of scorn was pointed at Mr Wordsworth from every journal in the land; and that we persisted in this homage at a period long enough removed to have revolutionized the public mind, and also long enough to have undermined the personal relations between us of confidential friendship. Did it ask no courage to come forward, in the first character, as solitary friends, holding up our protesting hands amidst a wilderness of chattering buffoons? Did it ask no magnanimity to stand firmly to the post we had assumed, not passively acquiescing in the new state of public opinion, but exulting in it and aiding it, long after we had found reason to think ourselves injuriously treated? Times are changed; it needs no courage, in the year of our Lord 1839,[15] to discover and proclaim a great poet in William Wordsworth; it needed none in the year 1815, to discover a frail power in the French empire, or an idol of clay and brass in the French Emperor. But, to make the first discovery in the years 1801–2, the other in 1808, those things were worthy of honour; and the first was worthy of gratitude from all the parties interested in the event. Let me not, however, be misunderstood – Mr Wordsworth is a man of unimpeached, unimpeachable integrity: he neither has done, nor could have done, consciously, any act in violation of his conscience. On the contrary, I am satisfied, Professor Wilson is satisfied, that injuries of a kind to involve an admitted violation of principle, cannot have occurred in Mr Wordsworth's intercourse with any man. But there are cases of wrong for which the conscience is not the competent tribunal. Sensibility to the just claims of another, power to appreciate these claims, power also to perceive the true mode of conveying and expressing the appreciation – in a case, suppose, where the claims to consideration are at once real, and even tangible, as to their ground, yet subtle and aerial as to the shape they have assumed – claims, for instance, founded on a personal devotion to the interests of the other party, when the rest of the world slighted them – this mode of appreciating skill may be utterly wanting, or may be crossed and thwarted by many a conflicting bias, where the conscience is quite incapable of going astray. I imagine a case such as this which follows: – The case of a man who, for many years, has connected himself closely with the domestic griefs and joys of another, over and above his primary service of giving to him the strength and the encouragement of a profound literary sympathy, at a time of universal scowling from the world; suppose this man to fall into a situation in which, from want of natural connexions and from his state of insulation in life, it might be most important to his feelings that some support should be lent to him by a family having a known place and acceptation, and what may be called a root in the country, by means of connexions, descent, and long settlement. To look for this, might be a most humble demand on the part of one who had testified his devotion in the way supposed. To miss it might – But enough. I murmur not; complaint is weak at all times; and the hour is passed irrevocably, and by many a year, in which an act of friendship so natural, and costing so little, (in both senses so priceless,) could have been availing. The ear is deaf that should have been solaced by the sound of welcome. Call, but you will not be heard; shout aloud, but your 'ave!' and 'all hail!' will now tell only as an echo of departed days, proclaiming the hollowness of human hopes. I, for my part, have long learned the lesson of suffering in silence; and also I have learned to know that, wheresoever female prejudices are concerned,[16] *there* it will be a trial more than Herculean, of a man's wisdom, if he can walk with an even step, and swerve neither to the right nor the left.

Notes ('Lake Reminiscences, No. I')

These extracts come from the first essay in De Quincey's 'Lake Reminiscences, from 1807 to 1830', a series of five articles signed by 'the English Opium-Eater'. It was published originally in *Tait's*, July 1839; called back to print in the two-volume *Literary Reminiscences* (1851), De Quincey's autobiography; and the 'Reminiscences reached their final form in the 1854 edition, retitled *Autobiographic Sketches*. The texts reprinted here are more candid, certainly more indiscreet, and more heart felt than the revised versions. (Both versions are available to the interested reader in Volumes XI and XIX of *The Works of Thomas De Quincey*, published in London by Pickering & Chatto, 2003.)

Wordsworth denied that he had ever read them, or ever would; he attributed the harshness of De Quincey's characterization of himself to 'wounded feelings'. Nevertheless, he tried to stop De Quincey's inclusion of the *Reminiscences* in his autobiography, and he never conceded that De Quincey, in the revised version, had considerably toned down what he had written about an erstwhile close friend and collaborator.

Notes

1 Wordsworth, 'Personal Talk' (1807), a free adaptation of line 12. In 1815 Wordsworth changed it to: 'In the loved presence of my cottage fire'.
2 David Masson identifies this as an omnibus review of 'Books of the Season', which commented on *Tilt's Medallion Portraits of Modern English Authors, with Illustrative Notices by H. F. Chorley*. The relevant sentence: 'The finest head, in every way, in the series, is that of Charles Lamb.' The review appeared in *Tait's Magazine* (December 1837), IV, 793.
3 'The elegant female judges of people's charms.'
4 Susan Edmonstone Ferrier (1782–1854), a quietly observant Scottish writer of fiction; her writings are marked by keen observation and a flair for satire. She made friends easily, and won the high praise of Sir Walter Scott, among many others of her countrymen and women. *Marriage*, her first novel, was completed in 1810, but not printed until 1818.
5 John Gibson Lockhart (1794–1854) wrote *Peter's Letters to his Kinfolk* (1819). The sketches took as subject-matter the behavior of members of Scottish society. Many of those satirized took offence. Lockhart later apologized for the sharpness of his remarks.
6 'Elegiac Stanzas suggested by a Picture of Peele Castle in a Storm' (1805). The painting is by George Beaumont.
7 Jonathan Richardson (*c.* 1665–1745) was a successful portrait painter. He influenced many important artists, among them William Hogarth and Sir Joshua Reynolds. Dr Johnson thought his writings superior to his paintings. Richardson's guide to works of art in England, the first to be compiled in England, and incisive comments about his own theory of art, bolster Johnson's judgment. The book De Quincey refers to is entitled *Explanatory Notes and Remarks on Paradise Lost* (1734), which Richardson co-wrote with his son.
8 Richard Carruthers (1792–1876). His oil painting of Wordsworth, completed in 1817, was engraved and printed in *New Monthly Magazine* (May 1819).
9 Wordsworth, 'Lament of Mary Queen of Scots/On the Eve of a New Year' (composed 1817; published 1820). The first line of the quotation should read, 'Those shocks of passion can prepare . . .'
10 *The Excursion* I, 291–300.
11 Archimedes (*c.* 287–212 BC) made important contributions to the developing disciplines of geometry, mechanics, and hydrostatics. Apollonius Rhodius (3rd C. BC) was a Greek poet and librarian at Alexandria. He quar-

reled with Callimachus about the viability of the epic form. De Quincey is
   quoting Byron's *Childe Harold's Pilgrimage* (1812), IV, 485.
12   Here De Quincey launches his strongly negative attack on Wordsworth's
   personality because of the slights that he believed Wordsworth had inflicted
   on him. The most remarkable aspect of the critique may be the fact that he
   has been fairly circumspect about his personal feelings until this point.
13   Wordsworth, 'A Complaint' (composed 1806; printed in 1807). De Quincey
   changed 'my need' (1. 6) to 'their need'.
14   Cf. Alexander Pope's note to *The Dunciad* (1728), II, 134.
15   A misprint for 1838, some eight months earlier; De Quincey was sufficiently
   annoyed that he wrote to *Blackwood's Magazine* to complain.
16   Julian North (617, fn. 53) believes that De Quincey refers to the way in
   which Margaret, his wife, was cold-shouldered by both Wordsworth's wife
   and sister.

DeQ, W, XI, Articles from Tait's Magazine and Blackwood's Magazine, 1838–1841, edited by Julian North (London: Pickering & Chatto, 2003), 'Lake Reminiscences, No. IV – William Wordsworth and Robert Southey', 110–13, 116–19

THAT night – the first of my personal intercourse with Wordsworth –
the first in which I saw him face to face – was (it is little, indeed, to say)
memorable: it was marked by a change even in the physical condition
of my nervous system. Long disappointment – hope for ever baffled,
(and why should it be less painful because *self*-baffled?) – vexation and
self-blame, almost self-contempt, at my own want of courage to face
the man whom of all since the Flood I most yearned to behold: – these
feelings had impressed upon my nervous sensibilities a character of
irritation – agitation – restlessness – eternal self-dissatisfaction – which
were gradually gathering into a distinct, well-defined type, that would,
but for youth – almighty youth, and the spirit of youth – have shaped
itself into some nervous complaint, wearing symptoms *sui generis*, (for
most nervous complaints, in minds that are at all eccentric, will be *sui
generis*;) and, perhaps, finally, have been immortalized in some medical
journal as the anomalous malady of an interesting young gentleman,
aged twenty-two, who was supposed to have studied too severely, and
to have perplexed his brain with German metaphysics. To this result
things tended; but, in one hour, all passed away. It was gone, never to
return. The spiritual being whom I had anticipated – for, like Eloise,

'My fancy fram'd him of th' angelic kind –
Some emanation of th' all beauteous mind' –[1]

this ideal creature had, at length, been seen – seen 'in the flesh' – seen with fleshly eyes; and now, though he did not cease for years to wear something of the glory and the *aureola* which, in Popish legends, invests the head of superhuman beings, yet it was no longer as a being to be feared – it was as Raphael, the 'affable' angel,[2] who conversed on the terms of man with man, that I now regarded him.

It was four o'clock, perhaps, when we arrived. At that hour the daylight soon declined; and, in an hour and a half, we were all collected about the teatable. This, with the Wordsworths, under the simple rustic system of habits which they cherished then, and for twenty years after, was the most delightful meal in the day; just as dinner is in great cities, and for the same reason – because it was prolonged into a meal of leisure and conversation.

That night, after hearing conversation superior by much, in its tone and subject, to any which I had ever heard before – one exception only being made, in favour of Coleridge, whose style differed from Wordsworth's in this, that being far more agile and more comprehensive, consequently more showy and surprising, it was less impressive and weighty; for Wordsworth's was slow in its movement, solemn, majestic. After a luxury so rare as this, I found myself, about eleven at night, in a pretty bedroom, about fourteen feet by twelve. Much I feared that this might turn out the best room in the house, and it illustrates the hospitality of my new friends, to mention that it was. Early in the morning, I was awoke by a little voice, issuing from a little cottage bed in an opposite corner, soliloquizing in a low tone. I soon recognised the words – 'Suffered under Pontius Pilate; was crucified, dead, and buried;'[3] and the voice I easily conjectured to be that of the eldest amongst Wordsworth's children, a son, and at that time about three years old. He was a remarkably fine boy in strength and size, promising (which has in fact been realized) a much more powerful person, physically, than that of his father. Miss Wordsworth I found making breakfast in the little sitting-room. No urn was there; no glittering breakfast service; a kettle boiled upon the fire, and everything was in harmony with these unpretending arrangements. I, the son of a merchant, and naturally, therefore, in the midst of luxurious (though not ostentatious) display from my childhood, had never seen so humble a *ménage*: and contrasting the dignity of the man with this honourable poverty, and this courageous avowal of it, his utter absence of all effort to disguise the simple truth of the case, I felt my admiration increase to the uttermost by all I saw. This, thought I to myself, is, indeed, in his own words –

'Plain living, and high thinking.'[4]

This is indeed to reserve the humility and the parsimonies of life for its bodily enjoyments, and to apply its lavishness and its luxury to its enjoyments of the intellect. So might Milton have lived; so Marvel. Throughout the day – which was rainy – the same style of modest hospitality prevailed. Wordsworth and his sister – myself being of the party – walked out in spite of the rain, and made the circuit of the two lakes, Grasmere and its dependancy Rydal – a walk of about six miles. On the third day, Mrs Coleridge having now pursued her journey northward to Keswick, and having, at her departure, invited me, in her own name as well as Southey's, to come and see them, Wordsworth proposed that we should go thither in company, but not by the direct route – a distance of only thirteen miles: this we were to take in our road homeward; our outward-bound journey was to be by way of Ulleswater – a circuit of forty-three miles.

At the foot of the lake, in a house called Ewsmere, we passed the night, having accomplished about twenty-two miles only in our day's walking and riding. The next day Wordsworth and I, leaving at Ewsmere the rest of our party, spent the morning in roaming through the woods of Lowther; and, towards evening, we dined together at Emont Bridge, one mile short of Penrith. Afterwards, we walked into Penrith. There Wordsworth left me in excellent quarters – the house of Captain Wordsworth, from which the family happened to be absent. Whither he himself adjourned, I know not, nor on what business; however, it occupied him throughout the next day; and, therefore, I employed myself in sauntering along the road, about seventeen miles, to Keswick. There I had been directed to ask for Greta Hall, which, with some little difficulty, I found; for it stands out of the town a few hundred yards, upon a little eminence overhanging the river Greta. It was about seven o'clock when I reached Southey's door; for I had stopped to dine at a little public-house in Threlkeld, and had walked slowly for the last two hours in the dark. The arrival of a stranger occasioned a little sensation in the house; and, by the time the front door could be opened, I saw Mrs Coleridge, and a gentleman whom I could not doubt to be Southey, standing, very hospitably, to greet my entrance. Southey was, in person, somewhat taller than Wordsworth, being about five feet eleven in height, or a trifle more, whilst Wordsworth was about five feet ten; and, partly from having slenderer limbs, partly from being more symmetrically formed about the shoulders than Wordsworth, he struck one as a better and lighter figure, to the effect of which his dress contributed; for he wore pretty constantly a short jacket and pantaloons, and had much the air of a Tyrolese mountaineer. On the next day arrived Wordsworth. I could read at once, in the manner of the two authors, that they were not on particularly friendly, or rather, I should say, confidential terms. It seemed to me as if both had silently said – we are too much men of sense to quarrel, because we do not happen particularly to like each other's writings: we are neighbours, or what passes for such in the country. Let us shew each other the courtesies which are becoming to men of letters; and, for any closer connexion, our distance of thirteen miles may be always sufficient to keep us from *that*. In after life, it is true – fifteen years, perhaps, from this time – many circumstances combined to bring Southey and Wordsworth into more intimate terms of friendship: agreement in politics, sorrows which had happened to both alike in their domestic relations, and the sort of tolerance for different opinions in literature, or, indeed, in anything else, which advancing years and experience are sure to bring with them. But, at this period, Southey and Wordsworth entertained a mutual esteem, but did not cordially like each other. Indeed, it would have been odd if they had. Wordsworth lived in the open air: Southey in his library, which Coleridge used to call his wife. Southey had particularly elegant habits (Wordsworth called them finical) in the use of books. Wordsworth, on the other hand, was so negligent, and so self-indulgent in the same case, that as Southey, laughing, expressed it to me some years afterwards, when I was staying at Greta Hall on a visit – 'To introduce Wordsworth into one's library, is like letting a bear into a tulip garden.' What I mean by self-indulgent is this: generally it happens that new books baffle and mock one's curiosity by their uncut leaves; and the trial is pretty much the same, as when, in some town, where you are utterly unknown, you meet the postman at a distance from your inn, with some letter for yourself from a dear, dear friend in foreign regions, without money to pay the postage. How is it with you, dear reader, in such a case? Are you not tempted (*I am* grievously) to snatch the letter from his tantalising hand, spite of the roar which you anticipate of 'Stop thief!' and make off as fast as you can for some solitary street in the suburbs, where you may instantly effect an entrance upon your new estate before the purchase-money is paid down? Such were Wordsworth's feelings in regard to new books; of which the first exemplification I had was early in my acquaintance with him, and on occasion of a book which (if any could) justified the too summary style of his advances in rifling its charms. On a level with the eye, when sitting at the tea-table in my little cottage at Grasmere, stood the collective works of Edmund Burke.[5] The book was to me an eye-sore and an ear-sore for many a year, in consequence of the cacophonous title lettered by the bookseller upon the back – 'Burke's Works.' I have heard it said, by the way, that Donne's intolerable defect of ear grew out of his own baptismal name, when harnessed to his own surname – *John Donne*. No man, it was said, who had listened to this hideous jingle from child-ish years, could fail to have his genius for discord, and the abominable in sound, improved to the utmost. Not less dreadful than *John Donne* was 'Burke's Works;' which, however, on the old principle, that every day's work is no day's work, continued to annoy me for twenty-one years. Wordsworth took down the volume; unfortunately it was uncut: fortunately, and by a special Providence as to him, it seemed, tea was proceeding at the time. Dry toast required butter; butter required knives; and knives then lay on the table; but sad it was for the virgin purity of Mr Burke's as yet un-sunned pages, that every knife bore upon its blade testimonies of the service it had rendered. Did *that* stop Wordsworth? Did that cause him to call for another knife? Not at all; he

'Look'd at the knife that caus'd his pain;
And look'd and sigh'd, and look'd and sigh'd again;'[6]

and then, after this momentary tribute to regret, he tore his way into the heart of the volume with this knife that left its greasy honours behind it upon every page: and are they not there to this day? This personal experience just brought me acquainted with Wordsworth's habits, and that particular, especially, with his intense impatience for one minute's delay which would have brought a remedy; and yet the reader may believe, that it is no affectation in me to say, that fifty such cases could have given me but little pain, when I explain, that what-ever could be made good by money at that time I did not regard. Had the book been an old black-letter book, having a value from its rarity, I should have been disturbed in an indescribable degree; but simply with reference to the utter impossibility of reproducing that mode of value. As to the Burke, it was a common book; I had bought the book, with many others, at the sale of Sir Cecil Wray's[7] library, for about two-thirds of the selling price: I could easily replace it; and I mention the case at all only to illustrate the excess of Wordsworth's outrages on books, which made him, in Southey's eyes, a mere monster; for Southey's beautiful library was his estate; and this difference of habits would alone have sufficed to alienate him from Wordsworth. And so I argued in other cases of the same nature. Meantime had Wordsworth done as Coleridge did, how cheerfully should I have acquiesced in his destruction (such it was, in a pecuniary sense) of books, as the very highest obligation he could confer. Coleridge often spoiled a book; but, in the course of doing this, he enriched that book with so many and so valuable notes, tossing about him with such lavish profusion, from such a cornucopia of discursive reading, and such a fusing intellect, commentaries so many-angled and so many-coloured, that I have envied many a man whose luck has placed him in the way of such injuries; and that man must have been a churl (though, God knows! too often this churl *has* existed) who could have found in his heart to complain. But Wordsworth rarely, indeed, wrote on the margin of books; and, when he did, nothing could less illustrate his intellectual superiority. The comments were such as might have been made by anybody. Once I remember, before I had ever seen Wordsworth – probably a year before – I met a person who had once enjoyed the signal honour of travelling with him to London. It was in a stage-coach. But the person in question well knew *who* it was that had been his *compagnon de voyage*. Immediately he was glorified in my eyes. 'And,' said I, to this glorified gentleman, (who, *par parenthèse*,[8] was also a donkey,) 'now, as you travelled nearly three hundred miles in the company of Mr Wordsworth, consequently, (for this was in 1805,) 'during two nights and two days, doubtless you must have heard many profound remarks that would inevitably fall from his lips.' Nay, Coleridge had also been of the party; and, if Wordsworth *solus* could have been dull, was it within human possibilities that these *gemini* should have been so? 'Was it possible?' I said; and, perhaps, my donkey, who looked like one that had been immoderately threatened, at last took courage; his eye brightened; and he intimated that he *did* remember something that Wordsworth had said – an 'observe,' as the Scotch call it.

'Ay, indeed; and what was it now? What did the great man say?'

'Why, sir, in fact, and to make a long story short, on coming near to London, we breakfasted at Baldock – you know Baldock? It's in Hertfordshire. Well, now, sir, would you believe it, though we were quite in regular time, the breakfast was precisely good for nothing?'

'And Wordsworth?'

'He observed' –

'What did he observe?'

'That the buttered toast looked, for all the world, as if it had been soaked in hot water.'

Ye heavens! *'buttered toast!'* And was it *this* I waited for? Now, thought I, had Henry Mackenzie been breakfasting with Wordsworth, at Baldock, (and, strange enough! in years to come, I *did* breakfast with Henry Mackenzie, for the solitary time I ever met him, and at Wordsworth's house, in Rydal,) he would have carried off one sole reminiscence from the meeting – namely, a confirmation of his creed, that we English are all dedicated, from our very cradle, to the luxuries of the palate, and peculiarly to this.[9]

Notes ('Lake Reminiscences, No. IV')

1 A loose adaptation of Alexander Pope's 'Eloisa to Abelard', 61–2.
2 John Milton, *Paradise Lost*, VII, 41.
3 Quoted from the Nicene Creed, which forms part of Anglican Church services.
4 William Wordsworth, 'Written in London, September, 1802', 11.
5 A 16-volume edition published between 1803 and 1827.
6 Loosely adapted from John Dryden's 'Alexander's Feast, or, The Power of Music', 112–13.
7 An independent-minded, and sometimes controversial, member of the House of Commons; he lived from 1734 to 1808.
8 'Incidentally', or 'By the way'.
9 Henry Mackenzie (1745–1831), a Scot, wrote the novel *The Man of Feeling* (1771), which was widely read; it was his greatest literary success. Sir Walter Scott called him 'the Northern Addison'.

William Hazlitt (1778–1830)

The alienation of Hazlitt and Wordsworth, taking place over a short period of time, bears a disquieting resemblance to the incidents leading eventually to De Quincey's fall from grace. (Hazlitt used the term 'estrangement' to characterize the shock he experienced when he discovered the human failings of a poet he had once admired greatly.)

The relationship, couched in mutually respectful language, had begun promisingly in May 1798, when Hazlitt, visiting Alfoxden, impressed by the quality of Wordsworth's contributions to *Lyrical Ballads*, offered to play a role in reprinting them separately from those of Coleridge. Wordsworth was receptive to the idea.

We are indebted to *My First Acquaintance with Poets* for Hazlitt's colorful description of Wordsworth as a rustic presence; but Hazlitt soon came to believe that Wordsworth's friendships were based, perhaps most importantly, on his need for an audience that approved both his political opinions and the poetical assumptions that underlay his literary work. Though Hazlitt took Wordsworth's side when the poet's problems with Coleridge developed during and shortly after the Scottish tour of 1803, the root causes of that alienation – Wordsworth's closeness to Dorothy and Mary, which left small room for an old friend's maneuvering to reestablish the free exchanges of only a few years earlier; profound disagreements about philosophical issues; Coleridge's drug addiction and physical collapse shortly before his departure for Sicily and Malta – loomed large in Coleridge's personal notebooks. Hazlitt, sensitively aware of what was happening, did not mistake Dorothy and Mary's loving ministrations during Coleridge's three-week illness for a true reconciliation.

Hazlitt's lengthy and carefully balanced review of *The Excursion*, published in *The Examiner* in 1814, irritated Wordsworth because it stressed his solipsism ('He lives in the busy solitude of his own heart; in the deep silence of thought', and much more to the same effect). Wordsworth regarded the review not merely as a literary critique, but took it as a personal attack. He had counted on the ability of favorable reviews to generate and accelerate sales, and Hazlitt had disappointed him. But he was to be stunned by an even more severe judgment, rendered by a magisterial Francis Jeffrey in the December 1814 issue of the *Edinburgh Review*: 'This will never do.' It is difficult to think of a more crushing single sentence written in an influential periodical by a highly respected critic, and published during the nineteenth century; Wordsworth soon thought of both Hazlitt and Jeffrey as his personal enemies.

The fallout affected Wordsworth's sense of who his real friends and enemies were. But, as in the case of De Quincey, from whom the Wordsworths turned away after his courtship of and marriage to a local farmer's daughter offended their sense of social proprieties, Hazlitt seems to have become involved in some sexual misbehavior in 1803. The Wordsworths neither forgot nor forgave what they thought was truly unforgivable. The evidence that might more clearly define what had happened at that time remains unclear to this day, and does not justify the lurid charges made in more than one biography. Nevertheless, many people knew that Wordsworth tried not to meet Hazlitt at social gatherings, and warned him well in advance of Hazlitt's turning up in his vicinity. He never responded affirmatively to Hazlitt's efforts to reestablish the friendship. Hazlitt, hurt by Wordsworth's taking serious umbrage at his review of *The Excursion* (which he had believed was a fair treatment of the poem's merits and failings), was to write more reviews, and have a great deal more to say about Wordsworth's publications and personality. His qualified judgments on what he regarded as the productions of a deteriorating talent were, perhaps inevitably, and certainly unfairly, interpreted by Wordsworth as sheer spitefulness. Each generation must judge anew whether Wordsworth or Hazlitt was more to blame for the disintegration of a notable friendship.

WH, *CW*, XI, 'A Reply to "Z" ',[1] 4–6

To return to your saying that I am a lounger in third-rate booksellers' shops. I answer I lounge in no booksellers' shops, third or first-rate. I sometimes indeed lounge away my time in the Fives' Court, and play at rackets, instead of answering your questions. But your not knowing me enables you to say what you please of me. It is not more likely to be true in fact, but it is not the less likely to answer your purpose on that account. You call me an essay, criticism, review and lecture manufac-turer. What of that? Where virtue is, these are most virtuous. You try to be a critic and reviewer: but you and I are critics and reviewers of a different sort; that I grant. You hate me; for that my 'name is Will.' What if I were to nickname Mr. Wordsworth 'Bill the Poet'; you would say of me what I think of you! But to our questions.

1. You ask me 'if I do not infamously vituperate and sneer at the character of Mr. Wordsworth, *videlicet*[2] his personal character; his genius even I dare not deny.' Why not: because I dare not deny my

own convictions: certainly I am bound by public opinion to acknowledge [it] in very unsparing terms, and I have in fact gone on the
forlorn hope in praising him. As to his personal character, I have said,
nothing about it: I have spoken of his intellectual egotism (and truly
and warrantably) as the bane of his talents and of his public principles.
It is because you cannot answer what I have said on the Lake School of
Poetry, that you ask me eight impertinent questions.

2. You want to know whether I do not get all my ideas about poetry
in the Lectures from gross misconceptions of Mr. Wordsworth's conversations. And I answer, No, for this reason, that I never got any idea,
at all from him, for the reason that he had none to give. All I remember of his conversation turned upon extreme instances of self-will and
self-adulation, as the following, which are given *verbatim*. 'That he
would hang up the whole house of Commons. That he wished Tierney
had shot out Mr. Pitt's tongue, to put an end to his gift of the gab.
That he saw nothing in Lord Chatham's and Lord Mansfield's speeches
to admire, and what did it end in, but their being made Lords? That
Sir Isaac Newton was a man of a little mind, if we could believe the
stories that Coleridge told about him. That as to poetry, there was
something in Shakespear that he could not make up his mind to, for
he hated those interlocutions between Lucius and Caius: and as to
Milton, the only great merit of the Paradise Lost was in the conception
or in getting rid of the horns and tail of the Devil, for as to the execution, he thought he could do as well or better himself.' There is
nothing like this in my Lectures. There is only one passage which I can
charge myself as having taken from his conversation, and I leave it to
his admirers to find it out. I have always spoken of it as a favourable
specimen of his powers of conversation on poetry, but I cannot say
that it has been remarked as a splendid patch on my 'coxcomb'
Lectures. Mr. Wordsworth's power is not that of analysis or illustration.
His head always puts me in mind of Dean Swift's reprimand to his
servant who was trying in vain to break a coal in pieces with the poker
– 'That's a stone, you blockhead!' – Mr. Wordsworth's natural aversion
to taking things in pieces, or looking into the reasons for them, and
desire of taking them in the mass, is shewn in one of the early poems,
which I hold to be authority still,

   – 'Our meddling intellect
Misshapes the beauteous forms of things:
We murder to dissect.'

3. You ask whether I do not owe my personal safety, perhaps existence, to the interference of that virtuous man in my behalf, &c. I beg
to be excused answering this question except as it relates to my
supposed ingratitude, and on that subject my answer is as follows.
Mr. Wilson tells, as I understand, in all companies the following story
of Mr. Wordsworth's particular benevolence and regard to me.

Some time in the latter end of the year 1814 Mr. Wordsworth
received an *Examiner* by the post, which annoyed him exceedingly
both on account of the expence and the paper. 'Why did they send
that rascally paper to him, and make him pay for it?' Mr. Wordsworth
is tenacious of his principles and not less so of his purse. 'Oh,' said
Wilson, 'let us see what there is in it. I dare say they have not sent it
you for nothing. Why here, there's a criticism upon the Excursion in
it.' This made the poet (*par excellence*) rage and fret the more. 'What
did they know about his poetry? What could they know about it? It
was presumption in the highest degree for these cockney writers to
pretend to criticise a Lake poet.' 'Well,' says the other, 'at any rate let
us read it.' So he began. The article was much in favour of the poet and
the poem. As the reading proceeded, 'Ha,' said Mr. Wordsworth, somewhat appeased, 'there's some sense in this fellow too: the Dog writes
strong.' Upon which Mr. Wilson was encouraged to proceed still
farther with the encomium, and Mr. Wordsworth continued his approbation; 'Upon my word very judicious, very well indeed.' At length,
growing vain with his own and the *Examiner*'s applause, he suddenly
seized the paper into his own hands, and saying 'Let me read it,
Mr. Wilson,' did so with an audible voice and appropriate gesture to
the end, when he exclaimed, 'Very well written indeed, Sir, I did not
expect a thing of this kind,' and strutting up and down the room in
high good humour kept every now and then wondering who could be
the author, 'he had no idea, and should like very much to know to
whom he was indebted for such pointed and judicious praise' — when
Mr. Wilson interrupting him with saying, 'Oh don't you know; it's
Hazlitt, to be sure, there are his initials to it,' threw our poor philosopher into a greater rage than ever, and a fit of outrageous incredulity
to think that he should be indebted for the first favourable account
that had ever appeared of any work he had ever written to a person on
whom he had conferred such great and unmerited obligations. I think
this statement will shew that there is very little love lost between me
and my benefactor. If farther proofs are called, I have them at hand,
and in a sufficient number.

WH, CW, IX, 103–6: *Uncollected Essays*: 'My First Acquaintance with Poets'

I returned home, and soon after set out on my journey with unworn heart and untired feet. My way lay through Worcester and Gloucester, and by Upton, where I thought of Tom Jones and the adventure of the muff. I remembered getting completely wet through one day, and stopping at an inn (I think it was at Tewkesbury) where I sat up all night to read Paul and Virginia. Sweet were the showers in early youth that drenched my body, and sweet the drops of pity that fell upon the books I read! I recollect a remark of Coleridge's upon this very book, that nothing could shew the gross indelicacy of French manners and the entire corruption of their imagination more strongly than the behaviour of the heroine in the last fatal scene, who turns away from a person on board the sinking vessel, that offers to save her life, because he has thrown off his clothes to assist him in swimming. Was this a time to think of such a circumstance? I once hinted to Wordsworth as we were sailing in his boat on Grasmere lake, that I thought he had borrowed the idea of his *Poems on the Naming of Places* from the local inscriptions of the same kind in Paul and Virginia. He did not own the obligation, and stated some distinction without a difference, in defence of his claim to originality. Any the slightest variation would be sufficient for this purpose in his mind; for whatever *he* added or omitted would inevitably be worth all that any one else had done, and contain the marrow of the sentiment. – I was still two days before the time fixed for my arrival, for I had taken care to set out early enough. I stopped these two days at Bridgewater, and when I was tired of sauntering on the banks of its muddy river, returned to the inn, and read Camilla. So have I loitered my life away, reading books, looking at pictures, going to plays, hearing, thinking, writing on what pleased me best. I have wanted only one thing to make me happy; but wanting that, have wanted every thing!

I arrived and was well received. The country about Nether Stowey is beautiful, green and hilly, and near the sea-shore. I saw it but the other day, after an interval of twenty years, from a hill near Taunton. How was the map of my life spread out before me, as the map of the country lay at my feet! In the afternoon, Coleridge took me over to All-Foxden, a romantic old family-mansion of the St Aubins, where Wordsworth lived. It was then in the possession of a friend of the poet's, who gave him the free use of it. Somehow that period (the time just after the

French Revolution) was not a time when *nothing was given for nothing*.
The mind opened, and a softness might be perceived coming over the
heart of individuals, beneath 'the scales that fence' our self-interest.
Wordsworth himself was from home, but his sister kept house, and set
before us a frugal repast; and we had free access to her brother's poems,
the *Lyrical Ballads*, which were still in manuscript, or in the form of
Sibylline Leaves. I dipped into a few of these with great satisfaction, and
with the faith of a novice. I slept that night in an old room with blue
hangings, and covered with the round-faced family-portraits of the age
of George I and II and from the wooded declivity of the adjoining park
that overlooked my window, at the dawn of day, could

hear the loud stag speak.

In the outset of life (and particularly at this time I felt it so) our
imagination has a body to it. We are in a state between sleeping and
waking, and have indistinct but glorious glimpses of strange shapes,
and there is always something to come better than what we see. As in
our dreams the fulness of the blood gives warmth and reality to the
coinage of the brain, so in youth our ideas are clothed, and fed, and
pampered with our good spirits; we breathe thick with thoughtless
happiness, the weight of future years presses on the strong pulses of
the heart, and we repose with undisturbed faith in truth and good. As
we advance, we exhaust our fund of enjoyment and of hope. We are
no longer wrapped in *lamb's-wool*, lulled in Elysium. As we taste the
pleasures of life, their spirit evaporates, the sense palls; and nothing is
left but the phantoms, the lifeless shadows of what *has been!*
That morning, as soon as breakfast was over, we strolled out into the
park, and seating ourselves on the trunk of an old ash-tree that
stretched along the ground, Coleridge read aloud with a sonorous and
musical voice, the ballad of *Betty Foy*. I was not critically or sceptically
inclined. I saw touches of truth and nature, and took the rest for
granted. But in the *Thorn*, the *Mad Mother*, and the *Complaint of a Poor
Indian Woman*, I felt that deeper power and pathos which have been
since acknowledged,

In spite of pride, in erring reason's spite,

as the characteristics of this author; and the sense of a new style and a
new spirit in poetry came over me. It had to me something of the

effect that arises from the turning up of the fresh soil, or of the first welcome breath of Spring,

> While yet the trembling year is unconfirmed.

Coleridge and myself walked back to Stowey that evening, and his voice sounded high

> Of Providence, foreknowledge, will, and fate,
> Fix'd fate, free-will, foreknowledge absolute,

as we passed through echoing grove, by fairy stream or waterfall, gleaming in the summer moonlight! He lamented that Wordsworth was not prone enough to belief in the traditional superstitions of the place, and that there was a something corporeal, a *matter-of-fact-ness*, a clinging to the palpable, or often to the petty, in his poetry, in consequence. His genius was not a spirit that descended to him through the air; it sprung out of the ground like a flower, or unfolded itself from a green spray, on which the gold-finch sang. He said, however (if I remember right) that this objection must be confined to his descriptive pieces, that his philosophic poetry had a grand and comprehensive spirit in it, so that his soul seemed to inhabit the universe like a palace, and to discover truth by intuition, rather than by deduction. The next day Wordsworth arrived from Bristol at Coleridge's cottage. I think I see him now. He answered in some degree to his friend's description of him, but was more gaunt and Don Quixote-like. He was quaintly dressed (according to the *costume* of that unconstrained period) in a brown fustian jacket and striped pantaloons. There was something of a roll, a lounge in his gait, not unlike his own Peter Bell. There was a severe, worn pressure of thought about his temples, a fire in his eye (as if he saw something in objects more than the outward appearance) an intense high-narrow forehead, a Roman nose, cheeks furrowed by strong purpose and feeling, and a convulsive inclination to laughter about the mouth, a good deal at variance with the solemn, stately expression of the rest of his face. Chantry's bust[3] wants the marking traits; but he was teazed into making it regular and heavy: Haydon's head of him, introduced into the *Entrance of Christ into Jerusalem*, is the most like his drooping weight of thought and expression. He sat down and talked very naturally and freely, with a mixture of clear gushing accents in his voice, a deep guttural intonation, and a strong tincture of the northern *burr*, like the crust on wine. He instantly began to make havoc of the half of a Cheshire cheese on the table, and said triumphantly that 'his marriage with experience had not been so unproductive as Mr Southey's in teaching him a knowledge of the good things of this life.' He had been to see the *Castle Spectre* by Monk Lewis, while at Bristol, and described it very well. He said 'it fitted the taste of the audience like a glove.'[4] This *ad captandum* merit was however by no means a recommendation of it, according to the severe principles of the new school, which reject rather than court popular effect. Wordsworth, looking out of the low, latticed window, said, 'How beautifully the sun sets on that yellow bank!' I thought within myself, 'With what eyes these poets see nature!' and ever after, when I saw the sun-set stream upon the objects facing it, conceived I had made a discovery, or thanked Mr Wordsworth for having made one for me! We went over to All-Foxden again the day following, and Wordsworth read us the story of Peter Bell in the open air; and the comment made upon it by his face and voice was very different from that of some later critics! Whatever might be thought of the poem, 'his face was as a book where men might read strange matters,' and he announced the fate of his hero in prophetic tones. There is a *chaunt* in the recitation both of Coleridge and Wordsworth, which acts as a spell upon the hearer, and disarms the judgment. Perhaps they have deceived themselves by making habitual use of this ambiguous accompaniment. Coleridge's manner is more full, animated, and varied; Wordsworth's more equable, sustained, and internal. The one might be termed more *dramatic*, the other more *lyrical*. Coleridge has told me that he himself liked to compose in walking over uneven ground, or breaking through the straggling branches of a copsewood; whereas Wordsworth always wrote (if he could) walking up and down a strait gravel-walk, or in some spot where the continuity of his verse met with no collateral interpretation. Returning that same evening, I got into a metaphysical argument with Wordsworth, while Coleridge was explaining the different notes of the nightingale to his sister, in which we neither of us succeeded in making ourselves perfectly clear and intelligible. Thus I passed three weeks at Nether Stowey and in the neighbourhood, generally devoting the afternoons to a delightful chat in an arbour made of bark by the poet's friend Tom Poole, sitting under two fine elm-trees, and listening to the bees humming round us, while we quaffed our *flip*.

WH, CW, XI, 91–5: 'Mr. Wordsworth' [subsection of *The Spirit of the Age, or Contemporary Portraits*, first published anonymously in one 8vo. volume by S. and R. Bentley, London, 1825; revised and expanded by Hazlitt, and reprinted by Henry Colburn, London, 1825, in two small 8vo. volumes]

Mr. Wordsworth, in his person, is above the middle size, with marked features, and an air somewhat stately and Quixotic. He reminds one of some of Holbein's heads, grave, saturnine, with a slight indication of sly humour, kept under by the manners of the age or by the pretensions of the person. He has a peculiar sweetness in his smile, and great depth and manliness and a rugged harmony, in the tones of his voice. His manner of reading his own poetry is particularly imposing; and in his favourite passages his eye beams with preternatural lustre, and the meaning labours slowly up from his swelling breast. No one who has seen him at these moments could go away with an impression that he was a 'man of no mark or likelihood.' Perhaps the comment of his face and voice is necessary to convey a full idea of his poetry. His language may not be intelligible, but his manner is not to be mistaken. It is clear that he is either mad or inspired. In company, even in a *tête-à-tête*, Mr. Wordsworth is often silent, indolent, and reserved. If he is become verbose and oracular of late years, he was not so in his better days. He threw out a bold or an indifferent remark without either effort or pretension, and relapsed into musing again. He shone most (because he seemed most roused and animated) in reciting his own poetry, or in talking about it. He sometimes gave striking views of his feelings and trains of association in composing certain passages; or if one did not always understand his distinctions, still there was no want of interest – there was a latent meaning worth inquiring into, like a vein of ore that one cannot exactly hit upon at the moment, but of which there are sure indications. His standard of poetry is high and severe, almost to exclusiveness. He admits of nothing below, scarcely of any thing above himself. It is fine to hear him talk of the way in which certain subjects should have been treated by eminent poets, according to his notions of the art. Thus he finds fault with Dryden's description of Bacchus in the *Alexander's Feast*, as if he were a mere good-looking youth, or boon companion—

'Flushed with a purple grace,
He shows his honest face'—

instead of representing the God returning from the conquest of India, crowned with vine-leaves, and drawn by panthers, and followed by troops of satyrs, of wild men and animals that he had tamed. You would think, in hearing him speak on this subject, that you saw Titian's picture of the meeting of *Bacchus and Ariadne*—so classic were his conceptions, so glowing his style. Milton is his great idol, and he sometimes dares to compare himself with him. His Sonnets, indeed, have something of the same high-raised tone and prophetic spirit. Chaucer is another prime favourite of his, and he has been at the pains to modernize some of the Canterbury Tales. Those persons who look upon Mr. Wordsworth as a merely puerile writer, must be rather at a loss to account for his strong predilection for such geniuses as Dante and Michael Angelo. We do not think our author has any very cordial sympathy with Shakespear. How should he? Shakespear was the least of an egotist of any body in the world. He does not much relish the variety and scope of dramatic composition. 'He hates those interlocutions between Lucius and Caius. Yet Mr. Wordsworth himself wrote a tragedy when he was young; and we have heard the following energetic lines quoted from it, as put into the mouth of a person smit with remorse for some rash crime:

——'Action is momentary,
The motion of a muscle this way or that;
Suffering is long, obscure, and infinite!'[5]

Perhaps for want of light and shade, and the unshackled spirit of the drama, this performance was never brought forward. Our critic has a great dislike to Gray, and a fondness for Thomson and Collins. It is mortifying to hear him speak of Pope and Dryden, whom, because they have been supposed to have all the possible excellences of poetry, he will allow to have none. Nothing, however, can be fairer, or more amusing, than the way in which he sometimes exposes the unmeaning verbiage of modern poetry. Thus, in the beginning of Dr. Johnson's *Vanity of Human Wishes*—

'Let observation with extensive view
Survey mankind from China to Peru'—

he says there is a total want of imagination accompanying the words, the same idea is repeated three times under the disguise of a different phraseology: it comes to this—'let *observation*, with extensive *observation*, *observe* mankind'; or take away the first line, and the second,

'Survey mankind from China to Peru,'

literally conveys the whole. Mr. Wordsworth is, we must say, a perfect Drawcansir[6] as to prose writers. He complains of the dry reasoners and matter-of-fact people for their want of *passion*; and he is jealous of the rhetorical declaimers and rhapsodists as trenching on the province of poetry. He condemns all French writers (as well of poetry as prose) in the lump. His list in this way is indeed small. He approves of Walton's Angler, Paley, and some other writers of an inoffensive modesty of pretension. He also likes books of voyages and travels, and Robinson Crusoe. In art, he greatly esteems Bewick's woodcuts, and Waterloo's sylvan etchings.[7] But he sometimes takes a higher tone, and gives his mind fair play. We have known him enlarge with a noble intelligence and enthusiasm on Nicolas Poussin's fine landscape-compositions, pointing out the unity of design that pervades them, the superintending mind, the imaginative principle that brings all to bear on the same end; and declaring he would not give a rush for any landscape that did not express the time of day, the climate, the period of the world it was meant to illustrate, or had not this character of *wholeness* in it. His eye also does justice to Rembrandt's fine and masterly effects. In the way in which that artist works something out of nothing, and transforms the stump of a tree, a common figure into an *ideal* object, by the gorgeous light and shade thrown upon it, he perceives an analogy to his own mode of investing the minute details of nature with an atmosphere of sentiment; and in pronouncing Rembrandt to be a man of genius, feels that he strengthens his own claim to the title. It has been said of Mr. Wordsworth, that 'he hates conchology, that he hates the Venus of Medicis.' But these, we hope, are mere epigrams and *jeux-d'esprit*, as far from truth as they are free from malice; a sort of running satire or critical clenches—

'Where one for sense and one for rhyme
Is quite sufficient at one time.'

We think, however, that if Mr. Wordsworth had been a more liberal and candid critic, he would have been a more sterling writer. If a greater number of sources of pleasure had been open to him, he would have communicated pleasure to the world more frequently. Had he been less fastidious in pronouncing sentence on the works of others, his own would have been received more favourably, and treated more leniently. The current of his feelings is deep, but narrow; the range of his understanding is lofty and aspiring rather than discursive. The force, the originality, the absolute truth and identity with which he feels some things, makes him indifferent to so many others. The simplicity and enthusiasm of his feelings, with respect to nature, renders him bigotted and intolerant in his judgments of men and things. But it happens to him, as to others, that his strength lies in his weakness; and perhaps we have no right to complain. We might get rid of the cynic and the egotist, and find in his stead a commonplace man. We should 'take the good the Gods provide us': a fine and original vein of poetry is not one of their most contemptible gifts, and the rest is scarcely worth thinking of, except as it may be a mortification to those who expect perfection from human nature; or who have been idle enough at some period of their lives, to deify men of genius as possessing claims above it. But this is a chord that jars, and we shall not dwell upon it.

Lord Byron we have called, according to the old proverb, 'the spoiled child of fortune': Mr. Wordsworth might plead, in mitigation of some peculiarities, that he is 'the spoiled child of disappointment.' We are convinced, if he had been early a popular poet, he would have borne his honours meekly, and would have been a person of great *bonhommie* and frankness of disposition. But the sense of injustice and of undeserved ridicule sours the temper and narrows the views. To have produced works of genius, and to find them neglected or treated with scorn, is one of the heaviest trials of human patience. We exaggerate our own merits when they are denied by others, and are apt to grudge and cavil at every particle of praise bestowed on those to whom we feel a conscious superiority. In mere self-defence we turn against the world, when it turns against us; brood over the undeserved slights we receive; and thus the genial current of the soul is stopped, or vents itself in effusions of petulance and self-conceit. Mr. Wordsworth has thought too much of contemporary critics and criticism; and less than he ought of the award of posterity, and of the opinion, we do not say of private friends, but of those who were made so by their admiration of his genius. He did not court popularity by a conformity to established models, and he ought not to have been surprised that his originality was not understood as a matter of course. He has *gnawed too much on the bridle*; and has often thrown out crusts to the critics, in mere defiance or as a point of honour when he was challenged, which otherwise his own good sense would have withheld. We suspect that Mr. Wordsworth's feelings are a little morbid in this respect, or that he resents censure more than he is gratified by praise. Otherwise, the tide has turned much in his favour of late years—he has a large body of determined partisans—and is at present sufficiently in request with the public to save or relieve him from the last necessity to which a man of genius can be reduced—that of becoming the God of his own idolatry!

Notes

1 'Z' is the pseudonym disguising the identities of John Gibson Lockhart and John Wilson. These two young barristers, not long out of Oxford, were hired by William Blackwood, in the Fall of 1817, to reinvigorate the literary coverage of his periodical: *Blackwood's*. Lockhart and Gibson vigorously attacked various writers who, they believed, were led by Leigh Hunt. Those being ridiculed constituted a 'conceited knot of superficial coxcombs', and were no better than 'superficial coxcombs' loosely organized into a 'cockney school of poetry'.

    Blackwood was pleased because the circulation of his periodical was steadily rising. In one diatribe 'Z' claimed that Wordsworth (whom Lockhart and Wilson admired) had been kept 'poor, miserably poor for twenty years' while he suffered from Jeffrey's 'malicious laughter'. (The assumption of 'Z' was that Hazlitt and Jeffrey shared similar low opinions of Wordsworth's talent.) These savage sneers crossed boundary lines of good taste.

    Hazlitt in the selection reprinted here attempted to answer by calling Lockhart and Wilson the 'Jackalls of the North'. He was especially irritated by the (untrue) charge that he was 'pimpled'. ('Z' repeated the charge several times.)

    Hazlitt's anger at such *ad hominem* attacks was genuine; he was not trying simply to continue a literary controversy. In addition to his 'Reply', he sued *Blackwood's*, and won a court judgment: his expenses were reimbursed, and he was understandably pleased by a private settlement of one hundred pounds.

    The incident of an *Examiner* review, singled out by Hazlitt as a prime example of the tactics used by 'Z', seems to have depended on details supplied by Wilson, who at the time was living at Elleray, above Windermere. It is probable that the publication of the anecdote permanently damaged the possibility of any reconciliation between Hazlitt and Wordsworth.

2 *videlicet*: clearly, plainly.

3 Sir Francis Legett Chantrey (1782–1841) switched from an unpromising life as a grocer's apprentice (he was sixteen years old) to what soon became a successful career in portrait painting, wood-carving, and modelling in clay. His busts are generally regarded as his finest works.

4 Matthew Gregory Lewis (1778–1818) wrote several 'Gothick' works of fiction. *The Monk* (1798) was so popular that he became known as 'Monk' for the rest of his life. He supplanted Ann Radcliffe as the creator of morally ambiguous villains. *Castle Spectre*, which he wrote after taking up a second career as a playwright, enjoyed a huge success. Wordsworth detested the play. Writing to James Webbe Tobin (6 March 1798), he began by conceding that he was

'perfectly easy about the theatre' if he had 'no other method of enjoying [himself]'. He continued: 'Lewis's success would have thrown me into despair. The *Castle Spectre* is a spectre indeed.' (Since he did not see the play in production until late May, he probably had read a printed copy.)

5   *The Borderers*, a drama first drafted by Wordsworth in 1796–97, available only in manuscript form until a heavily revised version was published (1841–42), is the play to which Hazlitt refers. The early version of the quoted lines – which Hazlitt may have quoted from memory – reads thus:

> Action is transitory, a step, a blow –
> 'Tis done – and in the after vacancy
> We wonder at ourselves like men betray'd.
> Suffering is permanent, obscure and dark,
> And has the nature of infinity.

This passage was slightly revised in the late version. For the texts of both versions, see the edition of *The Borderers*, edited by Robert Osborn (Ithaca: Cornell University Press, 1982).

6   In *The Rehearsal* (1670), by George Villiers, Duke of Buckingham (a burlesque of heroic dramas such as those written by John Dryden), Drawcansir enters a battle and kills all the combatants on both sides.

7   Thomas Bewick (1783–1828) was a largely self-educared wood engraver, whose illustrations for many books, especially that of *British Birds*, won him steady patronage and fame as a teacher of younger artists.

Antoni Waterloo (1609–90) was a Dutch painter, publisher, draughtsman, and acclaimed etcher. His prints, especially those which depicted forests and trees, enjoyed enormous popularity and respect over a period of two centuries.

James Henry Leigh Hunt (1784–1859)

Leigh Hunt's contributions to the development of the Romantic Movement were more significant than Wordsworth allowed in a number of patronizing comments. Placed within a context, Wordsworth's remarks may have been, more than anything else, repayments for Hunt's endorsement of his own work. Wordsworth repeated more than once his assessment: Hunt possessed 'Talents' rather than an ability to produce creative work of lasting importance. When he sent Hunt a copy of his *Poems*, he mentioned his 'pleasure' at hearing from Lord Brougham that his writings were 'valued by Mr Hunt'. The letter, dated 12 February 1815, did not accompany the volumes, which were sent on 26 April. Hunt took even longer to acknowledge the gift, delaying his response for three months. He neither wrote nor solicited the writing of a review that might have appeared in the *Examiner*. (Wordsworth wanted one.)

Almost fifteen years later Wordsworth praised Hunt's rendering of Chaucer's Mauncipal's Tale in *Chaucer's Poems Modernized* (1840), but could not resist adding that he himself had 'modernized' it 'many years ago', as if doing so foreclosed the issue, and even though he had decided not to add it to his other contributions to the anthology (demurring on the ground that it was 'too indelicate for pure taste to be offered to the world at this time').

Yet, after the publication of Hunt's first version of *The Feast of the Poets* in the *Reflector* (1811), Wordsworth had apparently noted the characterization of the Lake Poets – Southey ('Bob'), Wordsworth ('Billy'), and Coleridge ('Sam') – as 'asses'. Perhaps he decided to overlook it, or to forgive its injury to his self-regard. But it proved impossible to depend on continuing respect for himself in Hunt's writings, even though Hunt changed his mind (in Wordsworth's favor) after reading *The Excursion* and rereading Wordsworth's sonnets and shorter poems. In a reprinting of *The Feast of the Poets* he toned down his ridicule, and omitted the damning lines,

> And as to that Wordsworth! he'd been so benurst,
> Second childhood with him had come close on the first.

Henry Crabb Robinson noted (9 May 1815) that Wordsworth was 'by no means satisfied with Hunt's judgment of him'. On 13 June, Benjamin Robert Haydon and Wordsworth called on an ailing Hunt, who insisted that he had 'reformed in his opinions'. He told Wordsworth that he had become 'the most ardent' of his general admirers. The flattery, about which Hunt was entirely sincere, was enough, at least for that moment, and Wordsworth did not fail to notice that a copy of his poems was kept on a shelf next to a volume of Milton's works. (The second revision of *The Feast of the Poets*, with its notes, was published in 1815, after this visit.)

Hunt's opposition to Wordsworth's heavy emphasis on the theoretical underpinnings of his poetry grew from his sense that it did not, and could not, compensate for the choices Wordsworth made when he chose his subject matter: 'Idiot Boys, Mad Mothers, Wandering Jews, Visitations of Ague, (Indian Women left to die on the road . . .)'. Or, for that matter, Wordsworth's insistence on the kind of language that most appropriately suited these characters, presented without nuance, variety, or any distinction 'between natural and artificial associations'. Hunt acknowledged Wordsworth's greatness, even while adding codicils and reservations and indicating that his admiration could never be whole hearted.

The relationship between both men was strained still one more time when Hunt's review of *Peter Bell* appeared in the *Examiner* (1819). The book was described as 'another didactic little horror of Mr Wordsworth's'. Despite this summing-up, and similar negative verdicts by other reviewers, *Peter Bell* sold so briskly that Wordsworth chose not to make an issue of Hunt's airy dismissal.

Hunt's *Autobiography* states that he did not meet Wordsworth again for thirty years, without adding that plentiful opportunities to meet him had offered themselves. It was odd, at any rate, that Hunt, who revelled in his friendships with fellow-poets, was not exactly eager to develop a friendship with the man he had named 'the first poet of the day'. Hunt's *Poetical Works*, published by Edward Moxon, appeared in 1832, and perhaps the statement that Wordsworth had 'become a classic' indicates something of the strain which Hunt experienced every time he attempted to summarize Wordsworth's contribution to the age.

He knew that Wordsworth had very much liked his play, *A Legend of Florence* (1839); Richard Hengist Horne, a trustworthy friend, had written to tell him so (1 November 1839).

Yet the distance between Hunt and Wordsworth could not be permanently bridged. In 1844 Hunt edited an anthology of his favorite poems, and gave it a rollicking title: *Imagination and Fancy; or, Selections from the English Poets, illustrative of those First Requisites of their Art; with Markings of the best Passages, Critical Notices of the Writers, and an Essay in*

Answer to the Question, 'What is Poetry?' Hunt discoursed on the importance of poetry, and the ways in which it educated through the giving of
pleasure. His admiration of Coleridge, Shelley, and Keats was eloquently
expressed. Wordsworth, however, did not supply any of the 'best passages' that Hunt chose to illustrate either imagination or fancy.

Leigh Hunt, 'Note', attached to the text of the 1814 version of *The Feast of the Poets*; rpt, Robert Woof, ed., *William Wordsworth: the Critical Heritage*, Volume I, 1793–1820 (London: Routledge, Taylor and Francis Group, 2001), 332–9[1]

Whatever may be the faults of Mr. Wordsworth, it certainly appears to
me, that we have had no poet since the days of Spenser and Milton, –
so allied in the better part of his genius to those favoured men, not
excepting even Collins, who saw farther into the sacred places of
poetry than any man of the last age. Mr. Wordsworth speaks less of the
vulgar tongue of the profession than any writer since that period; he
always thinks when he speaks, has always words at command, feels
deeply, fancies richly, and never descends from that pure and elevated
morality, which is the native region of the first order of poetical spirits.

  To those who doubt the justice of this character, and who have hitherto seen in Mr. Wordsworth nothing but trifling and childishness, and
who at the same time speak with rapture of Spenser and Milton, I
would only recommend the perusal of such poems as the Female
Vagrant, a little piece on the Nightingale,* the three little exquisite
pieces ['Strange fits of passion', 'She dwelt among the untrodden ways',
'I travell'd among unknown Men' (in 1814 'A slumber did my spirit
seal')], another ['Three years she grew'], – the Old Cumberland Beggar
(a piece of perfect description philosophized), – Louisa, the Happy
Warrior, to H.C., the Sonnet entitled London, another on Westminster
Bridge, another beginning 'The World is too much with us,' the majestic simplicity of the Ode to Duty, a noble subject most nobly treated,
⟨and the simple, deep-felt, and calm yet passionate grandeur of the
poem entitled Laodamia.⟩ If after this, they can still see nothing beau-

---

⟨* Another poem on this bird mentioned in the former edition was, I afterwards found, Mr. Coleridge's; and I had to congratulate myself accordingly
on having said what I had, in a previous note, respecting his congeniality
with Mr. Wordsworth in point of real powers. It is a pity that all the poems
written by Mr. Coleridge are not collected in one publication.⟩

tiful or great in Mr. Wordsworth's writings, we must conclude that their insight into the beauties of Spenser and Milton is imaginary – and that they speak in praise of those writers as they do in dispraise of Mr. Wordsworth, merely by rote.

It may be asked me then, why, with such opinions as I entertain of the greatness of Mr. Wordsworth's genius, he is treated as he is in ⟨some of⟩ the verses before us; I answer, because he abuses that genius so as Milton or Spenser never abused it, and so as to endanger [destroy *1814*] those great ends of poetry, by which it should assist the uses and refresh the spirits of life. From him, to whom much is given, much shall be required. Mr. Wordsworth is capable of being at the head of a new and great age of poetry; and in point of fact, I do not deny that he is so already, as the greatest poet of the present; – but in point of effect, in point of delight and utility, he appears to me to have made a mistake unworthy of him, and to have sought by eccentricity and by a turning away from society, what he might have obtained by keeping to his proper and more neighbourly sphere. Had he written always in the spirit of the pieces above-mentioned, his readers would have felt nothing but delight and gratitude; but another spirit interferes, calculated to do good neither to their taste nor reflections; and after having been elevated and depressed, refreshed and sickened, pained, pleased, and tortured, we ⟨sometimes⟩ close his volumes, as we finish a melancholy day, with feelings that would go to sleep in forgetfulness, and full waking faculties too busy to suffer it.

The theory of Mr. Wordsworth, – if I may venture to give in a few words my construction of the curious and, in many respects, very masterly preface to the Lyrical Ballads, is this; – that owing to a variety of existing causes, among which are the accumulation of men in cities and the necessary uniformity of their occupations, – and the consequent craving for extraordinary incident, which the present state of the world is quick to gratify, the taste of society has become so vitiated and so accustomed to gross stimulants, such as 'frantic novels, *sickly* and stupid German tragedies, and deluges of *idle* and *extravagant* stories in verse,' as to require the counteraction of some simpler and more primitive food, which should restore to readers their true tone of enjoyment, and enable them to relish once more the beauties of simplicity and nature; – that, to this purpose, a poet in the present age, who looked upon men with his proper eye, as an entertainer and instructor, should chuse subjects as far removed as possible from artificial excitements, and appeal to the great and primary affections of our nature; – thirdly and lastly, that these subjects, to be worthily and effectively treated, should be clothed in language equally artless. I pass over the contingent parts of the Preface, though touching out, as they go, some beautiful ideas respecting poets and poetry in general, both because I have neither time nor room to consider them, and because they are not so immediate to my purpose. I shall merely observe, by the way, that Mr. Wordsworth ⟨though he has a fine Miltonic ear,⟩ does not seem to have exercised his reflections much on the subject of versification, and must protest against that attempt of his to consider perfect poetry as not essentially connected with metre, – an innovation, which would detract from the poet's properties, and shut up one of the finest inlets of his enjoyment and nourishers of his power – the sense of the harmonious.*

Now the object of the theory here mentioned has clearly nothing in the abstract, that can offend the soundest good sense or the best poetical ambition. In fact, it is only saying, in other words, that it is high time for poetry in general to return to nature and to a natural style, and that he will perform a great and useful work to society, who shall assist it to do so. I am not falling, by this interpretation, into the error which Mr. Wordsworth very justly deprecates, when he warns his readers against affecting to agree with him in terms, when they really differ with him in taste. The truth which he tells, however obvious, is necessary to be told and to be told loudly; and he should enjoy the praise which he deserves of having been the first, in these times, to proclaim it. But the question is (and he himself puts it at the end of his Preface,) has Mr. Wordsworth 'attained his object?' Has he acted up to his theory? Has he brought back that natural style, and restored to us those healthy and natural perceptions, which he justly describes as the proper state of our poetical constitution? I think not. He has shown that he could do it, and in many [some 1814] instances he has set the example; but the effect of at least many other passages in his poetry, and those, I believe, which he views with most partiality, appears to me to be otherwise: it tends, in my mind, to go to the other extreme of what he deprecates, and to substitute one set of diseased perceptions for another.

Delight or utility is the aim of the poet. Mr. Wordsworth, like one who has a true sense of the dignity of his profession, would unite both; and indeed, for their perfect ends, they cannot be separated. He finds then our taste for the one vitiated, and our profit of the other destroyed, and he says to us, 'Your complexion is diseased; – your blood fevered; you endeavour to keep up your pleasurable sensations by stimulants too violent to last, and which must be succeeded by

---

⟨* In the preface to the late edition of his poems, Mr. Wordsworth seems to have tacitly retracted on this head.⟩

others of still greater violence: – this will not do: your mind wants air and exercise, – fresh thoughts and natural excitements: – up, my friend; come out with me among the beauties of nature and the simplicities of life, and feel the breath of heaven about you.' – No advice can be better: we feel the call instinctively; we get up, accompany the poet into his walks, and acknowledge them to be the best and most beautiful; but what do we meet there? Idiot Boys, Mad Mothers, Wandering Jews, Visitations of Ague, ⟨Indian Women left to die on the road,⟩ and Frenzied Mariners, who are fated to accost us with tales that almost make one's faculties topple over.* – These are his refreshing thoughts, his natural excitements; and when you have finished with these, you shall have the smallest of your fugitive reflections arrested and embodied in a long lecture upon a thorn, or a story of a duffel-cloak, till thorns and duffel-cloaks absolutely confound you with their importance in life; – and these are his elementary feelings, his calm and counteracting simplicities.

Let the reader observe that I am not objecting to these subjects in behalf of that cowardly self-love falsely called sensibility, or merely because they are of what is termed a distressing description, but because they are carried to an *excess* that defeats the poet's intention, and distresses to no purpose. Nor should I select them as exhibiting a part of the character of Mr. Wordsworth's writings, rather than pass them over as what they really are, the defects of a great poet, – if the author himself had not especially invited our attention towards them as part of his system of counteraction, and if these and his occasional puerilities of style, in their disadvantageous effect upon his readers, did not involve the whole character and influence of his poetry.

But how is our passion for stimulants to be allayed by the substitution of stories like Mr. Wordsworth's? He wishes to turn aside our thirst for extraordinary intelligence to more genial sources of interest, and he gives us accounts of mothers who have gone mad at the loss of their children, of others who have killed their's [*sic*] in the most horrible manner, and of hard-hearted masters whose imaginations have revenged upon them the curses of the poor. In like manner, he would clear up and simplicize our thoughts; and he tells us tales of children that have no notion of death, of boys who would halloo to a landscape nobody knew why, and of an hundred inexpressible sensations, intended by nature no doubt to affect us, and even pleasurably so in the

---

⟨*   The last of these 'idle and extravagant stories' was written, it seems, by Mr. Coleridge. The pieces, by the way, supplied by this gentleman, have been left out of the late collection of Mr. Wordsworth's poems.⟩

general feeling, but only calculated to perplex or sadden us in our attempts at analysis. Now it appears to me, that all the craving after intelligence, which Mr. Wordsworth imagines to be the bane of the present state of society, is a healthy appetite in comparison to these morbid abstractions: the former tends, at any rate, to fix the eyes of mankind in a lively manner upon the persons that preside over their interests, and to keep up a certain demand for knowledge and public improvement; – the latter, under the guise of interesting us in the individuals of our species, turns our thoughts away from society and men altogether, and nourishes that eremitical vagueness of sensation, – that making a business of reverie, – that despair of getting to any conclusion to any purpose, which is the next step to melancholy or indifference.

It is with this persuasion, – a persuasion, which has not come to me through the want of acquaintance either with solitude or society, or with the cares of either, – that I have ventured upon the piece of ridicule in the text. Mr. Wordsworth has beautifully told us, that to him

> —the meanest flow'r that blows can give
> Thoughts that do often lie too deep for tears.

I have no doubt of it; and far be it from me to cast stones into the well in which they lie, – to disturb those reposing waters, – that freshness at the bottom of warm hearts, – those thoughts, which if they are too deep for tears, are also, in their best mood, too tranquil even for smiles. Far be it also from me to hinder the communication of such thoughts to mankind, when they are not sunk beyond their proper depth, so as to make one dizzy in looking down to them. The work of Shakespeare is full of them; but he has managed to apply them to their proper refreshing purposes; and has given us but one fond recluse in his whole works, – the melancholy Jaques. Shall we forget the attractions which this melancholy philosopher felt towards another kind of philosopher, whom he met in the forest, and who made a jest of every thing? Let us be sure, that this is one of the results of pushing our abstractions too far, and of that dangerous art which Mr. Wordsworth has claimed for his simpler pieces, – the giving importance to actions and situations by our feelings, instead of adapting our feelings to the importance they posses. The consequence of this, if carried into a system, would be, that we could make any thing or nothing important, just as diseased or healthy impulses told us; – a straw might awaken in us as many profound, but certainly not as useful reflections, as the fellow-creature that lay upon it; till at last, perplexed between the importance which every thing had obtained in our imaginations, and the little use of this new system of equality to the action and government of life, we might turn from elevating to depreciating, – from thinking trifling things important, to thinking important things trifling; and conclude our tale of extremes by closing in with expedience and becoming men of the world. – I would not willingly disturb the spirit, in which these remarks are written, by unpleasant allusions: but among the numerous acquaintances of Mr. Wordsworth, who have fallen in with his theories, perhaps he may be reminded of some, who have exemplified what I mean. He himself, though marked as government property, may walk about his fields uninjured, from the usual simplicity of his life and from very ignorance of what he has undergone; but those who never possessed the real wisdom of his simplicity, will hardly retain the virtue; and as in less healthy men, a turn for the worst taste of his reverie would infallibly be symptomatic of a weak state of stomach rather than of a fine strength of fancy, so in men of less intellect, the imitation of his smaller simplicities is little else but an announcement of that vanity and weakness of mind, which is open to the first skilful corrupter that wishes to make use of it.

With regard to the language in which Mr. Wordsworth says that poetry should be written, his mistake seems to be this, – that instead of allowing degrees and differences in what is poetical, he would have all poetry to be one and the same in point of style, and no distinction allowed between natural and artificial associations. Nobody will contend with him that the language of nature is the best of all languages, and that the poet is at his height when he can be most fanciful and most feeling in expressions the most neighbourly and intelligible; but the poet may sometimes chuse to show his art in a manner more artful, and appealing to more particular associations than what are shared by the world at large, as those of classical readers for instance. It is true, by so doing, he narrows his dominion, and gives up the glory of a greater and more difficult sway; but he still rules us by a legitimate title, and is still a poet. In the one instance, he must have all the properties of the greatest of his profession, – fancy, feeling, knowledge; – in the other, he requires less feeling, and for knowledge may substitute learning; – a great inferiority no doubt, but still only differing in degree, for learning is but the knowledge of books, as knowledge is the learning of things.

. . . [Wordsworth] talks of selection in the very midst of what appears to others an absolute contempt of it. Now selection has an eye to effect, and is an acknowledgment that what is always at hand, though it may be equally natural, is not equally pleasing. Who are to be the judges then between him and his faults? Those, I think, who, delighted with his nature, and happy to see and to allow that he has merits of his own superior to his felicitous imitations of Milton, (for the latter, after all, though admired by some as his real excellence, are only the occasional and perhaps unconscious tributes of his admiration,) are yet dissatisfied and mortified with such encounterings of the bellman, as 'Harry Gill and We are Seven;' – who think that in some of the effusions called 'Moods of My Own Mind,'* he mistakes the commonest process of reflection for its result, and the ordinary, every-day musings of any lover of the fields for original thinking; – who are of opinion, in short, that there is an extreme in nature as well as in art, and that this extreme, though not equally removed from the point of perfection, is as different from what it ought to be and what nature herself intended it to be, as the ragged horse in the desert is to the beautiful creature under the Arab, or the dreamer in a hermitage to the waking philosopher in society.

To conclude this inordinate note: Mr. Wordsworth, in objecting to one extreme, has gone to another, – the natural commencement perhaps of all revolutions. He thinks us over-active, and would make us over-contemplative, – a fault not likely to extend very widely, but which ought still to be deprecated for the sake of those to whom it would. We are, he thinks, too much crowded together, and too subject, in consequence, to high-fevered tastes and worldly infections. Granted: – he, on the other hand, lives too much apart and is subject, we think, to low-fevered tastes and solitary morbidities; – but as there is health in both of us, suppose both parties strike a bargain, – he to come among us a little more and get a true sense of our action, – we to go out of ourselves a little oftener and acquire a taste for his contemplation. We will make more holidays into nature with him; but he, in fairness, must earn them, as well as ourselves, by sharing our working-days: – we will emerge oftener into his fields; sit dangling our legs over his styles, and cultivate a due respect for his daffodils; but he, on the other hand, must grow a little better acquainted with our streets, must put up with our lawyers, and even find out a heart or so among our politicians: – in short, we will recollect that we have hearts and brains, and will feel and ponder a little more to purify us as spirits; but he will be good enough, in return, to cast an eye on his hands and muscles, and consider that the putting these to their purposes is necessary to complete our part in this world as organized bodies.

⟨* This title is omitted in the last edition. – Yet, in objecting to these pieces, it is impossible, I think, for any *poetical* mind not to [be] carried away with the enthusiasm of the song to a Skylark, or not to value the pure and exquisite sentiment wrapped up in the little piece on a Rainbow.⟩

Here is the good to be done on both sides; and as society, I believe, would be much bettered in consequence, so there is no man, I am persuaded, more capable than Mr. Wordsworth, upon a better acquaintance with society, to have done it the service. Without that acquaintance, his reputation in poetry, ⟨though very great,⟩ may be little more *salutary* than that of an Empedocles in philosophy or a Saint Francis in religion: – with it, he might have revived the spirit, the glory, and the utility of a Shakspeare.*

Leigh Hunt, *Essays (Selected) by Leigh Hunt*, edited by R. Brimley Johnson (London: Henry Frowde; Oxford University Press, 1929), 165–7

Wordsworth

[Autobiography][2]

MR. WORDSWORTH, whom Mr. Hazlitt designated as one that would have had the wide circle of his humanities made still wider, and a good deal more pleasant, by dividing a little more of his time between his lakes in Westmoreland and the hotels of the metropolis, had a dignified manner, with a deep and roughish but not unpleasing voice, and an exalted mode of speaking. He had a habit of keeping his left hand in the bosom of his waistcoat; and in this attitude, except when he turned round to take one of the subjects of his criticism from the shelves (for his contemporaries were there also), he sat dealing forth his eloquent but hardly catholic judgements. In his 'father's house' there were not 'many mansions.' He was as sceptical on the merits of all kinds of poetry but one, as Richardson was on those of the novels of Fielding.

⟨* Since this note, with little variation, was written, Mr. Wordsworth has collected his minor pieces into the two volumes so often referred to, and has published also two new and large poems, the 'Excursion,' and the 'White Doe of Rylstone.' It does not strike me, however, that I should alter it any further in consequence; though I confess I have risen, if possible, in my admiration of this great genius. The White Doe, it is true, which seems to have been written some time back, does not appear to be among his happiest performances, though containing, as almost all his performances do, touches of exquisite beauty. It is a narrative poem; and there is something in this kind of writing too much *out in the world* for the author's habitual powers. Reverie has been his delight; and the Excursion, with some objectionable parts on the old score, is a succession of noble reveries.⟩

Under the study in which my visitor and I were sitting was an archway, leading to a nursery-ground; a cart happened to go through it while I was inquiring whether he would take any refreshment; and he uttered, in so lofty a voice, the words, 'Anything which is *going forward*,' that I felt inclined to ask him whether he would take a piece of the cart. Lamb would certainly have done it. But this was a levity which would neither have been so proper on my part, after so short an acquaintance, nor very intelligible, perhaps, in any sense of the word, to the serious poet. There are good-humoured warrants for smiling, which lie deeper even than Mr. Wordsworth's thoughts for tears.

I did not see this distinguished person again till thirty years afterwards; when, I should venture to say, his manner was greatly superior to what it was in the former instance; indeed, quite natural and noble, with a cheerful air of animal as well as spiritual confidence; a gallant bearing, curiously reminding me of the Duke of Wellington, as I saw him walking some eighteen years ago by a lady's side, with no unbecoming oblivion of his time of life. I observed, also, that the poet no longer committed himself in scornful criticisms, or, indeed, in any criticisms whatever, at least as far as I knew. He had found out that he could, at least, afford to be silent. Indeed, he spoke very little of anything. The conversation turned upon Milton, and I fancied I had opened a subject that would have 'brought him out,' by remarking, that the most diabolical thing in all *Paradise Lost* was a feeling attributed to the angels. 'Aye!' said Mr. Wordsworth, and inquired what it was. I said it was the passage in which the angels, when they observed Satan journeying through the empyrean, let down a set of steps out of heaven, on purpose to add to his misery—to his despair of ever being able to re-ascend them; they being angels in a state of bliss, and he a fallen spirit doomed to eternal punishment. The passage is as follows:—

Each stair was meant mysteriously, nor stood
There always, but, drawn up to heaven, sometimes
Viewless; and underneath a bright sea flow'd
Of jasper, or of liquid pearl, whereon
Who after came from earth sailing arriv'd
Wafted by angels, or flew o'er the lake
Rapt in a chariot drawn by fiery steeds.
The stairs were then let down, whether to dare
The fiend by easy ascent, *or aggravate*
His sad exclusion from the doors of bliss.

Mr. Wordsworth pondered, and said nothing. I thought to myself, what pity for the poor devil would not good Uncle Toby have expressed! Into what indignation would not Burns have exploded! What knowledge of themselves would not have been forced upon those same coxcombical and malignant angels by Fielding or Shakespeare!

Walter Scott said that the eyes of Burns were the finest he ever saw. I cannot say the same of Mr. Wordsworth's; that is, not in the sense of the beautiful, or even of the profound. But certainly I never beheld eyes that looked so inspired or supernatural. They were like fires half burning, half smouldering, with a sort of acrid fixture of regard, and seated at the further end of two caverns. One might imagine Ezekiel or Isaiah to have had such eyes. The finest eyes, in every sense of the word, which I have ever seen in a man's head (and I have seen many fine ones) are those of Thomas Carlyle.

Notes

1   *The Feast of the Poets*, insofar as it referred to Wordsworth, satirized his poems on the basis of reviews by other writers for periodicals rather than on the basis of direct reading that might allow Hunt to judge for himself. At least so Haydon claimed. If true, Hunt's attack amounted to a lazy way of pretending more acute knowledge of Wordsworth's publications than he actually possessed in 1811, when the poem was first published. (Hunt's editorship of *The Examiner* and then of *The Reflector*, in which *The Feast of the Poets* was first published, had elevated him to a position of considerable power in literary circles.) Some of the digs amounted to sweeping insults:

> What! think ye a bard's a mere gossip who tells
> Of the ev'ry-day feelings of ev'ry one else;
> And that poetry lies, not in something select,
> But in gath'ring the refuse that others reject?

Hunt repented within a matter of months, and he added to reprints of this poem in 1814 and 1815 several fairly long Notes that demonstrated his eagerness to make amends; Wordsworth became – if not a veritable God – 'the Prince of the Bards of his Time'. Wordsworth's subject matter was eulogized:

> Of nature it told, and of simple delights
> On days of green sunshine, and eye-lifting nights;
> Of summer-sweet isles and their noon-shaded bowers,
> Of mountains, and valleys, trees, water, and flowers,
> Of hearts, young and happy, and all that they show
> For the home that we came from and whither we go;
> Of wisdom in age by this feeling renewed,
> Of hopes that stand smiling o'er passions subdued,
> Of the springs of sweet waters in evil that lie; —

Of all, which, in short, meets the soul's better eye
When we go to meek nature our hearts to restore,
And bring down the Gods to walk with us once more.

Not far from doggerel, this tribute to Wordsworth nevertheless accomplished its purpose, that is, 'to do justice to Mr. Wordsworth', and to make sure that Wordsworth knew he had done so. Wordsworth repressed his doubts about the 'weathercock', and Hunt was later to quote Byron to the effect that he had made Wordsworth 'popular upon town'. (Byron approved of the text's '*good* humour in every sense of the word', and praised Hunt's Notes, especially those dealing with Wordsworth.)

In this extract, taken from his longest and most fully developed analysis of Wordsworth's achievement (added to the 1814 version), Hunt bowed his knee to acknowledge 'the greatest poet of the present', and agreed with him that the growth of cities had debased the taste of their inhabitants; he found common ground on a number of related issues. Nevertheless, his serious reservations remained intact in the 1815 recension.

2 Hunt's *Autobiography* was published in 1850, the year of Wordsworth's death.

Robert Southey (1774–1843)

In 1795 Wordsworth was pleased to be invited to become a tenant at Racedown Lodge in Dorset. The property belonged to John Pretor Pinney, a Bristol sugar merchant. The offer required Wordsworth to act as host for occasional visits by John Frederick and Azariah Pinney, John Pinney's two sons, and to supervise the activities of Basil Montagu. Wordsworth had already lived with Basil for a short time in London, and he did not hesitate to agree to the stipulated responsibilities. (The rental fee was waived.) He thus was able, with minimal financial expense, to expand his circle of acquaintances to include Robert Southey, whom he met in Bristol (September 1795).

War between France and England, begun in 1793, had already soured the expectations of many English radicals. Their hopes that the blazing fire of revolution in France might spread to England and in some ill-defined ways lead to the amelioration of conditions pressing down on the working class and the intelligentsia had already been shattered; Godwin's teachings had become for many, including Wordsworth, much less attractive. Southey's views on the execution of Louis XVI, Edmund Burke's defence of the British monarchical system, Thomas Paine's denunciation of the divine right of kings, and the trial of William Frend at Cambridge for the propagation of seditious views were modified, on Southey's part, by a growing interest in domestic life, a recognition that life at Oxford was too narrowly based for his literary interests, and a sharpened awareness of the need for earning a living.

In important respects this increasingly pragmatic transformation in Southey's outlook moved him closer to Wordsworth. A Pantisocratic scheme which would have involved Southey's moving to the banks of the Susquehanna in America and earning a living by means of manual labor (tilling the soil) petered out. Southey's enthusiasm for the establishment of this idealistic community, shared and even heightened by Coleridge, a close friend, became entangled in the complications of personal life. Coleridge's impulsive offer of marriage to Sara Fricker and Southey's secret marriage to Edith Fricker, Sara's sister (14 November 1795), constituted two sensational elements in the doomed project known as Pantisocracy, which soon receded into the past.

Southey's attitude toward Wordsworth began as a respectful recognition of a superior talent, though he recognized intermittent failures in Wordsworth's execution of an over-ambitious agenda. Even before he became an active champion of his new acquaintance, he foresaw the eventual recognition by lovers of poetry – perhaps as many as 'two or three generations' – that Wordsworth's work would rank among 'the finest poems in our language'. He was enthusiastic about *The Borderers*, and enjoyed it far more than he did Coleridge's *Osorio* (later, called *Remorse*). He characterized Wordsworth as 'a man of real genius', and compared him to Milton and Shakespeare sooner than most of his contemporaries. Seeing the poet as inseparable from his poetry, for example, he marveled that Wordsworth's personal demeanor, gravely reserved, was Miltonic.

Wordsworth's attitude toward Southey was much more qualified, though he often professed to hold Southey high in his affection. There was, for one thing, an instinctive recoil against Southey's excesses, particularly when the emotions had not been held at a distance and examined before being turned into poetry. Wordsworth read faithfully whatever Southey sent him, but remained mildly dismayed that Southey wrote too much. To call Southey 'one of the cleverest men that is now living' (a remark recorded by Henry Crabb Robinson around 1812) was double-edged, and perhaps was meant to be so. Aubrey de Vere quoted Wordsworth as saying that Southey was a man 'deficient in felicity and comprehension'. Wordsworth may never have forgiven Southey for a review published in the *Critical Review* (October 1798), one that strongly praised *Tintern Abbey* but did so along with a series of damning comments on Wordsworth's contributions to the first edition of *Lyrical Ballads*. In general, he rated Southey's prose far above his poetry. Uninvited to Southey's funeral, probably because his comment that Southey 'had had the misfortune to outlive his faculties' had been widely circulated, he nevertheless showed up. Caroline Bowles, Southey's second wife, was deeply offended by what she regarded as 'utterly heartless & spiritless' lines of verse written by Wordsworth for a monumental tablet in Crosthwaite Church.

Southey's praise, coming in the early years of Wordsworth's efforts to make a living from the publication of his poems, counted for a great deal. It is at least arguable that Wordsworth tried, in a number of awkward ways, and relatively late in their relationship, to make amends for his carping comments.

RS, NL, I, 148–9: letter from Robert Southey to C. W. Williams Wynn, 22 September 1797

Coleridge has written a tragedy – by request of Sheridan.[1] It is uncommonly fine—the very character appears to me to possess qualities which can not possibly exist in the same mind. But there is a man, whose

name is not known in the world—Wordsworth – who has written great
part of tragedy, upon a very strange and unpleasant subject—but it is
equal to my dramatic pieces [whic]h I have ever seen.[2] God bless you.

RS, NL, I, 448–9: letter from Robert Southey to John Rickman, mid-April 1807

What you have heard of Coleridge is true, he is about to seperate from
his wife, and as he chuses to do every thing in a way different from the
rest of the world, is first going with her to visit his relations where
however she has long since been introduced. The seperation is a good
thing—his habits are so murderous of all domestic comfort that I am
only surprized Mrs C. is not rejoiced at being rid of him. He besots
himself with opium, or with spirits, till his eyes look like a Turks who
is half reduced to idiotcy by the practise—he calls up the servants at all
hours of the night to prepare food for him—he does in short all things
at all times except the proper time—does nothing which he ought to
do, and every thing which he ought not. His present scheme is to live
with Wordsworth—it is from his idolatry of that family that this has
begun—they have always humoured him in all his follies, listened to
his complaints of his wife, and when he has complained of his itch,
helped him to scratch, instead of covering him with brimstone oint-
ment, and shutting him up by himself.[3] Wordsworth and his sister
who pride themselves upon having no selfishness, are of all human
beings whom I have ever known the most intensely selfish. The one
thing to which W. would sacrifice all others is his own reputation, concerning which his anxiety is perfectly childish—like a woman of her
beauty: and so he can get Coleridge to talk his own writings over with
him, and critise [sic] them, and (without amending them) teach him
how to do it—to be in fact the very rain and air and sunshine of his
intellect, he thinks. C. is very well employed and this arrangement a
very good one. I myself, as I have told Coleridge, think it highly fit that
the seperation should take place, but by no means so that it should
ever have been necessary.

RS, SL, I, 216: letter from Robert Southey to John May, 1803
[Southey begins by promising to refute criticisms of himself printed in a recent issue of the *Scotch Review*]

With regard to that part of the review which relates to Wordsworth, it
has obviously no relation whatever to 'Thalaba,' nor can there be a

stronger proof of want of discernment, or want of candour, than in grouping together three men so different in style as Wordsworth, Coleridge, and myself, under one head. The fault of Coleridge has been a too-swelling diction; you who know his poems know whether they ought to be abused for mean language. Of 'Thalaba,' the language rises and falls with the subject, and is always in a high key. I wish you would read the Lyrical Ballads of Wordsworth; some of them are very faulty; but, indeed, I would risk my whole future fame on the assertion that they will one day be regarded as the finest poems in our language. I refer you particularly to 'The Brothers,' a poem on 'Tintern Abbey,' and 'Michael.' Now, with Wordsworth I have no intimacy; scarcely any acquaintance. In whatever we resemble each other, the resemblance has sprung, not, I believe, from chance, but because we have both studied poetry—and indeed it is no light or easy study—in the same school,—in the works of nature, and in the heart of man.

RS, *SL*, I, 245: letter from Robert Southey to John King, 19 November 1803

By this time you have probably seen and detected William Taylor's articles in the 'Annual Review.' I am hard at work for my next year's *quantum*, killing and slaying, or rather, in your way, anatomising the dead. One most complete scoundrel has been by God's judgment consigned over to my tribunal, some fellow, who writes under the assumed name of Peter Bayley, Jun., Esq. He has stolen from Wordsworth in the most wholesale way and most artfully, and then at the end of his book thinks proper to abuse Wordsworth by name. I mean to prove his thefts one by one, and then call him rascal.

RS, *SL*, I, 254: letter from Robert Southey to Miss Barker, 1804

Oh! do you know who is the man who has published a volume of poems under the assumed name of Peter Bayley, Jun. Esq.: he talks of his native Wever, which may be a sham; but that, you know, is in your part of the world. The Lord in heaven have mercy on that gentleman-scoundrel, whosoever he be! for I have got him upon my thumb-nail, and shall crack him, Senhora, for a *fidalgo*. He hath committed high treason against me in the first place; but what he is to be damned for is, first, having stolen by wholesale from the 'Lyrical Ballads,' and then abusing Wordsworth by name. I will break him upon the wheel, and then hook him up alive, *in terrorem*, and make his memory stink in the noses of all readers of English, present and to come. I wish he could know that his book has been sent to me to be reviewed, and that Wordsworth has now got it to claim his own whenever he finds it. Every peacock's feather shall be plucked out; and then his tail will be left in a very fit and inviting condition for a cat o'nine tails.

RS, *SL*, I, 271: letter from Robert Southey to Miss Barker, February 1804

[Coleridge] has been sitting to Northcote for Sir George Beaumont. There is a finely painted, but dismal picture of him here, with a companion of Wordsworth. I enjoy the thought of your emotion when you will see that portrait of Wordsworth. It looks as if he had been a month in the condemned hole, dieted upon bread and water, and debarred the use of soap, water, razor, and combs, then taken out of prison, placed in a cart, carried to the usual place of execution, and had just suffered Jack Ketch to take off his cravat. The best of this good joke is, that the Wordsworths are proud of the picture, and that his face is the painter's ideal of excellence; and how the devil the painter has contrived to make a likeness of so well-looking a man so ridiculously ugly poozles everybody.

RS, *SL*, II, 15: letter from Robert Southey to C. W. Williams Wynn, 11 June 1807

Have you also seen Wordsworth's new poems?[4] Some are very childish, some very obscure, though not so to me, who understand his opinions; others of first rate excellence — nothing comparable to them is to be found anywhere except in Shakspeare and Milton. Of this character are most of the sonnets which relate to the times. I never saw poetry at once so truly philosophical and heroic.

RS, *SL*, II, 409: letter from Robert Southey to J. W. White, 8 May 1815

Wordsworth is in town. Have you seen the new edition of his poems? I do not hesitate to say that in the whole compass of poetry, ancient or modern, there is no collection of miscellaneous poems comparable to them, nor any work whatever which discovers greater strength of mind or higher poetical genius.

RS, *SL*, III, 109–10: letter from Robert Southey to John Rickman, mid-April 1807

I was quite certain that you would appreciate Wordsworth justly. Nations, you say, are not proud of living genius. They are proud of it only as far as they understand it; and the majority, being incapable of understanding it, can never admire it, till they take it upon trust: so that two or three generations must pass before the public affect to admire such poets as Milton and Wordsworth. Of such men the world scarcely produces one in a millennium; — has it, indeed, ever produced more than two? for Shakspeare is of a different class. But of all inferior degrees of poets no age and no country was ever so prolific as our own: every season produces some half dozen poems, not one of which obtains the slightest attention, and any one of which would have the author celebrated above all contemporaries five-and-twenty years ago.

Notes

1 *Osorio*, a Spanish tragedy written on the basis of a commission from Sheridan, was rejected ('because of the obscurity of the last three acts'), much to Coleridge's chagrin. A full decade later, Coleridge asked Godwin to locate and rescue the only extant copy from 'any chance rubbish-corner'. Godwin was successful in his search, but years passed before the play, renamed *Remorse*, received a stage production (1813).
2 *The Borderers* (1795–96) was not produced in the theatre until the final decade of Wordsworth's life (1842).
3 The Wordsworths gently but firmly dissuaded Coleridge from coming to live with them; the question that had to be answered (as Dorothy Wordsworth wrote to Catherine Clarkson in February 1807) was *'where?'*. They did not have the space for Coleridge and his two sons, and it would have been 'unpleasant (not to say indelicate)' because of their friendship for Mrs Coleridge. They did encourage Coleridge to visit them, however.
4 *Poems, in Two Volumes* (1807) was published without a preface or an explanation of the poetic theory which Wordsworth had carefully formulated to justify his choices of language and subject matter. As a consequence many of the reviewers, and even some of Wordsworth's friends, censured what seemed to them to be an unbecoming unwillingness to separate the better poems from those that were less successful. (Francis Jeffrey's attack on 'such trash', 'an insult on the public taste', etc., printed in the *Edinburgh Review*, October 1807, was especially vehement.) Southey's enthusiasm, as expressed in these excerpts from letters to Wynn and White, represented a minority view at the time.

John Keats (1795–1821)

In Benjamin Robert Haydon's letter to Wordsworth (31 December 1816), a poem by Keats was enclosed. Haydon wrote that the young poet who had written it wanted to convey his 'Reverence' (Haydon was not exaggerating). The opening lines illustrated Keats's strong and sincere desire to please Wordsworth:

> Great Spirits now on Earth are sojourning
> He of the Cloud, the Cataract, the Lake
> Who on Helvellyn's summit wide awake
> Catches his freshness from archangels wing . . .

Keats had been overwhelmed by the true music of poetry that he found in *The Excursion*, the ode on *Intimations of Immortality*, *Tintern Abbey*, and the Lucy poems; but his uncritical acceptance of Wordsworth's genius would yield, within a year, to a more qualified admiration.

At least part of the reason can be traced to Wordsworth's patronizing of Keats on one memorable occasion, after Haydon had gone to some trouble to arrange a meeting of the poets in the home of Thomas Monkhouse (very late in the year 1817, though the exact date is unclear). Wordsworth's dismissal of Keats's recitation of 'an exquisite ode to Pan' (Haydon's description) with the remark that it was 'a Very pretty piece of Paganism' offended Haydon: 'This was unfeeling, & unworthy of his high Genius to a young Worshipper like Keats — & Keats felt it *deeply*.'

Perhaps not, since Keats met Wordsworth on at least four subsequent occasions, and Walter Jackson Bate, in his fine biography, *John Keats* ([Cambridge, Mass.: The Belknap Press of Harvard University Press, 1963], 261), lists several reasons why Keats might have taken it in his stride: Keats kept to himself any chagrin he may have felt; the stress placed on different words, even the possibility that Wordsworth smiled as he spoke, may have softened the offence; Haydon had, after all, begun his account with the statement that Wordsworth received Keats 'kindly'; and Keats may not have taken the remark personally.

Wordsworth, who took pride in his own literary dicta, could not have been completely unaware of the impact such a verdict might have. But there were other offhand comments by Wordsworth – such as a condemnation of 'the sorry company' Keats kept, or of an 'over-lusciousness' of diction (which Wordsworth declared Keats shared with the younger Tennyson). These suggest that Wordsworth never raised by much his original estimate of Keats's talent; he thought of it as minor, and certainly compared it unflatteringly to his own. When Keats thought he might comment on Wordsworth's opinion of a particular point having to do with the craft of poetry, Wordsworth's wife 'put a hand upon his arm, saying—"Mr. Wordsworth is never interrupted"' – a sure way to fracture still further Keats's sense of 'Reverence'. Perhaps at that moment he intended to take exception to what Wordsworth was saying, or he may only have intended to insinuate 'a confirmatory suggestion', as Charles Clarke wrote (in *Recollections of Writers*, 1878, 149–50). Keats may have been unduly irritated by his learning that Wordsworth actively campaigned for Lord Lowther, a reactionary politician who was fighting to defeat Henry Brougham, a Whig. (Lowther was responsible for the calling-out of troops to maintain order in Lancaster, an industrial city; Brougham had defended John and Leigh Hunt in the legal proceedings of 1811–12, focusing on their seditious libel against the Prince Regent.) Keats wrote to his brother Tom while on his way to visit Wordsworth in late June 1818: 'Sad—sad—sad—and yet the [Lowther] family has been his friend always. What can we say?' Charles Armitage Browne, who accompanied Keats on this trip, wrote in his journal the next day: 'The younger poet looked thoughtfull at this exposure of his elder', and decided, on second thought, to cross out the word 'exposure' as an over-statement. Keats's political beliefs, consistently anti-Tory, were bound to color his view of Wordsworth's character.

At any rate, Keats found Wordsworth's self-centeredness useful in his formulation of an aesthetic argument about the higher value of a 'camelion Poet' who lost himself in his art. He had been inspired by Hazlitt's *Lectures on the English Poets*, given at the Surrey Institution in London during the winter months (January–March) of 1818. Keats's definition of Negative Capability, defined, in its earliest version, in a letter to George and Tom Keats dated 27 December 1817, is a statement of belief in the essence of Shakespeare's triumph. The formulation – 'when man is capable of being in uncertainties, Mysteries, doubts, without any irritable reaching after fact & reason' – proved especially helpful to him as he moved toward the great poems of his liberated imagination. The self-confident feeling it inspired more than compensated for the disillusionment caused by his recognition of Wordsworth's character flaws. These he listed, in a letter to his brothers dated 21 February 1818, as 'egotism, Vanity and bigotry'. Keats added that Wordsworth, even with such shortcomings, remained 'a great Poet if not a Philosopher'.

(An odd opinion expressed in several recent writings on Keats is that the phrase 'egotistical sublime' should be taken as a generic abstraction, and that Keats intended to posit it against the kind of poetry he, following the example of Shakespeare, was attempting to write. If ever Keats intended a phrase to be understood in its *ad hominem* application, this was it.)

Writing to J. H. Reynolds (3 February 1818), Keats reacted strongly against what he interpreted as a conviction held firmly by Wordsworth, that is, that his opinions deserved assent from all right-thinking artists. No one set of opinions could legitimately demand such allegiance. Rather, human life might be profitably considered as 'a large Mansion of Many Apartments'. Keats was about to embark on his own glorious year, from October 1818 to October 1819, in which he would write many of his major poems. He had already paid the debt that he owed Wordsworth. Wordsworth's path was not the one he should be following, nor did he ever again repeat the word 'Reverence' as a description of his own attitude toward Wordsworth.

JK, L, I, 102–4: letter from John Keats to John Hamilton Reynolds, 3 February 1818

I thank you for your dish of Filberts—Would I could get a basket of them by way of des[s]ert every day for the sum of two-pence.[1] Would we were a sort of ethereal Pigs, and turn'd loose to feed upon spiritual Mast and Acorns—which would be merely being a squirrel and feed[ing] upon filberts, for what is a squirrel but an airy pig, or a filbert but a sort of archangelical acorn[?] About the nuts being worth cracking, all I can say is that where there are a throng of delightful Images ready drawn simplicity is the only thing. The first is the best on account of the first line, and the 'arrow—foil'd of its antler'd food', and moreover (and this is the only word or two I find fault with, the more because I have had so much reason to shun it as a quicksand) the last has 'tender and true'. We must cut this, and not be rattlesnaked into any more of the like. It may be said that we ought to read our contemporaries, that Wordsworth & c. should have their due from us. But, for the sake of a few fine imaginative or domestic passages, are we to be bullied into a certain Philosophy engendered in the whims of an Egotist[?] Every man has his speculations, but every man does not brood and peacock over them till he makes a false coinage and deceives himself. Many a man can travel to the very bourne of Heaven, and yet want confidence to put down his half-seeing. Sancho will invent a

Journey heavenward as well as any body. We hate poetry that has a palpable design upon us, and if we do not agree, seems to put its hand in its breeches pocket. Poetry should be great and unobtrusive, a thing which enters into one's soul, and does not startle it or amaze it with itself, but with its subject.—How beautiful are the retired flowers! how would they lose their beauty were they to throng into the highway crying out, 'admire me I am a violet!—dote upon me I am a primrose!' Modern poets differ from the Elizabethans in this. Each of the moderns like an Elector of Hanover governs his petty state, and knows how many straws are swept daily from the Causeways in all his dominions and has a continual itching that all the Housewives should have their coppers well scoured: the antients were Emperors of vast Provinces, they had only heard of the remote ones and scarcely cared to visit them.—I will cut all this—I will have no more of Wordsworth or Hunt in particular. Why should we be of the tribe of Manasseh, when we can wander with Esau? why should we kick against the Pricks, when we can walk on Roses? Why should we be owls, when we can be Eagles? Why be teased with 'nice Eyed wagtails',[2] when we have in sight 'the Cherub Contemplation'?[3] Why with Wordsworth's 'Matthew with a bough of wilding in his hand'[4] when we can have Jacques 'under an oak &c.'?[5] The secret of the Bough of Wilding will run through your head faster than I can write it. Old Matthew spoke to him some years ago on some nothing, and because he happens in an Evening Walk to imagine the figure of the Old Man, he must stamp it down in black and white, and it is henceforth sacred. I don't mean to deny Wordsworth's grandeur and Hunt's merit, but I mean to say we need not be teazed with grandeur and merit when we can have them uncontaminated and unobtrusive. Let us have the old Poets, and Robin Hood. Your letter and its sonnets gave me more pleasure than will the Fourth Book of Childe Harold and the whole of anybody's life and opinions. In return for your Dish of filberts, I have gathered a few Catkins. I hope they'll look pretty.

JK, *L*, I, 115–16: letter from John Keats to George and Thomas Keats, 21 February 1818

The thrushes are singing now as if they would speak to the winds, because their big brother Jack—the Spring—was not far off. I am reading Voltaire and Gibbon, although I wrote to Reynolds the other day to prove reading of no use; I have not seen Hunt since. I am a good deal with Dilke and Brown; we are very thick; they are very kind to me, they are well; I don't think I could stop in Hampstead but for their neighbourhood. I hear Hazlitt's lectures regularly, his last was on Gray, Collins, Young, &c., and he gave a very fine piece of discriminating Criticism on Swift, Voltaire, and Rabelais. I was very disappointed at his treatment of Chatterton. I generally meet with many I know there. Lord Byron's 4th Canto is expected out, and I heard somewhere, that Walter Scott has a new Poem in readiness. I am sorry that Wordsworth has left a bad impression where-ever he visited in town by his egotism, Vanity, and bigotry. Yet he is a great poet if not a philosopher. I have not yet read Shelley's Poem,[6] I don't suppose you have it yet, at the Teignmouth libraries. These double letters must come rather heavy, I hope you have a moderate portion of cash, but don't fret at all, if you have not—Lord! I intend to play at Cut and run as well as Falstaff, that is to say, before he got so lusty.

I remain praying for your health my dear Brothers

Your affectionate Brother

John

JK, *L*, I, 244–6: letter from John Keats to Richard Woodhouse, 27 October 1818

Your Letter gave me a great satisfaction; more on account of its friendliness, than any relish of that matter in it which is accounted so acceptable in the 'genus irritabile'. The best answer I can give you is in a clerklike manner to make some observations on two principle points, which seem to point like indices into the midst of the whole pro and con, about genius, and views and atchievements and ambition and cœtera. 1st As to the poetical Character itself (I mean that sort of which, if I am any thing, I am a Member; that sort distinguished from the wordsworthian or egotistical sublime; which is a thing per se and stands alone) it is not itself—it has no self—it is every thing and nothing—It has no character—it enjoys light and shade; it lives in gusto, be it foul or fair, high or low, rich or poor, mean or elevated—It has as much delight in conceiving an Iago as an Imogen. What shocks the virtuous philosopher, delights the camelion Poet. It does no harm from its relish of the dark side of things any more than from its taste for the bright one; because they both end in speculation. A Poet is the most unpoetical of any thing in existence; because he has no Identity—he is continually in for and filling some other Body—The Sun, the Moon, the Sea and Men and Women who are creatures of impulse are poetical and have about them an unchangeable attribute—

the poet has none; no identity—he is certainly the most unpoetical of all God's Creatures. If then he has no self, and if I am a Poet, where is the Wonder that I should say I would write no more? Might I not at that very instant have been cogitating on the Characters of Saturn and Ops? It is a wretched thing to confess; but is a very fact that not one word I ever utter can be taken for granted as an opinion growing out of my identical nature—how can it, when I have no nature? When I am in a room with People if I ever am free from speculating on creations of my own brain, then not myself goes home to myself: but the identity of every one in the room begins to to [*sic*] press upon me that I am in a very little time an[ni]hilated—not only among Men; it would be the same in a Nursery of children: I know not whether I make myself wholly understood: I hope enough so to let you see that no dependence is to be placed on what I said that day.

In the second place I will speak of my views, and of the life I purpose to myself. I am ambitious of doing the world some good: if I should be spared that may be the work of maturer years—in the interval I will assay to reach to as high a summit in Poetry as the nerve bestowed upon me will suffer. The faint conceptions I have of Poems to come brings the blood frequently into my forehead. All I hope is that I may not lose all interest in human affairs—that the solitary indifference I feel for applause even from the finest spirits, will not blunt any acuteness of vision I may have. I do not think it will. I feel assured I should write from the mere yearning and fondness I have for the Beautiful even if my night's labours should be burnt every morning, and no eye ever shine upon them. But even now I am perhaps not speaking from myself: but from some character in whose soul I now live. I am sure however that this next sentence is from myself. I feel your anxiety, good opinion and friendliness in the highest degree, and am

Your's most sincerely

John Keats

Notes

1 Keats was responding to two sonnets on Robin Hood enclosed in Reynolds's letter.
2 Leigh Hunt, 'The Nymphs', Part II, l. 170.
3 John Milton, 'Il Penseroso', l. 54.
4 Wordsworth's 'The Two April Mornings', ll. 59–60.
5 *As You Like It*, II, i, 31.
6 *The Revolt of Islam* (10 January 1818), 244–6.

Sir Walter Scott (1771–1832)

John G. Lockhart's biography of Sir Walter Scott (his father-in-law) was but recently published when Wordsworth, responding to a gift copy, wrote to Lockhart describing Scott as a man who lived 'a favored and happy life', who had carried on his anonymity too long; alas, 'the burthen of secrecy' had been contrary to his 'open genial nature'. The misfortunes plaguing the latter part of his life constituted a moral lesson, since Scott had responded to adversity in a way that provided 'much consolation both for those that loved him, and for Persons comparatively indifferent to his fate'. Wordsworth did not praise the biography, and chose not to discuss it in any detail. Lockhart thought that Wordsworth had seen the book as a broad-brush tribute to Scott, and (though he had raised the possibility that the book might be considered too long) he resented Wordsworth's willingness to agree that it was. He was annoyed by Wordsworth's correction of 'a few trifling inaccuracies'.

Unfortunately, Wordsworth's disdain for Lockhart's biography was closely related to his low opinion of Scott's novels and poetry. Scott's phenomenal popularity had been purchased at too high a cost: he too readily descended to the level of his large and growing public. Though he and Scott appreciated each other's abilities, they differed wildly in their assessment of each other's poetry. Scott, writing to Anna Seward (18 April 1806), disparaged the 'New School of Poetry' established by Wordsworth and Southey. 'They sometimes lose their energy in trying to find a better but a different path from what has been travelld by their predecessors.'

He found Wordsworth, as a man, 'virtuous, simple, and unaffectedly restricting every want & wish to the bounds of a very narrow income...' When Sir George Beaumont died, Scott wondered whether in fact he had understood Wordsworth's poetry, a poetry which he himself found too much given to abstractions. 'I do not at all acquiesce in his system of poetry and I think he had injured his own fame by adhering to it', he wrote in his *Journal* (12 May 1828). Another *Journal* entry (26 May 1828) noted that Wordsworth seemed to be a poet who continually denied himself the opportunity to become popular. Scott, who abided happily by 'the established rules of criticism' (letter to Southey, November 1807), brushed aside Wordsworth's carping at his poems. When in the neighborhood, he enjoyed walks with his boon companion. Never did he trigger an outburst that might have imperilled their friendship.

Yet one wonders if Scott really understood how much Wordsworth disliked his publications. Wordsworth spoke of Scott's poems with 'contempt' – a harsh word that he used when speaking to Aubrey de Vere and Henry Crabb Robinson on different occasions. If Scott and Lord Byron flourished, it was at the expense of 'an honest Poet', who as a consequence could not hope to thrive. Scott pleased the public by 'the vulgarity of his conceptions'.

We cannot accurately judge whether Wordsworth reached such conclusions because Scott, in his free-wheeling comments on Wordsworth's poetry, misquoted him, or because Scott attracted a large audience eager to cheer him on no matter what he wrote. Wordsworth certainly was irritated by Scott's failure to respond immediately to a complimentary copy of *The Excursion* that he had sent him. He repeated, in various conversations, his objections to what he called Scott's 'commonplace contrivances, worthy only of the Minerva press, and such bad vulgar English as no gentleman of education ought to have written'. If Scott's prose was superior to his poetry, the reason was that his own feelings were more conspicuously shown in his novels, but over-all 'very little productive power was exerted in popular creations'. And, perhaps most galling, Scott could spend freely because more money would flood in whenever he needed it. 'This', Wordsworth said, 'was marvellous to me, who had never written a line with a view to profit.'

WW, *L*, III, 180: letter from William Wordsworth to Robert Pearse Gillies, 22 December 1814

I am delighted to learn that your Edinburgh Aristarch[1] has declared against the *Excursion*, as he will have the mortification of seeing a book enjoy a high reputation, to which he has not contributed. Do not imagine that my principles lead me to condemn Scott's method of pleasing the public, or that I have not a very high respect for his various talents and extensive attainments. I sent him the *Excursion*, and am rather surprised that I have had no letter from him to acknowledge the receipt of it. Pray, present my regards to him when you see him.

WW, *L*, III, 232: letter from William Wordsworth to Robert Pearse Gillies, 25 April 1815.

You ought to have received my two volumes of poems long before this, if Longman has done his duty. I ordered a copy likewise to be sent to Walter Scott. I cannot but flatter myself that this publication will interest you. The pains which I have bestowed on the composition can never be known but to myself, and I am very sorry to find, on reviewing the work, that the labour has been able to do so little for it. You mentioned *Guy Mannering* in your last. I have read it. I cannot say that I was disappointed, for there is very considerable talent displayed in the performance, and much of that sort of knowledge with which the author's mind is so richly stored. But the adventures I think not well chosen or invented, and they are still worse put together; and the characters, with the exception of Meg Merrilies, excite little interest. In the management of this lady the author has shown very considerable ability, but with that want of taste, which is universal among modern novels of the Radcliffe school, which, as far as they are concerned, this is. I allude to the laborious manner in which everything is placed before your eyes for the production of picturesque effect. The reader, in good narration, feels that pictures rise up before his sight, and pass away from it unostentatiously, succeeding each other. But when they are fixed upon an easel for the express purpose of being admired, the judicious are apt to take offence, and even to turn sulky at the exhibitor's officiousness. But these novels are likely to be much overrated on their first appearance, and will afterwards be as much undervalued. *Waverley* heightened my opinion of Scott's talents very considerably, and if *Mannering* has not added much, it has not taken much away. Infinitely the best part of *Waverley* is the pictures of Highland manners at Mac Ivor's castle, and the delineation of his character, which are done with great spirit. The Scotch baron, and all the circumstances in which he is exhibited, are too peculiar and *outré*. Such caricatures require a higher condiment of humour to give them a relish than the author of *Waverley* possesses. But too much of this gossip.

WW, *PrW*, III, 442–3: Mrs Davy's reminiscence of Wordsworth, 11 July 1844

Mr. Wordsworth, in his best manner, with earnest thoughts given out in noble diction, gave his reasons for thinking that as a poet Scott would not live. 'I don't like,' he said, 'to say all this, or to take to pieces some of the best reputed passages of Scott's verse, especially in presence of my wife, because she thinks me too fastidious; but as a poet Scott *cannot* live, for he has never in verse written anything addressed to the immortal part of man. In making amusing stories in verse, he will be superseded by some newer versifier; what he writes in the way of natural description is merely rhyming nonsense.' As a prose writer, Mr. Wordsworth admitted that Scott had touched a higher vein, because there he had really dealt with feeling and passion. As historical novels, professing to give the manners of a past time, he did not attach much value to those works of Scott's so called, because that he held to be an attempt in which success was impossible. This led to some remarks on historical writing, from which it appeared that Mr. Wordsworth has small value for anything but contemporary history.

WW, PrW, III, 445: Lady Richardson's reminiscence of Wordsworth, 12 July 1844

[Wordsworth] discoursed at great length on Scott's works. His poetry he considered of that kind which will always be in demand, and that the supply will always meet it, suited to the age. He does not consider that it in any way goes below the surface of things; it does not reach to any intellectual or spiritual emotion; it is altogether superficial, and he felt it himself to be so. His descriptions are not true to Nature; they are addressed to the ear, not to the mind. He was a master of bodily movements in his battle-scenes; but very little productive power was exerted in popular creations.

WS, J, 278, 473–4, 482

14 WEDNESDAY [February 1827] 'Death's gi'en the art an unco devel.' Sir George Beaumont's dead. By far the most sensible and pleasing man I ever knew, kind too in his nature and generous—gentle in society and of those mild manners which tend to soften the causticity of the general London [tone] of persiflage and personal satire. As an amateur he was a painter of the very [highest rank]. Though I know nothing of the matter yet I should hold him a perfect critic on painting for he always made his criticisms intelligible and used no slang. I am very sorry, as much as is in my nature to be for one whom I could see but seldom. He was the great friend of Wordsworth and understood his poetry, which is a rare thing for it is more easy to see his peculiarities than to feel his great merit or follow his abstract ideas.[1]

12 MONDAY [May 1828] Old George II was as is well known extremely passionate. On these occasions his small stock of English totally faild him and he used to express his indignation in the following form 'G— d—n me who I am? Got d—n you who you be?' Lockhart and I visited a Mrs. Quillinan[2] with whom Wordsworth and his wife have pitched their tent. I was glad to see my old friend whose conversation has so much that is fresh and manly in it. I do not at all acquiesce in his system of poetry and I think he has injured his own fame by adhering to it. But a better or more sensible man I do not know than W. W.

26 MONDAY [May 1828] An awful confusion with paying of bills, writing of cards and all species of trumpery business. Southey who is just come to town breakfasted with us. He looks I think but poorly, but it may be owing to family misfortune. One is always tempted to compare Wordsworth and Southey—The latter is unquestionably the greater scholar, I mean possesses the most extensive stock of information, but there is a freshness, vivacity and spring about Wordsworth's mind which if we may compare two men of uncommon powers shows more originality. I say nothing of their poetry. Wordsworth has a system which disposes him to take the bull by the horns and offend public taste, which right or wrong will always be the taste of the public, yet he could be popular if he would witness the feast at Brougham castle—'Song of the Cliffords' I think is the name.

Notes

1   Francis Jeffrey, editor of the *Edinburgh Review*. Wordsworth was shocked by the harshness of Jeffrey's review of *The Excursion* (November 1814).
2   Thirteen years later, on 11 May 1841, Edward Quillinan, her son, would marry Dora, Wordsworth's daughter.

John Hamilton Reynolds (1794–1852)

John Hamilton Reynolds's career began with a series of precocious publications that drew the respectful attention of Lord Byron (who characterized him as 'a youngster, and a clever one'), and created a stir leading to Leigh Hunt's bracketing his name with those of Shelley and Keats. Several of his contributions to *The Inquirer, or Literary Miscellany*, *The Champion* (a Sunday newspaper), *The Yellow Dwarf*, the influential *London Magazine*, and his authorship of a large number of literary notices for the *Edinburgh Review*, the *Retrospective Review*, and the *Westminster Review*, saw print before he reached the age of 20. His personality charmed many who knew him and worked with him (Hazlitt, Hood, De Quincey, and Lamb, among many other journalists and critics). Above all, the services he rendered to the younger Keats – the greater part of Keats's finest literary criticism may be found in letters Keats wrote to Reynolds, who had recognized his genius immediately – have earned him an important place in the hierarchy of Romantic writers. On his gravestone the telling phrase, 'The Friend of Keats', was added (in 1917, as part of a cemetery clean-up).

Remembering the significance of his close relationship to Keats helps to balance the emphasis of literary historians on how much Reynolds, for multiple and sometimes unclear reasons, suffered during his final years; how his work as a solicitor suffocated his literary interests; how his financial problems became increasingly serious; and how much his drinking to excess worried his friends. Ill health forced him, finally, to retreat to Newport on the Isle of Wight, where he intermittently and unhappily fulfilled the duties of a clerk of the court until he died in relative obscurity.

Awed by Wordsworth's poetry and from what he could learn about the man who had written pastorals with heart, Reynolds foresaw as early as 1816 the revolutionary implications of Wordsworth's contribution to English literature for the rest of the century. Despite what he called Wordsworth's lack of popular appeal, he appreciated the fact that the artificial diction of a non-philosophical interpretation of Nature, which had dominated the subject matter of poetry for decades, could no longer be sustained. He reviewed Wordsworth's contribution in several essays – even in one which ostensibly dealt with the current condition of the theatre – and in his own work ('Margaret', for instance, an imitation of the Lucy poems, and *The Eden of Imagination*). He was evidently trying on Wordsworth's manner to see whether it fit.

Reynolds's admiration of Wordsworth may be traced in at least three of his literary meditations prior to his sending on to Wordsworth a copy of *The Naiad: A Tale, with Other Poems* (1816), his new publication. He invited Wordsworth to pass judgment upon its degree of artistic success: 'Should you have leisure to point out any passages which you think objectionable, I shall be happy at being able to benefit the Poem by your suggestions' (August 1816). He probably was not ready for Wordsworth's largely negative response, with its sharply honed comments on the poem's excessive length, and a recommendation that Reynolds should trim the first 57 lines and 'the last 146'. Reynolds's fancy, in Wordsworth's judgment (28 November 1816), ran much too freely in *The Naiad*.[1]

An announcement, three years later, of the impending publication of Wordsworth's *Peter Bell* stimulated Reynolds to write his zestful parody, *Peter Bell: Lyrical Ballad* (1819). Reynolds's *Preface* does real damage to Wordsworth's carefully monitored self-image. The satire, attacking Wordsworth's rustic poetry as if no other subject matter had ever been deemed worthy of poetic treatment at Grasmere, so delighted the public that several reprints were called for. Even so, tracing a direct line of causation from the letter Wordsworth wrote to Reynolds in 1816 to the enthusiastic thrust-and-parry of Reynolds's parody must be qualified. Even though Reynolds soon turned his hero-worshipping gaze on Keats, going so far as to write adaptations of Boccaccio in a collaborative scheme, he continued to believe that Wordsworth had performed a great liberating service for English poetry.

Wordsworth was understandably offended by his satire, however. Matters were not mended when parodies by other poets, written immediately after the publication of his own *Peter Bell*, rolled off the presses. He never wrote again to Reynolds.

JHR, L, 5

The Book is at any rate a well dressed One. The Naiad is a truly respectable woman as far as personal appearance goes:—I shall leave it to the world to decide on the beauty of her voice & the fascination of her Song. I wish some of the Critics may be lured into an admiration of her,—if she could but charm with her warblings, the bony heart of a Scotch literary Surgeon,—what might not be looked for at my hands, & in my hopes. If the Naiad is to be ⟨hacked⟩ dissected;—Heaven knows what complaint, the Operator may say occasioned her decease. But I will not talk of death now,—nor of the damnation which may tread

on the heels of it—'We know the End will come,—& there's an End.'
I am glad you have sent the Copy to Wordsworth for me:—Oh Haydon
when I think of the sunlike genius, & fine firm principle of that Noble
Poet;—I think higher of human nature, of the age in which I live. He is
the Milton of our day. He has twined the pillars of the Temple of
Philosophy with the loveliest flowers of Poetry. He has turned by the
touch of his genius, the mountain air of his country into words.
Liberty breathes through his Poetry, as the wind wanders over his Hills.
Thought is the friend of his retirement. I long to see Wordsworth.

John Hamilton Reynolds, *Peter Bell: Lyrical Ballad* (London: Taylor and Hessey, 1819), vi–viii [published anonymously]

'I do affirm that I am the REAL SIMON PURE.'
  – Susanna Centlivre, *Bold Stroke for a Wife* (1718)[2]

Preface

IT is now a period of one-and-twenty years since I first wrote some of
the most perfect compositions (except certain pieces I have written in
my later days) that ever dropped from poetical pen. My heart hath
been right and powerful all its years. I never thought an evil or a weak
thought in my life. It has been my aim and my achievement to deduce
moral thunder from buttercups, daisies*, celandines, and (as a poet,
scarcely inferior to myself, hath it) 'such small deer.'[3] Out of sparrows'
eggs I have hatched great truths,[4] and with sextons' barrows have I
wheeled into human hearts, piles of the weightiest philosophy. I have
persevered with a perseverance truly astonishing, in persons of not the
most pursy purses;—but to a man of my inveterate morality and independent stamp, (of which Stamps I am proud to be a Distributor)[5] the
sneers and scoffings of impious Scotchmen, and the neglect of my poor
uninspired countrymen, fall as the dew upon the thorn, (on which
plant I have written an immortal stanza or two)[6] and are as fleeting as
the spray of the waterfall, (concerning which waterfall I have composed some great lines which the world will not let die.)—Accustomed
to mountain solitudes, I can look with a calm and dispassionate eye

---

* A favourite flower of mine. It was a favourite with Chaucer, but he did not
  understand its moral mystery as I do.
    'Little Cyclops, with one eye.'
                  Poems by ME.

upon that fiend-like, vulture-souled, adder-fanged critic, whom I have not patience to name, and of whose Review I loathe the title, and detest the contents.[7]—Philosophy has taught me to forgive the misguided miscreant, and to speak of him only in terms of patience and pity. I love my venerable Monarch and the Prince Regent.* My Ballads are the noblest pieces of verse in the whole range of English poetry: and I take this opportunity of telling the world I am a great man. Milton was also a great man. Ossian was a blind old fool.[8] Copies of my previous works may be had in any numbers, by application at my publisher.

Of PETER BELL I have only thus much to say: it completes the simple system of natural narrative, which I began so early as 1798. It is written in that pure unlaboured style, which can only be met with among labourers;—and I can safely say, that while its imaginations spring beyond the reach of the most imaginative, its occasional meaning occasionally falls far below the meanest capacity. As these are the days of counterfeits, I am compelled to caution my readers against them, "for such are abroad." However, I here declare this to be the true Peter; this to be the old original Bell. I commit my Ballad confidently to posterity. I love to read my own poetry: it does my heart good.

W. W.

N. B. The novel of Rob Roy is not so good as my Poem on the same subject.[9]

Supplementary Essay.

I BEG leave, once for all, to refer the Reader to my previous Poems, for illustrations of the names of the characters, and the severe simplicity contained in this affecting Ballad. I purpose, in the course of a few years, to write laborious lives of all the old people who enjoy sinecures in the text, or are pensioned off in the notes, of my Poetry. The Cumberland Beggar is dead. He could not crawl out of the way of a fierce and fatal post chaise, and so fell a sacrifice to the Philosophy of Nature. I shall commence the work in heavy quarto, like the Excursion, with that "old, old Man," (as the too joyous Spenser saith.)—If ever I should be surprised into a second edition, I shall write an extra-supplementary Essay on the principles of simple Poetry. I now conclude, with merely

---

* Mr. Vansittart, the great Chancellor of the Exchequer, is a noble character:— and I consecrate this note to that illustrious financier.

extracting (from my own works) the following eloquent and just passage (my Prose is extremely good) contained in the two volumes lately published, and not yet wholly disposed of:—

"A sketch of my own notion of the Constitution of Fame has been given; and as far as concerns myself, I have cause to be satisfied.—The love, the admiration, the indifference, the slight, the aversion, and even the contempt, with which these Poems have been received, knowing, as I do, the source within my own mind, from which they have proceeded; and the labour and pains which, when labour and pains appeared needful, have been bestowed upon them,—must all, if I think consistently, be received as pledges and tokens, bearing the same general impression though widely different in value;—they are all proofs that for the present time I have not laboured in vain; and afford assurances, more or less authentic, that the products of my industry will endure."

Lyrical Ballads, Vol. i, p. 368.

Notes

1   Francis Jeffrey did not review *The Naiad and Other Poems* in the *Edinburgh Review*, and its publication was ignored by that periodical. Eight periodicals did review it, however.

   Reynolds had asked Haydon to give to Wordsworth, when Haydon next visited him, a copy of *The Naiad* along with a brief letter that he had written. (Wordsworth did not mention Haydon as a go-between when he responded; his thoughtful letter pinpointed, in some detail, what he considered to be the poem's failings. Reynolds's reaction to Wordsworth's criticism, which was doubtless intended to be taken as constructive, was ambivalent.)

2   In *Bold Stroke for a Wife*, Isabella Centlivre (*c.* 1667–1723) was depicting the moment when a man who had impersonated Simon Pure, a Quaker preacher, was unmasked by 'the real Simon Pure'. Another of her plays, *The Wonder! a Woman keeps a Secret* (1714), provided Garrick with one of his hit roles; he played a jealous husband.

   This tag-line (from V, i, of *Bold Stroke for a Wife*) was used by Reynolds to set the mood for his satirizing Wordsworth's egoism, choice of subject matter, and simplified diction, in the *Preface* to *Peter Bell*.

3   *King Lear*, III, iv, 137.

4   A reference to Wordsworth's 'The Sparrow's Nest', 1–4 (published in 1807).

5   Wordsworth was Distributor of Stamps for Westmorland.

6   'The Thorn', by Wordsworth.

7   Francis Jeffrey, editor of the *Edinburgh Review*.

8   Wordsworth's 'Essay, Supplementary to the Preface' (1820), rpt, *The Prose Works of William Wordsworth*, edited by W. J. B. Owen and Jane Worthington (Oxford: Clarendon Press, 1974), III, 77: 'Having had the good fortune to be born and reared in a mountainous country, from my very

childhood I have felt the falsehood that pervades the volumes imposed upon the world under the name of Ossian. From what I saw with my own eyes, I knew that the imagery was spurious.' Wordsworth continues in this vein for several hundred more words.

9   Charles Cowden Clarke (1787–1877), in *Recollections of Writers* (1878), which he co-wrote with Mary Victoria (1809–98) (both were noted Shakespeare scholars), tells the story of how Wordsworth, while conversing with Keats, responded to the news that Sir Walter Scott's *Rob Roy* would soon be published: he 'read to the Company "Rob Roy's Grave"; then, returning it to the shelf, observed, "I do not know what more Mr. Scott can have to say upon the subject." '

Alfred, Lord Tennyson (1809–92)

Wordsworth was aware, from 1830 on, that the two Tennyson brothers (Charles and Alfred) were writing poetry that deserved a serious reading. For several years he believed that Charles was the superior craftsman. His praise of Alfred was, more often than not, hedged round with reservations. In 1848, shortly before his death, he told Ralph Waldo Emerson that Alfred Tennyson (who would succeed him as Poet Laureate) was 'a right poetic genius, though with some affectation'. The assessment echoed an earlier statement, expressed in 1840, that Tennyson and Keats shared an 'over-lusciousness'. Nevertheless, the right hand gave what the left took away, since Wordsworth thought well of the 'music in syllables' that both poets had mastered. His distaste for Tennyson's first performance – probably *Poems, chiefly Lyrical* (1830), rather than *Poems* (1833) – may be sensed in a number of slighting remarks that he kept making until his death.

Tennyson, like his fellow Apostles at Cambridge, regarded Wordsworth as pre-eminent among the poets of the first half of the century, though he also appreciated and praised the extraordinary achievement of Keats, who had died at too young an age, before his ambitions could be achieved. An oddity often remarked by Tennyson's friends was his reluctance to take advantage of several opportunities to meet Wordsworth. For example, when Wordsworth, accompanying his brother, visited the Lodge at Trinity, where he stayed for several weeks (1830), he enjoyed conversations with numerous undergraduates, but Tennyson was not among them. It is unclear whence the timidity originated. He may have been unwilling to inflict himself on a poet so much older than himself, a patriarch who was well known for his grave and courteous manners. It is at least equally possible that he knew of Wordsworth's dislike of the 'new style of beauty' marking his own poetry. In the mid-1830s Tennyson lived in Ambleside, but refused to travel the short distance to Rydal Mount to meet Wordsworth despite the repeated urging of his friend James Spedding. The entry of Tennyson's name in the visitors' book at Wordsworth's home may (or may not) provide proof of the first meeting of the two poets; nobody knows for sure.

Not until May 1845 did Tennyson willingly accompany Aubrey de Vere on a visit to the aged Wordsworth. Tennyson afterward complained that his effort to stimulate an exchange of views on the bright scarlet leaves he had seen on a tropical island he had once visited foundered on Wordsworth's unwillingness to respond directly. This conversational strain was lightened two days later, when Wordsworth, on the verge of entering the dining room of Edward Moxon's home, took Tennyson's arm and, in an ingratiating way that was irresistible, said, 'Come, brother bard, to dinner.' Tennyson responded, later that evening, by telling Wordsworth of how much pleasure he had experienced while reading his poetry. Wordsworth confessed that he could not maintain his indifference any longer, even though he was convinced that Tennyson entertained little sympathy for what he prized most highly in his own work, 'viz the spirituality with which [he had] endeavoured to invest the material Universe', and 'the moral relation' under which he had wished to exhibit 'its most ordinary appearance'.[1]

He hoped, nevertheless, that Tennyson would 'give the world still better things'. Tennyson, a poet forty years younger than himself, had graduated to become 'the first of our living Poets'. And, even if each of them continued to confide to friends that technical deficiencies prevented complete enjoyment of the other's poetry, a new civility prevailed.

WW, L, VII, 686–8: letter from William Wordsworth to Henry Reed, 1 July 1845[2]

I have as usual been long in your debt, which I am pretty sure you will excuse as heretofore. It gave me much pleasure to have a glimpse of your Brother, under circumstances which no doubt he will have described to you. He spoke of his health as improved, and I hope it will continue to do so. I understood from him that it was probable he should call at Rydal before his return to his own Country. I need not say to you I shall be glad, truly glad to see him both for his own sake and as so nearly connected with you. My absence from home lately was of more than three weeks. I took the journey to London solely to pay my respects to the Queen upon my appointment to the Laureatship upon the decease of my Friend Mr Southey. The weather was very cold, and I caught an inflammation in one of my eyes which rendered my stay in the South very uncomfortable. I nevertheless did in respect to the object of my journey all that was required. The reception given me by the young Queen at her Ball was most gracious. Mrs Everett the wife of your minister among many others was a witness to it; without knowing who I was. It moved her to the shedding of tears. This effect was in part produced, I suppose by American habits of feeling, as pertaining to a republican government like yours. To see a grey haired Man 75 years of age kneeling down in a large assembly, to kiss the hand of a young Woman is a sight for which institutions essentially democratic do not prepare a spectator of either sex, and must naturally place the opinions upon which a Republic is founded, and the sentiments which support it, in strong contrast with a government based and upheld as our's is. I am not therefore surprized that Mrs Everett was moved as she herself described to persons of my acquaintance, among others to Mr Rogers the Poet. By the bye this Gentleman, now I belive in his 83^d year I saw more of than of any other Person except my Host Mr Moxon, while I was in London. He is singularly fresh and strong for his years, and his mental faculties (with the exception of his memory a little) not at all impaired. It is remarkable that he and the Revd W. Bowles were both distinguished as Poets when I was a schoolboy, and they have survived almost all their eminent contemporaries, several of whom came into notice long after them. Since they became known Burns, Cowper, Mason the author of Caractacus and friend of Gray have died. Thomas Warton Laureate, then Byron, Shelley, Keats, and a good deal latter Scott, Coleridge, Crabbe, Southey, Lamb, the Ettrick Shepherd, Cary the Translator of Dante, Crowe the author of Lewesdon Hill, and others of more or less distinction have disappeared. And now of English Poets advanced in life, I cannot recall any but James Montgomery, Thomas Moore, and myself who are living, except the Octogenarian with whom I began. I saw Tennyson when I was in London, several times. He is decidedly the first of our living Poets, and I hope will live to give the world still better things. You will be pleased to hear that he expressed in the strongest terms his gratitude to my writings. To this I was far from indifferent though persuaded that he is not much in sympathy with what I should myself most value in my attempts, viz the spirituality with which I have endeavored to invest the material Universe, and the moral relation under which I have wished to exhibit its most ordinary appearances.

AT, L, II, 162–3: letter from Alfred Tennyson to William Allingham, 21 October 1856

I daresay you have cursed me in your heart[3] for not sending your book[4] before now.

I have been away travelling for more than two months in Wales and did not receive your book till long after you had sent it.

My opinion of your poem is that Georgy Levison is very good and graphic—the man I mean. The poem seems in parts too fine, in the style of the last century, and some of the worst parts of Wordsworth, a style which he inherited and could not quite shake off.

For instance your Corinthian bush means currants—why not say 'currant bush' at once. Wordsworth has 'the fragrant beverage drawn from China's herb' for tea.[5] This sort of avoidance of plain speaking is the more ungrateful to me in your poem because other parts of it are quite unadorned and justly simple. Georgy himself as I said is well-drawn and remains, a picture upon the memory, and will remain I hope to do you honour in men's eyes.

The other poems I have had scarce time to look at since my return, but I may tell you that my little boy, four years old, repeats your 'Robin' with great unction.

> Yours ever, in all haste, but very truly
> A. Tennyson

Mind, I like your Poem and therefore I say about it what I have said. It is *worth* correction. I said I had not read the others; I meant so as to give them their due consideration. 'Mea culpa' I admire much. My wife's kind regards to you.

Notes

1   Mary Moorman, *William Wordsworth: a Biography: the Later Years 1803–1850* (London: Oxford University Press, 1968, 2 vols., II, 572n, 575. Cf. Stephen Gill, *William Wordsworth: a Life* (Oxford: Clarendon Press, 1989), 412. Both Gill and Moorman are paraphrasing the descriptions of Tennyson's two meetings with Wordsworth that are recorded in one of the (unpublished) diaries of Aubrey de Vere. See Wilfrid Ward's biography, *Aubrey de Vere: a Memoir Based on His Unpublished Diaries and Correspondence* (London: Longmans, Green, 1904), 73–4, 373.

2   Wordsworth's letter to Henry Reed, Professor of English Literature at 'the University of Philadelphia' (1 July 1845), was written after he received a visit from William B. Reed, Henry's brother. Wordsworth's high praise of Tennyson, and an expression of his hope that better poems were yet to be written, is carefully worded. *WW, L*, VII, 687–8.

3   Job, i:v.

4   The unnamed 'book' that Tennyson mentions is a collection of poems in manuscript form, later collected and printed in Allingham's *Poems* (Boston: Ticknor and Fields, 1861).

5   Wordsworth, in the 1828 draft of *The Excursion*, described tea as 'the beverage drawn from China's fragrant herb'. Concerned that readers might think the wording 'somewhat too pompous', he changed it to a simpler version for the 1837 edition.

John Stuart Mill (1806–73)

Two autobiographical statements, amounting to a confession of a great debt owed to Wordsworth, are worth remembering. One describes Mill's first encounter with Wordsworth's poems, as printed in the two-volume edition of 1815. Reading them rescued Mill from a period of deep depression, which had begun in August 1826 and lasted through the autumn of 1828.

The other records (briefly) his personal impressions of Wordsworth. Mill, touring the Lakes in 1831, probably met Wordsworth and Southey for the first time at a breakfast given by Henry Taylor (14 November 1830). Almost immediately he scored Southey's personality and intellect, though pleasant enough, as inferior to Wordsworth's ability to render balanced opinions on issues of the day, his eloquent exposition of poetry as an art, and his 'admirable and delightful' conversation. Mill added that he had heard many first-rate talkers, but, he believed, Wordsworth surpassed them all. Perhaps more surprising, given the abundance of contrary opinions then in circulation, is Mill's observation that Wordsworth was generous in his praise of 'good poetry however dissimilar to his own'.

The Victorian Age is rich in instances of mid-life crisis, but Mill's angst remains special. Many biographers and historians have noted the significance (to Mill) of the death of a father, and the subsequent grief of his son, in Jean François Marmontel's *Mémoires d'un père* (1805). Mill's relationship to his own father, who inflicted on him a stern and emotionally desiccated upbringing, is often cited as sufficient cause for, and a plausible explanation of, the depression that, in its worst moments, may even have invited Mill to think of committing suicide.

However, Mill's strong reaction against the moods expressed in the poetry of Byron ('too like my own') resembles the repudiation of Byronism recorded by an impressive number of his contemporaries, including Aubrey de Vere and Tennyson. Perhaps any explanation of Mill's despair that Freudianizes its origin oversimplifies the reasons for his loss of all hope and self-confidence. Taught by his father to collect and weigh evidence for himself, he investigated statements that he could not accept as true simply because they originated from higher authority; this on-going struggle to test seemingly self-evident truisms (i.e., commonly accepted platitudes) required vast expenditures of energy.

Mill himself did not regard his childhood as unhappy, and said so. But, even before his entering India House as a clerk in the examiner's office (1821), his circle of acquaintances did not provide him with the stimulation that might be created by a broad cross-section of views; he yearned for closer friendships; his ambitions were vast and, he increasingly realized, impossible to achieve within a reasonable time period; and during the 1820s, the first decade of his long service as a trusted manager of the company's relations with the native states, he was baffled by the challenge of redefining a concept of human happiness that might more fully engage his own capabilities. Hence, it is understandable why eventually he should turn toward Wordsworth, who wrote the kind of poetry that celebrated a realm of experience he had seen only from afar, namely, the beauties of the natural world, and earn for himself a more sanguine view of unselfish human conduct.

Mill sensed immediately that he had little use for Wordsworth's philosophy as expressed in the 'Ode: Intimations of Immortality', but he expressed, with gratitude, his appreciation of what Wordsworth had done for him. 'The result', Mill wrote, 'was that I gradually, but completely, emerged from my habitual depression, and was never again subject to it.' This candid confession of how he had been rescued by poetry that taught him how to live was appreciated, in equal measure, by many of his contemporaries. They, too, had experienced similar frustrations as they toiled toward what Thomas Carlyle, in *Sartor Resartus*, famously called the Everlasting Yea.

JSM, EL, XII, 80–2: letter from John Stuart Mill to John Sterling, 20 October 1831

I have done nothing in this letter but talk to you about the world in general and about myself. I must now talk to you about other people, and particularly about several new acquaintances of mine that I had not made or had only just begun to make when you left this white world. First of all, I went this summer to the Lakes, where I saw much splendid scenery, and also saw a great deal both of Wordsworth and Southey; and I must tell you what I think of them both. In the case of Wordsworth, I was particularly struck by several things. One was, the extensive range of his thoughts and the largeness & expansiveness of his feelings. This does not appear in his writings, especially his poetry, where the contemplative part of his mind is the only part of it that appears: & one would be tempted to infer from the peculiar character of his poetry, that real life & the active pursuits of men (except of farmers & other country people) did not interest him. The fact however is that these very subjects occupy the greater part of his thoughts, & he talks on no subject more instructively than on states of society & forms of government. Those who best know him, seem to be most impressed with the catholic character of his ability. I have been told that Lockhart[1] has said of him that he would have been an admirable country attorney. Now a man who could have been either Wordsworth or a country attorney, could certainly have been anything else which circumstances had led him to desire to be. The next thing that struck me was the extreme comprehensiveness and philosophic spirit which is in him. By these expressions I mean the direct antithesis of what the Germans most expressively call onesidedness. Wordsworth seems always to know the pros and the cons of every question; & when you think he strikes the balance wrong, it is only because you think he estimates erroneously some matter of fact. Hence all my differences with him, or with any other philosophic Tory, would be differences of matter-of-fact or detail, while my differences with the radicals & utilitarians are differences of principle: for *these see* generally only one side of the subject, & in order to convince them, you must put some entirely new idea into their heads, whereas Wordsworth has all the ideas there already, & you have only to discuss with him concerning the 'how much', the more or less of weight which is to be attached to a certain cause or effect, as compared with others: thus the difference with him turns upon a question of varying or fluctuating quantities, where what is *plus* in one age or country is *minus* in another & the whole question is one of observation & testimony & of the value of particular articles of evidence. I need hardly say to you that if one's own conclusions & his were at variance on every question which a minister or a Parliament could to-morrow be called upon to solve, his is nevertheless the mind with which one would be really in communion: our principles would be the same, and we should be like two travellers pursuing the same course on the opposite banks of a river.— Then when you get Wordsworth on the subjects which are peculiarly his, such as the theory of his own art—if it be proper to call poetry an art, (that is, if art is to be defined the expression or embodying in words or forms, of the highest & most refined parts of nature) no one can converse with him without feeling that he has advanced that great subject beyond any other man, being probably the first person who ever combined, with such eminent success in the practice of the art, such high powers of generalization & habits of meditation on its principles. Besides all this, he seems to me the best talker I ever heard (& I have heard several first-rate ones); & there is a benignity & kindliness about his whole demeanour which confirms what his poetry would lead one to expect, along with a perfect simplicity of character which is delightful in any one, but most of all in a person of first-rate intellect. You see I am somewhat enthusiastic on the subject of Wordsworth, having found him still more admirable & delightful a person on a nearer view than I had figured to myself from his writings; which is so seldom the case that it is impossible to see it without having one's faith in man greatly increased & being made greatly happier in consequence. I also was very much pleased with Wordsworth's family—at least the female part of it. I am convinced that the proper place to see him is in his own kingdom—I call the whole of that mountain region his kingdom, as it will certainly be as much thought of hereafter by the people of Natchitoches or of Swan River, as Mænalus and the Cephissus, or Baiae and Soracte by ourselves, and this from the fortuitous circumstance that he was born there & lived there. I believe it was not there that you were acquainted with him, & therefore I am not telling you an old story in talking about the little palace or pavilion which he occupies in this poetic region, & which is perhaps the most delightful residence in point of situation in the whole country. The different views from it are a sort of abstract or abridgment of the whole Westmoreland side of the mountains, & every spot visible from it has been immortalised in his poems. I was much pleased with the universality of his relish for all good poetry however dissimilar to his own: & with the freedom & unaffected simplicity with which every person about him seemed to be in the habit of discussing & attacking any passage or poem in his own works which did not please them.—I also saw a great deal of Southey, who is a very different kind of man, very inferior to Wordsworth in the higher powers of intellect, & entirely destitute of his philosophic spirit, but a remarkably pleasing & likeable man . . .

JSM, A, I, 138–9, 141, 143, 145, 147, 149, 151, 153: 'A Crisis in My Mental History. One Stage Onward'

FOR SOME YEARS after this time I wrote very little, and nothing regularly, for publication: and great were the advantages which I derived from the intermission. It was of no common importance to me, at this period, to be able to digest and mature my thoughts for my own mind only, without any immediate call for giving them out in print. Had I gone on writing, it would have much disturbed the important transformation in my opinions and character, which took place during those years. The origin of this transformation, or at least the process by which I was prepared for it, can only be explained by turning some distance back.

From the winter of 1821, when I first read Bentham, and especially from the commencement of the *Westminster Review*, I had what might truly be called an object in life; to be a reformer of the world. My conception of my own happiness was entirely identified with this object. The personal sympathies I wished for were those of fellow labourers in this enterprise. I endeavoured to pick up as many flowers as I could by the way; but as a serious and permanent personal satisfaction to rest upon, my whole reliance was placed on this: and I was accustomed to felicitate myself on the certainty of a happy life which I enjoyed, through placing my happiness in something durable and distant, in which some progress might be always making, while it could never be exhausted by complete attainment. This did very well for several years, during which the general improvement going on in the world and the idea of myself as engaged with others in struggling to promote it, seemed enough to fill up an interesting and animated existence. But the time came when I awakened from this as from a dream. It was in the autumn of 1826. I was in a dull state of nerves, such as everybody is occasionally liable to; unsusceptible to enjoyment or pleasurable excitement; one of those moods when what is pleasure at other times, becomes insipid or indifferent; the state, I should think, in which converts to Methodism usually are, when smitten by their first 'conviction of sin'. In this frame of mind it occurred to me to put the question directly to myself, 'Suppose that all your objects in life were realized; that all the changes in institutions and opinions which you are looking forward to, could be completely effected at this very instant: would this be a great joy and happiness to you?' And an irrepressible self-consciousness distinctly answered, 'No!' At this my heart sank within me: the whole foundation on which my life was constructed fell down. All my happiness was to have been found in the continual pursuit of this end. The end had ceased to charm, and how could there ever again be any interest in the means? I seemed to have nothing left to live for.

At first I hoped that the cloud would pass away of itself; but it did not. A night's sleep, the sovereign remedy for the smaller vexations of life, had no effect on it. I awoke to a renewed consciousness of the woful fact. I carried it with me into all companies, into all occupations. Hardly anything had power to cause me even a few minutes oblivion of it. For some months the cloud seemed to grow thicker and thicker. The lines in Coleridge's 'Dejection'—I was not then acquainted with them—exactly describe my case:

> A grief without a pang, void, dark and drear,
> A drowsy, stifled, unimpassioned grief,
> Which finds no natural outlet or relief
> In word, or sigh, or tear.

In vain I sought relief from my favourite books; those memorials of past nobleness and greatness, from which I had always hitherto drawn strength and animation. I read them now without feeling, or with the accustomed feeling *minus* all its charm; and I became persuaded, that my love of mankind, and of excellence for its own sake, had worn itself out. I sought no comfort by speaking to others of what I felt. If I had loved any one sufficiently to make confiding my griefs a necessity, I should not have been in the condition I was. I felt, too, that mine was not an interesting, or in any way respectable distress. There was nothing in it to attract sympathy. Advice, if I had known where to seek it, would have been most precious. The words of Macbeth to the physician often occurred to my thoughts.[2] But there was no one on whom I could build the faintest hope of such assistance. My father, to whom it would have been natural to me to have recourse in any practical difficulties, was the last person to whom, in such a case as this, I looked for help. Everything convinced me that he had no knowledge of any such mental state as I was suffering from, and that even if he could be made to understand it, he was not the physician who could heal it. My education, which was wholly his work, had been conducted without any regard to the possibility of its ending in this result; and I saw no use in giving him the pain of thinking that his plans had failed, when the failure was probably irremediable, and at all events, beyond the power of *his* remedies. Of other friends, I had at that time none to whom I had any hope of making my condition intelligible. It was however abundantly intelligible to myself; and the more I dwelt upon it, the more hopeless it appeared.

My course of study had led me to believe, that all mental and moral feelings and qualities, whether of a good or of a bad kind, were the results of association; that we love one thing and hate another, take pleasure in one sort of action or contemplation, and pain in another sort, through the clinging of pleasurable or painful ideas to those things, from the effect of education or of experience. As a corollary from this, I had always heard it maintained by my father, and was myself convinced, that the object of education should be to form the strongest possible associations of the salutary class; associations of pleasure with all things beneficial to the great whole, and of pain with all things hurtful to it. This doctrine appeared inexpugnable; but it now seemed to me on retrospect, that my teachers had occupied themselves but superficially with the means of forming and keeping up these salutary associations. They seemed to have trusted altogether to the old familiar instruments, praise and blame, reward and punishment. Now I did not doubt that by these means, begun early and applied unremittingly, intense associations of pain and pleasure, especially of pain, might be created, and might produce desires and aversions capable of lasting undiminished to the end of life. But there must always be something artificial and casual in associations thus produced. The pains and pleasures thus forcibly associated with things, are not connected with them by any natural tie; and it is therefore, I thought, essential to the durability of these associations, that they should have become so intense and inveterate as to be practically indissoluble, before the habitual exercise of the power of analysis had commenced. For I now saw, or thought I saw, what I had always before received with incredulity—that the habit of analysis has a tendency to wear away the feelings: as indeed it has when no other mental habit is cultivated, and the analysing spirit remains without its natural complements and correctives. The very excellence of analysis (I argued) is that it tends to weaken and undermine whatever is the result of prejudice; that it enables us mentally to separate ideas which have only casually clung together: and no associations whatever could ultimately resist this dissolving force, were it not that we owe to analysis our clearest knowledge of the permanent sequences in nature; the real connexions between Things, not dependent on our will and feelings; natural laws, by virtue of which, in many cases, one thing is inseparable from another in fact; which laws, in proportion as they are clearly perceived and imaginatively realized, cause our ideas of things which are always joined together in Nature, to cohere more and more closely in our thoughts. Analytic habits may thus even strengthen the associations between causes and effects, means and ends, but tend altogether to weaken those which are, to speak familiarly, a *mere* matter of feeling. They are therefore (I thought) favourable to prudence and clearsightedness, but a perpetual worm at the root both of the passions and of the virtues; and above all, fearfully undermine all desires, and all pleasures, which are the effects of association, that is, according to the theory I held, all except the purely physical and organic; of the entire insufficiency of which to make life desirable, no one had a stronger conviction than I had. These were the laws of human nature by which, as it seemed to me, I had been brought to my present state. All those to whom I looked up, were of opinion that the pleasure of sympathy with human beings, and the feelings which made the good of others, and especially of mankind on a large scale, the object of existence, were the greatest and surest sources of happiness. Of the truth of this I was convinced, but to know that a feeling would make me happy if I had it, did not give me the feeling. My education, I thought, had failed to create these feelings in sufficient strength to resist the dissolving influence of analysis, while the whole course of my intellectual cultivation had made precocious and premature analysis the inveterate habit of my mind. I was thus, as I said to myself, left stranded at the commencement of my voyage, with a well equipped ship and a rudder, but no sail; without any real desire for the ends which I had been so carefully fitted out to work for: no delight in virtue or the general good, but also just as little in anything else. The fountains of vanity and ambition seemed to have dried up within me, as completely as those of benevolence. I had had (as I reflected) some gratification of vanity at too early an age: I had obtained some distinction, and felt myself of some importance, before the desire of distinction and of importance had grown into a passion: and little as it was which I had attained, yet having been attained too early, like all pleasures enjoyed too soon, it had made me *blasé* and indifferent to the pursuit. Thus neither selfish nor unselfish pleasures were pleasures to me. And there seemed no power in nature sufficient to begin the formation of my character anew, and create in a mind now irretrievably analytic, fresh associations of pleasure with any of the objects of human desire.

These were the thoughts which mingled with the dry heavy dejection of the melancholy winter of 1826–7. During this time I was not incapable of my usual occupations. I went on with them mechanically, by the mere force of habit. I had been so drilled in a certain sort of mental exercise, that I could still carry it on when all the spirit had gone out of it. I even composed and spoke several speeches at the debating society, how, or with what degree of success I know not. Of four years continual speaking at that society, this is the only year of which I remember next to nothing. Two lines of Coleridge, in whom alone of all writers I have found a true description of what I felt, were often in my thoughts, not at this time (for I had never read them), but in a later period of the same mental malady:

Work without hope draws nectar in a sieve,
And hope without an object cannot live.[3]

In all probability my case was by no means so peculiar as I fancied it, and I doubt not that many others have passed through a similar state; but the idiosyncracies of my education had given to the general phenomenon a special character, which made it seem the natural effect of causes that it was hardly possible for time to remove. I frequently asked myself, if I could, or if I was bound to go on living, when life must be passed in this manner. I generally answered to myself, that I did not think I could possibly bear it beyond a year. When, however, not more than half that duration of time had elapsed, a small ray of light broke in upon my gloom. I was reading, accidentally, Marmontel's *Memoirs*,[4] and came to the passage which relates his father's death, the distressed position of the family, and the sudden inspiration by which he, then a mere boy, felt and made them feel that he would be everything to them— would supply the place of all that they had lost. A vivid conception of the scene and its feelings came over me, and I was moved to tears. From this moment my burthen grew lighter. The oppression of the thought that all feeling was dead within me, was gone. I was no longer hopeless: I was not a stock or a stone. I had still, it seemed, some of the material out of which all worth of character, and all capacity for happiness, are made. Relieved from my ever present sense of irremediable wretchedness, I gradually found that the ordinary incidents of life could again give me some pleasure; that I could again find enjoyment, not intense, but sufficient for cheerfulness, in sunshine and sky, in books, in conversation, in public affairs; and that there was, once more, excitement, though of a moderate kind, in exerting myself for my opinions, and for the public good. Thus the cloud gradually drew off, and I again enjoyed life: and though I had several relapses, some of which lasted many months, I never again was as miserable as I had been.

The experiences of this period had two very marked effects on my opinions and character. In the first place, they led me to adopt a theory of life, very unlike that on which I had before acted, and having much in common with what at that time I certainly had never heard of, the anti-self-consciousness theory of Carlyle.[5] I never, indeed, wavered in the conviction that happiness is the test of all rules of conduct, and the end of life. But I now thought that this end was only to be attained by not making it the direct end. Those only are happy (I thought) who have their minds fixed on some object other than their own happiness; on the happiness of others, on the improvement of mankind, even on some art or pursuit, followed not as a means, but as itself an ideal end. Aiming thus at something else, they find happiness by the way. The enjoyments of life (such was now my theory) are sufficient to make it a pleasant thing, when they are taken *en passant*, without being made a principal object. Once make them so, and they are immediately felt to be insufficient. They will not bear a scrutinizing examination. Ask yourself whether you are happy, and you cease to be so. The only chance is to treat, not happiness, but some end external to it, as the purpose of life. Let your self-consciousness, your scrutiny, your self-interrogation, exhaust themselves on that; and if otherwise fortunately circumstanced you will inhale happiness with the air you breathe, without dwelling on it or thinking about it, without either forestalling it in imagination, or putting it to flight by fatal questioning. This theory now became the basis of my philosophy of life. And I still hold to it as the best theory for all those who have but a moderate degree of sensibility and of capacity for enjoyment, that is, for the great majority of mankind.

The other important change which my opinions at this time underwent, was that I, for the first time, gave its proper place, among the prime necessities of human well-being, to the internal culture of the individual. I ceased to attach almost exclusive importance to the ordering of outward circumstances, and the training of the human being for speculation and for action. I had now learnt by experience that the passive susceptibilities needed to be cultivated as well as the active capacities, and required to be nourished and enriched as well as guided. I did not, for an instant, lose sight of, or undervalue, that part of the truth which I had seen before; I never turned recreant to intellectual culture, or ceased to consider the power and practice of analysis as an essential condition both of individual and of social improvement. But I thought that it had consequences which required to be corrected, by joining other kinds of cultivation with it. The maintenance of a due balance among the faculties, now seemed to me of primary importance. The cultivation of the feelings became one of the cardinal points in my ethical and philosophical creed. And my thoughts and inclinations turned in an increasing degree towards whatever seemed capable of being instrumental to that object.

I now began to find meaning in the things which I had read or heard about the importance of poetry and art as instruments of human culture. But it was some time longer before I began to know this by personal experience. The only one of the imaginative arts in which I had from childhood taken great pleasure, was music; the best effect of which (and in this it surpasses perhaps every other art) consists in exciting enthusiasm; in winding up to a high pitch those feelings of an elevated kind which are already in the character, but to which this excitement gives a glow and a fervour, which though transitory at its utmost height, is precious for sustaining them at other times. This effect of music I had often experienced; but, like all my pleasurable susceptibilities, it was suspended during the gloomy period. I had sought relief again and again from this quarter, but found none. After the tide had turned, and I was in process of recovery, I had been helped forward by music, but in a much less elevated manner. I at this time first became acquainted with Weber's *Oberon*,[6] and the extreme pleasure which I drew from its delicious melodies did me good, by shewing me a source of pleasure to which I was as susceptible as ever. The good however was much impaired by the thought, that the pleasure of music (as is quite true of such pleasure as this was, that of mere tune) fades with familiarity, and requires either to be revived by intermittence, or fed by continual novelty. And it is very characteristic both of my then state, and of the general tone of my mind at this period of my life, that I was seriously tormented by the thought of the exhaustibility of musical combinations. The octave consists only of five tones and two semitones, which can be put together in only a limited number of ways, of which but a small proportion are beautiful: most of these, it seemed to me, must have been already discovered, and there could not be room for a long succession of Mozarts and Webers, to strike out as these had done, entirely new and surpassingly rich veins of musical beauty. This source of anxiety may perhaps be thought to resemble that of the philosophers of Laputa, who feared lest the sun should be burnt out.[7] It was, however, connected with the best feature in my character, and the only good point to be found in my very unromantic and in no way honorable distress. For though my dejection, honestly looked at, could not be called other than egotistical, produced by the ruin, as I thought, of my fabric of happiness, yet the destiny of mankind in general was ever in my thoughts, and could not be separated from my own. I felt that the flaw in my life, must be a flaw in life itself; that the question was, whether, if the reformers of society and government could succeed in their objects, and every person in the community were free and in a state of physical comfort, the pleasures of life, being no longer kept up by struggle and privation, would cease to be pleasures. And I felt that unless I could see my way to some better hope than this for human happiness in general, my dejection must continue; but that if I could see such an outlet, I should then look on the world with pleasure; content as far as I was myself concerned, with any fair share of the general lot.

This state of my thoughts and feelings made the fact of my reading Wordsworth for the first time (in the autumn of 1828) an important event in my life. I took up the collection of his poems from curiosity, with no expectation of mental relief from it, though I had before resorted to poetry with that hope. In the worst period of my depression I had read through the whole of Byron (then new to me) to try whether a poet, whose peculiar department was supposed to be that of the intenser feelings, could rouse any feeling in me. As might be expected, I got no good from this reading, but the reverse. The poet's state of mind was too like my own. His was the lament of a man who had worn out all pleasures, and who seemed to think that life, to all who possess the good things of it, must necesarily be the vapid uninteresting thing which I found it. His Harold and Manfred had the same burthen on them which I had; and I was not in a frame of mind to derive any comfort from the vehement sensual passion of his Giaours, or the sullenness of his Laras. But while Byron was exactly what did not suit my condition, Wordsworth was exactly what did. I had looked into *The Excursion* two or three years before, and found little in it; and should probably have found as little, had I read it at this time. But the miscellaneous poems, in the two-volume edition of 1815 (to which little of value was added in the latter part of the author's life), proved to be the precise thing for my mental wants at that particular juncture.

In the first place, these poems addressed themselves powerfully to one of the strongest of my pleasurable susceptibilities, the love of rural objects and natural scenery; to which I had been indebted not only for much of the pleasure of my life, but quite recently for relief from one of my longest relapses into depression. In this power of rural beauty over me, there was a foundation laid for taking pleasure in Wordsworth's poetry; the more so, as his scenery lies mostly among mountains, which, owing to my early Pyrenean excursion, were my ideal of natural beauty. But Wordsworth would never have had any great effect on me, if he had merely placed before me beautiful pictures of natural scenery. Scott does this still better than Wordsworth, and a very second-rate landscape does it more effectually than any poet. What made Wordsworth's poems a medicine for my state of mind, was that they expressed, not mere outward beauty, but states of feeling, and of thought coloured by feeling, under the excitement of beauty. They seemed to be the very culture of the feelings, which I was in quest of. In them I seemed to draw from a source of inward joy, of sympathetic and imaginative pleasure, which could be shared in by all human beings; which had no connexion with struggle or imperfection, but would be made richer by every improvement in the physical or social condition of mankind. From them I seemed to learn what would be the perennial sources of happiness, when all the greater evils of life shall have been removed. And I felt myself at once better and happier as I came under their influence. There have certainly been, even in our own age, greater poets than Wordsworth; but poetry of deeper and loftier feeling could not have done for me at that time what his did. I needed to be made to feel that there was real, permanent happiness in tranquil contemplation. Wordsworth taught me this, not only without turning away from, but with a greatly increased interest in, the common feelings and common destiny of human beings. And the delight which these poems gave me, proved that with culture of this sort, there was nothing to dread from the most confirmed habit of analysis. At the conclusion of the Poems came the famous 'Ode', falsely called Platonic, 'Intimations of Immortality': in which, along with more than his usual sweetness of melody and rhythm, and along with the two passages of grand imagery but bad philosophy so often quoted, I found that he too had had similar experience to mine; that he also had felt that the first freshness of youthful enjoyment of life was not lasting; but that he had sought for compensation, and found it, in the way in which he was now teaching me to find it. The result was that I gradually, but completely, emerged from my habitual depression, and was never again subject to it. I long continued to value Wordsworth less according to his intrinsic merits, than by the measure of what he had done for me. Compared with the greatest poets, he may be said to be the poet of unpoetical natures, possessed of quiet and contemplative tastes. But unpoetical natures are precisely those which require poetic cultivation. This cultivation Wordsworth is much more fitted to give, than poets who are intrinsically far more poets than he.

It so fell out that the merits of Wordsworth were the occasion of my first public declaration of my new way of thinking, and separation from those of my habitual companions who had not undergone a similar change. The person with whom at that time I was most in the habit of comparing notes on such subjects was Roebuck,[8] and I induced him to read Wordsworth, in whom he also at first seemed to find much to admire: but I, like most Wordsworthians, threw myself into strong antagonism to Byron, both as a poet and as to his influence on the character. Roebuck, all whose instincts were those of action and struggle, had, on the contrary, a strong relish and great admiration of Byron, whose writings he regarded as the poetry of human life, while Wordsworth's, according to him, was that of flowers and butterflies.

Notes

1　John Gibson Lockhart (1794–1854), author of an important biography of Sir Walter Scott; Lockhart was his son-in-law.
2　*Macbeth*, V, iii, 40–5.
3　Samuel Taylor Coleridge, 'Work without Hope', in *Poetical Works*, Vol. II (London: Pickering, 1828), 81.
4　John François Marmontel, *Mémoires d'un père*, Vol. I (London: Peltier, 1805), 87–8.
5　Thomas Carlyle, *Sartor Resartus*, Book II, Chapters i and ix.
6　Karl Maria von Weber, *Oberon; or, The Elf-King's Oath* (first performed in London in April 1826).
7　Mill refers to Voyage III, Chapter ii, in Jonathan Swift's *Gulliver's Travels*.
8　John Arthur Roebuck (1801–79), a politician whose radical opinions dismayed Mill. A lengthy consideration of Roebuck's views formed an important part of an early draft of Mill's *Autobiography*.

Walter Savage Landor (1775–1864)

The intersection of Walter Savage Landor's interests with those of Wordsworth began promisingly enough. Robert Southey – a close friend, and one whose literary merits were given high praise by Landor on several occasions – passed on to Wordsworth several flattering messages from Landor. Wordsworth responded several times, again through the mediation of Southey's good will. Landor paid a high tribute to Wordsworth in *Idyllia Heroica Decem* (1820), a collection of Latin poems. Longmans, Landor's publisher, was reluctant to print and distribute the book because the firm foresaw limited sales, and Landor was forced to publish it in Pisa. Wordsworth, responding to the compliment, wrote back (3 September 1821) that 'It could not but be grateful to me to be praised by a Poet who has written verses of which I would rather have been the Author than of any produced in our time. What I now write to you, I have frequently said to many.' Wordsworth was alluding to 'Gebir' and 'Count Julian', which he could conjure up from his capacious memory; at the time he wrote his letter, however, his eye inflammation had prevented him from reading the Latin poems themselves.

Landor's praise was a spontaneous reaction to Wordsworth's poetry, a body of work that he considered 'stupendous'. When he wrote to Southey that 'In thoughts, feelings, and images not one amongst the ancients equals him, and his language (a rare thing) is English', he was expressing a genuine delight in an era he believed was very close to a Golden Age – his own. 'Wordsworth, Southey, Miss Bailie, what a class! Even the breakfast-table poets, Campbell, Ld Biron, Scott, Crabbe, Rogers, put all the continent to shame.'

Landor, nevertheless, did not like in equal measure the poems that Wordsworth published only a few years later, and found much to criticize. He became angry when he thought he heard Wordsworth scoff at Southey's talent (Wordsworth, he claimed, had flippantly declared that he would not give five shillings for all Southey's poetry). His imaginary conversation between Robert Southey and Richard Porson (1759–1808), the astonishingly erudite classical scholar, published first in *Blackwood's Magazine* (December 1842), ridiculed Wordsworth as an instrument which had 'no trumpet-stop'. More aggravating still, Landor wrote parodies of Wordsworth; Porson delivered them with gusto, and even imagined that Wordsworth, on an occasion when he had been invited to read from one of the Waverley Novels, became so entranced by Scott's partial quotation of one of his own poems that, totally ignoring Scott's novel, he then proceeded to recite the rest of his own poem.

Four months later Edward Quillinan, Wordsworth's son-in-law, angrily responded in the same forum to what he considered *lèse-majesté*. He attacked Landor as a garrulous sexagenarian and, even worse, a plagiarist. (Landor was more incensed by the second charge than by the first.)

Wordsworth, writing to Sir William Rowan Hamilton (April 1843), said that he had not paid attention to Landor's attack, and, if he had known about it, would have tried to dissuade Quillinan from yielding to a temptation to defend his father-in-law. He added a strong denunciation of Landor, betraying his anger at Landor's other writings about himself.

The breach was destined to widen: matters could not be patched up, as, to some extent, the arguments between Wordsworth and Coleridge, Hazlitt, and Southey were eventually smoothed over. Years later Landor wrote an imaginary conversation between Julius Charles Hare and himself, which allowed the character named Landor to deliver some sincere comments about the 'due honours' that Wordsworth deserved. But the conversation was very carefully phrased; the tribute to Wordsworth's poetical genius was accompanied by serious qualifiers. Even if the conversation had been written and published before Wordsworth's death on 23 April 1850, it would doubtless have been dismissed by Wordsworth as too little and too late.

Landor was consistent in his belief that Wordsworth's faults prevented a conscientious critic (he thought himself to be one) from indulging in hero worship. He loved *The Prelude*, and thought that 'Michael' was a finer poem than anything written by the 'classic poets'; but, when he wrote to Emerson about his changing opinion of the Grasmere sage, he felt compelled to defend Sir Walter Scott against Wordsworth's strictures, and to scoff at Wordsworth's dismissal of Virgil as a poet inferior to Lucretius. He had met Wordsworth relatively late (in 1832), and Wordsworth's conversation on that occasion, which lasted longer than at any subsequent meeting, astonished Landor because so many questions of literary preference were delivered as final judgments. The true strangeness of this relationship may well have been the length of time the friendship lasted before Wordsworth and Landor went their separate ways.

WW, *L*, V, 536: letter from William Wordsworth to William Rowan Hamilton, 25 June 1832

A fortnight ago I came hither to my son and Daughter who are living a gentle, happy, quiet and useful life together. My daughter Dora is also with us. On this day I should have returned but an inflammation in my eyes makes it unsafe for me to venture in an open carriage, the weather being exceedingly disturbed. A week ago appeared here Mr W. S. Landor the Poet and author of the *Imaginary Conversations*, which probably have fallen in your way. We had never met before tho' several letters had passed between us, and as I had not heard that he was in England my gratification in seeing him was heightened by surprise. We passed a day together at the house of my friend Mr Rawson, on the banks of Wastwater. His conversation is lively and original, his learning great tho' he will not allow it and his laugh the heartiest I have heard for a long time. It is I think not much less than 20 years since he left England for France and afterwards Italy where he hopes to end his days, nay [he has] fixed n^r Florence upon the spot where he wishes to be buried. Remember me most kindly to y^r Sisters. Dora begs her love and thanks to y^r Sister Eliza for her last most interesting letter w^h she will answer when she can command a frank.

WW, *L*, VII, 438: letter from William Wordsworth to Sir William Rowan Hamilton, April 1843

The attack upon W. S. L. to which you allude was written by my Son in Law; but without any sanction from me, much less encouragement; in fact I knew nothing about it or the preceding Article of Landor that had called it forth, till after Mr Qu's had appeared. He knew very well that I should have disapproved of his condescending to notice anything that a man so deplorably tormented by ungovernable passion as that unhappy creature might eject. His character may be given in two or three words; a mad-man, a bad-man, yet a man of genius, as many a madman is.—I have not eyesight to spare for Periodical Literature, so with exception of a Newspaper now and then, I never look into anything of the kind, except some particular article may be recommended to me by a Friend upon whose judgement I can rely.

You are quite at liberty to print when and where you like any verses you may do me the honor of writing upon, or addressing to, me—

WSL, *CW*, V, 139–40, 152–3, 154, 155: 'Southey and Porson'

SOUTHEY AND PORSON

PORSON. I suspect, Mr Southey, you are angry with me for the freedom with which I have spoken of your poetry and Wordsworth's.

SOUTHEY. What could have induced you to imagine it, Mr Professor? You have indeed bent your eyes upon me, since we have been together, with somewhat of fierceness and defiance: I presume you fancied me to be a commentator. You wrong me in your belief that any opinion on my poetical works hath molested me; but you afford me more than compensation in supposing me acutely sensible of injustice done to Wordsworth. If we must converse on these topics, we will converse on him. What man ever existed who spent a more inoffensive life, or adorned it with nobler studies?

PORSON. I believe so; and they who attack him with virulence are men of as little morality as reflection.

SOUTHEY. Let Wordsworth prove to the world that there may be animation without blood and broken bones, and tenderness remote from the stews. Some will doubt it; for even things the most evident are often but little perceived and strangely estimated. Swift ridiculed the music of Handel and the generalship of Marlborough; Pope the perspicacity and the scholarship of Bentley; Gray the abilities of Shaftesbury and the eloquence of Rousseau. Shakespeare hardly found those who would collect his tragedies; Milton was read from godliness; Virgil was antiquated and rustic; Cicero, Asiatic. What a rabble has persecuted my friend! An elephant is born to be consumed by ants in the midst of his unapproachable solitudes: Wordsworth is the prey of Jeffrey. Why repine? Let us rather amuse ourselves with allegories, and recollect that God in the creation left his noblest creature at the mercy of a serpent. . . .

PORSON. Wordsworth goes out of his way to be attacked; he picks up a piece of dirt, throws it on the carpet in the midst of the company, and cries, *This is a better man than any of you!* He does indeed mould the base material into what form he chooses; but why not rather invite us to contemplate it than challenge us to condemn it? Here surely is false taste.

SOUTHEY. The principal and the most general accusation against him is, that the vehicle of his thoughts is unequal to them. Now did ever the judges at the Olympic games say, 'We would have awarded to you the meed of victory, if your chariot had been equal to your horses: it is true they have won; but the people are displeased at a car neither new nor richly gilt, and without a gryphon or sphinx engraved on the axle?' You admire simplicity in Euripides; you censure it in Wordsworth: believe me, sir, it arises in neither from penury of thought—which seldom has produced it—but from the strength of temperance, and at the suggestion of principle. . . .

Take up a poem of Wordsworth's and read it—I would rather say, read them all; and, knowing that a mind like yours must grasp closely what comes within it, I will then appeal to you whether any poet of our country, since Milton, hath exerted greater powers with less of strain and less of ostentation. I would, however, by his permission, lay before you for this purpose a poem which is yet unpublished and incomplete.

PORSON. Pity, with such abilities, he does not imitate the ancients somewhat more.

SOUTHEY. Whom did they imitate? If his genius is equal to theirs he has no need of a guide. He also will be an ancient; and the very counterparts of those who now decry him will extol him a thousand years hence in malignity to the moderns.

WSL, L:BA, 356–9

We are now at Rydal Mount.

Wordsworth's bite is less fervid than Carlyle's: it comes with more saliva about it, and with a hoarser expectoration. 'Lucretius he esteems a far *higher* poet than Virgil.'

The more fool he! 'not in his system, which is nothing, but in his power of illustration.'

Does a power of illustration imply the *high* poet? It is in his system (which, according to Wordsworth, *is nothing*), that the power of Lucretius consists. Where then is its use? But what has Virgil in his *Eclogues,* in his *Georgics,* or in his *Æneid,* requiring illustration? Lucretius does indeed well illustrate his subject; and few even in prose among the philosophers have written so intelligibly; but the quantity of his poetry does not much exceed three hundred lines in the whole: one of the noblest specimens of it is a scornful expostulation against the fear of death. Robert Smith, brother of Sidney, wrote in the style of Lucretius such Latin poetry as is fairly worth all the rest in that language since the banishment of Ovid. Even Lucretius himself nowhere hath exhibited such a continuation of manly thought and of lofty harmony.

We must now descend to Wordsworth once again.

He often gave an opinion on authors which he never had read, and on some which he could not read. Plato, for instance. He speaks contemptuously of the Scotch. The first time I ever met him, and the only time I ever conversed with him longer than a few minutes, he spoke contemptuously of Scott, and violently of Byron. He chattered about them incoherently and indiscriminately. In reality, Scott had singularly the power of imagination and of construction: Byron little of either; but this is what Wordsworth neither said nor knew. His censure was hardened froth. I praised a line of Scott's on the dog of a traveller lost in the snow (if I remember) on Skiddaw. He said it was the only good one in the poem, and began instantly to recite a whole one of his own upon the same subject. This induced me afterwards to write as follows on a fly-leaf in Scott's poems,

> Ye who have lungs to mount the Muse's hill,
> Here slake your thirst aside their liveliest rill:
> Asthmatic Wordsworth, Byron piping-hot,
> Leave in the rear, and march with manly Scott.

I was thought unfriendly to Scott for one of the friendliest things I ever did toward an author. Having noted all the faults of grammar and expression in two or three of his volumes, I calculated that the number of them, in all, must amount to above a thousand. Mr. Lockhart, who married his daughter, was indignant at this, and announced at the same time (to prove how very wrong I was) that they were corrected in the next edition.

Poor Scott! he bowed his high intellect and abased the illustrious rank conferred on him by the unanimous acclaim of nations, before a prince who was the approbrium of his country for enduring so quietly and contentedly his Neronianism.

Scott's reading was extensive, but chiefly within the range of Great Britain and France; Wordsworth's lay, almost entirely, between the near grammar school and Rydal Mount. He would not have scorned, although he might have reviled, the Scotch authors, if he ever had read Archibald Bower, or Hume, or Smollett, or Adam Smith; he would have indeed hated Burns; he would never have forgiven Beattie that incomparable stanza,

> O how canst thou renounce the boundless store
> Of charms that Nature to her votary yields,
> The warbling woodlands, the resounding shore,
> The pomp of groves and garniture of fields,
> All that the genial ray of morning gilds,
> And all that echoes to the song of even,
> All that the mountain's sheltering bosom shields,
> And all the dread magnificence of heaven;
> O how canst thou renounce and hope to be forgiven?

Nor would he have endured that song of Burns, more animated than the odes of Pindar,

> Scots wha hae wi' Wallace bled.

He would have been horrified at the Doric-Scotch of 'wha hae'; yet what wool in the mouth were *have* and *with*! Gerald Massey too must have fared ill with him; and the gentle and graceful Tennyson's dress-shoes might have stood in danger of being trodden on by the wooden. Wordsworth's walk was in lowlands of poetry, where the wooden shoe is commodious. The vigorous and animated ascend their high battle-field neither in that not in the slipper, but press on, and breathe hard, ευκνημιδες.

When Hazlitt was in Tuscany he often called on me, and once asked me whether I had ever seen Wordsworth. I answered in the negative, and expressed a wish to know something of his appearance.

'Sir,' said Hazlitt, 'have you ever seen a horse?' 'Assuredly.' 'Then, Sir, you have seen Wordsworth.'

When I met him some years after at a friend's on the lake of Waswater, I found him extremely civil. There was *equinity* in the lower part of his face: in the upper was much of the contemplative, and no little of the calculating. This induced me, when, at a breakfast where many were present, he said he 'would not give five shillings for all Southey's poetry,' to tell a friend of his that he might safely make such an investment of his money and throw all his own in. Perhaps I was too ill-humoured, but my spirit rose against his ingratitude toward the man who first, and with incessant effort and great difficulty, brought him into notice. He ought to have approached his poetical benefactor as he did the

> illustrious peer,
> With high respect and gratitude sincere.

Southey would have been more pleased by the friendliness of the senti-ment than by the intensity of the poetry in which it is expressed; for Southey was the most equitable, the most candid, the most indulgent of mankind. I was unacquainted with him for many years after he had commended in the *Critical Review*, my early poem, *Gebir*. In the letters now edited by Mr. Water, I find that in the *Whitehaven Journal* there was inserted a criticism, in which, on the strength of this poem, I am compared and preferred to Goethe. I am not too much elated. Neither

in my youthful days nor in any other have I thrown upon the world
such trash as 'Werther' and 'Wilhelm Meister,' nor flavoured my poetry
with the corrugated spicery of metaphysics. Nor could he have written
in a lifetime any twenty, in a hundred or thereabout, of my *Imaginary
Conversations*. My poetry I throw to the Scotch terriers growling at my
feet. Fifty pages of Shelley contain more of pure poetry than a hundred
of Goethe, who spent the better part of his time in contriving a puzzle,
and in spinning out a yarn for a labyrinth. How different in features,
both personal and poetical, are Goethe and Wordsworth! In the countenance of Goethe there was something of the elevated and august;
less of it in his poetry: Wordsworth's physiognomy was entirely rural.
With a rambling pen he wrote admirable paragraphs in his longer
poems, and sonnets worthy of Milton: for example,

'Two voices are there,' etc.

which is far above the highest pitch of Goethe. But his unbraced and
unbuttoned impudence in presence of our grand historians, Gibbon
and Napier, must be reprehended and scouted. Of Gibbon I have delivered my opinion; of Napier too, on whom I shall add nothing more at
present than that he superseded the Duke, who intended to write the
history of his campaign, and who (his nephew Capt. William Wellesley
tells me) has left behind him 'Memoirs'.

WSL, L, 63, 155–61

'Cowper was grave and intellectual, but never is prosaic as Wordsworth often is, for example in his dedication to Lord Lonsdale:

' "Illustrious peer
With high respect and gratitude sincere."

'Moore is caught gilding refined gold, yet in the midst of pleasantry
there is tenderness and grace. . . . The " Lays of Rome " are vigorous;
his [Macaulay's] criticism and history are diluted epigrams, and are
more ingenious than just. I have not spoken of Scott, Wordsworth, and
Byron. Scott superseded Wordsworth, and Byron superseded Scott,
unjustly in both instances. Scott had a wider range than either, and
excelled in more qualities.'

With Wordsworth Landor was not always in touch. At first, and when
Wordsworth's merits were eclipsed by the popularity of Byron, Landor

was loud in his praise. 'In thoughts, feelings, and images not one amongst the antients equals him, and his language (a rare thing) is English.'* No poet since Milton, he makes Southey say, had exerted greater powers with less of strain and less of ostentation. 'Laodamia' was 'a composition such as Sophocles might have exulted to own.' This admiration was repaid in kind. 'It could not but be grateful to me,' Wordsworth wrote, 'to be praised by a poet who has written verses of which I would rather have been the author than of any produced in our time; and what I now write to you I have frequently said to many.' The verses referred to were 'Gebir' and 'Count Julian.'

But Landor's liking for Wordsworth, as they grew older, underwent diminution. At a breakfast party, where both were present, Wordsworth said, or Landor fancied he said, that he would not give five shillings for all Southey's poetry. 'My spirit,' Landor afterwards wrote, 'rose against his ingratitude toward the man who first, and with incessant effort and great difficulty, brought him into notice.'† In a second conversation between Southey and Porson, published originally in *Blackwood's Magazine*,‡ Landor's disapproval of what he held to be flaws in Wordsworth's poetry was put in a shape that could hardly fail to vex and grieve the future Laureate's admirers. Porson is made to say that 'among all the bran in the little bins of Mr. Wordsworth's beer-cellar there is not a legal quart of that stout old English beverage with which the good Bishop of Dromore regaled us.' The insinuation is not outrageously unfair. After a course of 'Chevy Chase' and 'Otterburne' a good many people might find even the 'Excursion' a trifle flat. Nor is Porson so very wide of the mark when he says that Wordsworth's is an instrument which has no trumpet-stop. Descending to particulars, he lays his finger on inanities which even a devout Wordsworthian must deplore. Landor also makes Porson the vehicle for some parodies of Wordsworth. One of them begins:

I.

'Hetty, old Dinah Mitchell's daughter,
Had left the side of Derwentwater
   About the end of Summer.
I went to see her at her cot,
Her and her mother, who were not
   Expecting a new comer.

---

*   Landor to Southey, 1818.
†   'Letter to Emerson.'
‡   December, 1842.

II.

'They both were standing at one tub,
You might have heard their knuckles rub
    The hempen sheet they wash'd.
The mother suddenly turn'd round,
The daughter cast upon the ground
    Her eyes, like one abasht.'

And so on. The whole tone of Porson's remarks rather suggests that Landor regretted having praised Wordsworth so highly in former conversations.

However this may be, it served to make Wordsworth's son-in-law, Edward Quillinan, exceedingly angry. Four months later there appeared in *Blackwood's* an Imaginary Conversation written by Mr. Quillinan, who referred, in a note, to Landor as a garrulous sexagenarian. Landor possibly would have pocketed this affront had not a charge of plagiarism been added thereto; of plagiarism, moreover, from the very writer who, as the garrulous sexagenarian was never tired of reiterating, had stolen a sea shell from ' Gebir.' Landor had made Southey say : ' Wit appears to require a certain degree of unsteadiness in the character. Diamonds sparkle the most brilliantly on heads stricken by the palsy.' Now Wordsworth, in a little poem written in 1818, and called ' Inscriptions in a Hermit's Cell,' had said :

' Diamonds dart their brightest lustre
From a palsy-shaken head.'

The resemblance was indisputable, but Landor never told his mortification. He only hastened to cancel the passage; and when the dialogue was reprinted in 1846, not only had all traces of the plagiarism disappeared, but some of Porson's sharpest criticisms, together with the parody quoted above, had been cut out.

' The trumpet blast of Marmion' delighted him [Landor]. No large poem of the time, not even Southey's ' Roderick' was so animated, or so truly heroic. The battle scene, he declared, was one of the four epic pieces transcending all others; the other three being the colloquy of Achilles and Priam in Homer's ' Iliad,' the contention of Ulysses and Ajax in Ovid's ' Metamorphoses,' and the first book of Milton's ' Paradise Lost.' He was no less ready to praise the Waverley Novels. At first, the ' Heart of Midlothian ' was his favourite; but in his old age, it was 'Kenilworth' that he liked best. There is a freshness in all Scott's scenery, he makes Porson say to Southey, and a vigour and distinction in all his characters. 'He seems the brother in arms of Froissart,' and it would not be easy to hit on a happier comparison. He also puts into Porson's mouth a wicked story about Wordsworth, who, being invited to read one of the Waverley Novels, and finding at the commencement a quotation from his own poetry, totally forgot the novel, and recited the poem from end to end, with many comments and more commendations. No doubt there are some people who will laugh at Landor for ranking Scott above Byron as a poet; but a good deal might be said in favour of his choice, and he was always ready to vindicate it.

Robert Browning (1812–89)

The ironic tone of a comment made in Wordsworth's letter to Edward Moxon (12 October 1846) guaranteed its rapid circulation in literary circles. Learning of Elizabeth Barrett's marriage to Robert Browning (12 September), Wordsworth, after expressing a hope that it would be a happy union, added that he did not doubt that 'they will speak more intelligibly to each other than, not withstanding their abilities, they have yet done to the Public'. (*Sordello*, notorious for its complex and often obscure language, had been published six years earlier.)

In 1845 Browning published *Dramatic Romances and Lyrics*, which included 'The Lost Leader'. There is no record that Wordsworth had read it before writing his barbed comment to Moxon (he often refused to read hostile criticism). His reaction to the Browning marriage might have been more strongly worded if he had been aware of the attitude toward himself that Browning held at the time.

Browning tinkered slightly with the wording in subsequent printings, but he thought well enough of the poem to keep it as one of his *Dramatic Lyrics*. Browning found occasion to regret its popularity; age and experience conspired to alter his opinion of Wordsworth's acceptance of the stamp distributorship for Westmorland, vigorous espousal of a number of Tory lines of argument, and acceptance of the post of Poet Laureate as a suitable reward for services rendered. As the years passed, Browning admitted in several letters and conversations that he had Wordsworth in mind when he wrote the poem, but blamed the heat of the moment and his own youthfulness for the insinuation that Wordsworth had changed his politics for 'a handful of silver' and 'a riband to stick in his coat'. Wordsworth, he confessed in a letter to Alexander Grosart, was 'never influenced' by such showy trifles.

The letter reprinted here was sent by Browning to a Miss Lee of West Peckham, Maidstone, who had written to him, in verse, so charmingly that he felt himself obliged to respond. His recantation of the opinion he had held three decades earlier does not seem to settle the question of what the 'unlucky juncture' at that time may have been, either in Wordsworth's life or his own. The poem, at any rate, darkened Wordsworth's image for many Victorians.

Wordsworth first met Browning at the home of Sir Thomas Noon ('Sergeant') Talfourd, who was celebrating the success of his play *Ion* (May 1836). The evening may have been memorable to Browning for another reason; he volunteered to write a play on the Earl of Strafford for Charles Macready, the actor-manager. The subject seemed promising to both men: Strafford had served Charles I as his emissary to Ireland

(1633–39) and was a harsh supporter of the policy of 'Thorough' there. His strongly held opinions and controversial executive actions after his return to England led ultimately to his execution.

Browning met Wordsworth socially on several later evenings at parties given by John Kenyon, a cousin of Elizabeth Barrett, who, as a wealthy bon vivant, made a habit of befriending poets. The relationship between the two poets was not cultivated by either side, and beyond ordinary courtesies did not amount to much. Browning attended meetings of the Wordsworth Society, and once, in the absence of the regular Chair, conducted the Society's business. Though he tried hard ('with the best will in the world') to like Wordsworth's late poems, his heart went out more willingly and frequently to the early ones.

Robert Browning, *The Poems*, Vol. I, edited by Thomas J. Collins (New Haven, Conn.: Yale University Press, 1981), 410–11

The Lost Leader

I
Just for a handful of silver he left us,
    Just for a riband to stick in his coat –
Found the one gift of which fortune bereft us,
    Lost all the others she lets us devote;
They, with the gold to give, doled him out silver,
    So much was theirs who so little allowed:
How all our copper had gone for his service!
    Rags – were they purple, his heart had been proud!
We that had loved him so, followed him, honoured him,
    Lived in his mild and magnificent eye,
Learned his great language, caught his clear accents,
    Made him our pattern to live and to die!
Shakespeare was of us, Milton was for us,
    Burns, Shelley, were with us, – they watch from their graves!
He alone breaks from the van and the freemen,
    – He alone sinks to the rear and the slaves!

II
We shall march prospering, – not through his presence;
    Songs may inspirit us, – not from his lyre;
Deeds will be done, – while he boasts his quiescence,
    Still bidding crouch whom the rest bade aspire:

Blot out his name, then, record one lost soul more,
    One task more declined, one more footpath untrod,
One more devils'-triumph and sorrow for angels,
    One wrong more to man, one more insult to God!
Life's night begins: let him never come back to us!
    There would be doubt, hesitation and pain,
Forced praise on our part – the glimmer of twilight,
    Never glad confident morning again!
Best fight on well, for we taught him – strike gallantly,
    Menace our heart ere we master his own;
Then let him receive the new knowledge and wait us,
    Pardoned in heaven, the first by the throne!

Mrs Sutherland Orr, *Life and Letters of Robert Browning* (London: Smith, Elder, 1908), 122–3

The Lost Leader has given rise to periodical questionings continued until the present day, as to the person indicated in its title. Mr. Browning answered or anticipated them in a letter to Miss Lee, of West Peckham, Maidstone. It was his reply to an application in verse made to him in their very young days by herself and two other members of her family, the manner of which seems to have unusually pleased him.

Villers-sur-mer, Calvados, France: September 7, '75.
    Dear Friends,—Your letter has made a round to reach me—hence the delay in replying to it—which you will therefore pardon. I have been asked the question you put to me—tho' never asked so poetically and so pleasantly—I suppose a score of times: and I can only answer, with something of shame and contrition, that I undoubtedly had Wordsworth in my mind—but simply as 'a model;' you know, an artist takes one or two striking traits in the features of his 'model,' and uses them to start his fancy on a flight which may end far enough from the good man or woman who happens to be 'sitting' for nose and eye.

    I thought of the great Poet's abandonment of liberalism, at an unlucky juncture, and no repaying consequence that I could ever see. But—once call my fancy-portrait *Wordsworth*—and how much more ought one to say,—how much more would not I have attempted to say!

    There is my apology, dear friends, and your acceptance of it will confirm me

Truly yours,
Robert Browning.

Aubrey Thomas de Vere (1814–1902)

De Vere's legacy to the Victorian Age owes much to his admiration of Wordsworth, who in turn praised generously (and perhaps beyond their merits) the poems that were submitted to him for judgment. Wordsworth, focusing on de Vere's sonnets, called them 'the most perfect of the age'. Despite his austere manner and a strong tendency to approve his own work above that of almost any other contemporary, he could make and keep friends – like De Vere – over a long period of time.

De Vere, in addition to his poetry, wrote several dramas and books of travel, literary criticism, and commentaries on Greek literature. *Legends of St. Patrick*, a readable treatment of Irish legends, was one of many such studies that enjoyed a wide readership, and his influence on the Celtic Revival was important and long lasting. He wrote consistently from a religious perspective after his conversion to Roman Catholicism. Richard Hutton, known for his ability to evaluate carefully the role that religious conviction played in the countless volumes of Victorian verse that he reviewed week after week, thought that de Vere's Catholic Church was not the Roman Catholic Church which actually existed; but it was impossible for anyone who knew de Vere to want to find fault with his deep religious beliefs. Not that Wordsworth, who discussed religion frequently with him, ever tried.

The two men immediately liked each other, partly because of shared interests in the role that religion played in uplifting the human spirit. De Vere, in conversation with Wilfrid Ward (who became his biographer), named Wordsworth and Newman as the two great souls who had most impressed him over a long lifetime. Wordsworth, well aware of de Vere's loyalty to him (which Ward called 'a passion'), told de Vere that he rejoiced at having met someone who seemed 'so capable of appreciating his poetry'. More strikingly, he paid close attention to de Vere's suggestions for improving troubling passages in his poems; according to de Vere's memoir, Wordsworth improved his wording at least three times because of recommendations he made.

Writing to his sister Ellen not long after meeting Wordsworth (in early 1841), de Vere characterized Wordsworth's manner of talking in a memorable sentence: 'He murmurs like a tree in the breeze; as softly and as incessantly; it seems as natural to him to talk as to breathe.' In 1845, de Vere succeeded in persuading a reluctant Tennyson to meet Wordsworth. When Wordsworth died, de Vere, in one of several letters he wrote to Isabella Fenwick, lamented the loss of England's 'greatest man', and added, 'He had done his work, however. Perhaps no other poet has ever as completely done what was given him to do, and surely few have ever drunk so deeply of all that is best and deepest in our human lot.'

Wilfrid Ward, *Aubrey de Vere: a Memoir Based on his Unpublished Diaries and Correspondence*, Second Impression (London: Longmans, Green, 1904), 62–6, 105, 265, 392

DURING the years 1845–46 Aubrey de Vere kept a diary. They were years in which he associated much with his friends. They were years, too, of varied and in part painful interest. They witnessed his early intimacy with Wordsworth, the object of his life-long veneration, and with Tennyson, the poet friend of his later years. They saw the ripening of the great friendship of his life with Henry Taylor, who was now drawn closer to him by his marriage to Aubrey's cousin, Theodosia Alice Spring Rice. These years witnessed, too, the crisis of the Oxford Movement and the conversion of Newman. The time in Ireland was critical. English statesmen had at last become alive to the injustice of refusing to give state aid towards the education of Catholic Irishmen. The Maynooth Grant was proposed and passed. Peel introduced his bill for establishing the Queen's Colleges, in which for the first time Catholics might receive University education on equal terms with their Protestant fellow-countrymen. Again 1846 saw the beginning of the great Irish famine which left an indelible impression on Aubrey de Vere. He and his brother Stephen devoted themselves heart and soul to measures of relief, and I cannot doubt that personal contact with the suffering poor, and the strenuous effort to aid his countrymen at that terrible crisis permanently deepened and strengthened the poet's nature.

But perhaps a deeper landmark still in his life-story was the loss in this year (1846) of his dearly loved father. Constant intercourse and similarity of tastes had made the bond between these two a specially close one. The story of the father's illness, which brought out, by the haunting dread of separation, the son's passionate love; the last months of tender intercourse; the short-lived pang of relief when danger seemed past; the final catastrophe—in the end quite unexpected—these belong to the time at which the diary was kept, and give it a deep personal interest.

The earlier part of the diary, however, is chiefly valuable as giving, with the aid of contemporary correspondence, a very vivid picture of

Aubrey's intercourse with his friends. And in this picture Wordsworth naturally claims our first attention.

De Vere first came to know the Bard of Rydal during a visit to London in 1841. In that year, too, he first met Sara Coleridge, the object of perhaps the most ideal friendship of his life. She was the daughter of Samuel Taylor Coleridge, and the widow of her cousin, Henry Nelson Coleridge. The following contemporary letter from Aubrey to his sister gives a graphic word-picture of the Bard, and records his first impressions of the woman whose friendship was so much to him while her life lasted :—

London : June 25, 1841.

My dearest Sister,—I found on opening my desk the beginning of a letter to you which ought to have reached you long ago. You must forgive my long delay in finishing the said epistle in consideration of the extreme difficulty one finds in commanding a quarter of an hour in this great Babel.

I have been seeing and hearing such a multitude of things since my arrival here that it is really difficult to know what to tell you about first. You will not quarrel, however, with my giving precedence to Wordsworth. I have been almost as much with him as if I had been living at his house. When he was with the Marshalls[1] they were not only constantly asking me to meet him, but also contrived in the kindest way to find a place for me in their different excursions. I need not say to you who know him that ' familiarity has not bred contempt ' or even lessened the respect I had always felt for the old Druid. It is true I have discovered that he wears a coat and not singing robes—that he gets hot and dusty like other people, &c., and in this sense it is impossible to meet anyone without something being taken from the ideal, which is not only without faults, but is also, as you used to say, *denuded of impertinences*. This is necessarily true, but beyond this, Wordsworth is all that an admirer of his writings should expect. He strikes me as the kindest and most simple-hearted old man I know, and I did not think him less sublime for enquiring often after you, and saying that you were not a person to be forgotten. He talks in a manner very peculiar. As for duration, it is from the rising up of the sun to the going down of the same. As for quality, a sort of thinking aloud, a perpetual purring of satisfaction. He murmurs like a tree in the breeze ; as softly and as incessantly ; it seems as natural to him to talk as to breathe. He is by nature audible, as well as visible, and goes on thus uttering his being just as a fountain continues to flow, or a star to

shine. In his discourse I was at first principally struck by the extraordinary purity of his language, and the absolute perfection of his sentences; but by degrees I came to find a great charm in observing the
exquisite balance of his mind, and the train of associations in which
his thoughts followed each other. He does not put forward thoughts
like those of Coleridge which astonished his hearers by their depth or
vastness, but you gradually discover that there is a sort of inspiration
in the mode in which his thoughts flow out of each other, and connect
themselves with outward things. He is the voice and Nature the instrument; and they always keep in perfect tune. We went together to
Windsor, and you may imagine the interest with which I saw the old
bard, so thoroughly English in his feelings, looking upon those historical towers as old and grey as himself. We enjoyed all the pictures,
wandered in the courts thinking of the Edwards and Harrys, and paced
the terraces, looked forth over Eton and that glorious expanse of country beyond, and ended the day by hearing the full Cathedral service
chaunted in St. George's Chapel, including the prayer for the 'Knights
Companions of the Noble Order of the Garter,' and an anthem unusually fine, in compliment to Wordsworth. Amongst other subjects, we
talked frequently on the Church. He is greatly interested about the
Oxford Highchurchmen; but says that he has not yet had time to
study their writings sufficiently to come to a conclusion.

I like his wife also very much. She is as sweet-tempered as possible—
single-hearted and full of a spirit of enjoyment and desire to make
others enjoy themselves. His daughter I have met also—and she
enquired much for you. She is just married to a person called
Mr. Quillinan. They were in love with each other fifteen years before
Wordsworth, who saw them always together, thought it possible. He
was much vexed, because the lover is very poor, a holy Roman, and a
person whom his family had taken up to console, on occasion of his
first wife being burned to death. After some years more of patient
waiting, however, [the poet] consented, and the bride seemed very
happy.[2] Wordsworth said once to me that he was very glad to have met
a person who seemed so 'capable of appreciating his poetry' as I did.
I thought the expression would amuse you. His entire simplicity often
makes him say those things which are in truth as far removed from
vanity as possible. I wish I could send you a list of even the subjects we
have talked over, but this is impossible. He is in good spirits about politics—he says he does not wish to be called either Conservative or
Reformer, but an 'improver.' He says that Landor is mad, adding that
he himself heard him advising a lady not to teach her daughters to read
much, but to be careful about their dancing and singing. He calls

Mr. Sydney Smith a 'miserable old man.' He calls Miss Wyndham 'his little rose-bud.' He says that ladies ought to be very particular about their dress, considering it as part of the fine arts. He says that he will publish a volume next year. He says that the 'Recluse' has never been written except a few passages—and probably never will. He says that the poem on the 'Individual Mind' consists of fifteen books, having been lately added to and quite perfected. He says also (and you must tell my father this, as I forgot it) that no copies are to be given of the sonnet he sent him, though he is quite at liberty to print it as a motto.

And now I must really say no more about him.

A little later Aubrey de Vere stayed with Miss Fenwick, Wordsworth's neighbour and dear friend, and saw the bard in his mountain home. De Vere's own tender friendship for Miss Fenwick also laid its foundations at this time. It was, he tells us, a case of 'friendship at first sight.' In 1842 he stayed in Wordsworth's own house—'the greatest honour,' he often declared, of his life.

The worst line in Wordsworth is that in which he calls our great Mahometan Poet 'Holiest of Men.' I thought for a long time that he meant *himself*, and as such admired the line as a piece of poetical parrhesia. What a *low* conception of the Supreme Being, that of making him a Theologian! I would rather he called him a 'cloud-compeller' than made him a wielder of theological clouds, which evidently rise from the swamps of our fallen humanity when Apollo chooses to play with it. Dante's conception of God was a thousand times loftier and purer. Just observe the feeling of the *Infinite* which belongs to the last few lines of his poem—the one great Christian Poem. Advancing from height to height in eminence of beatific vision he last comes within sight of the Mystery of the Trinity. Then he said, the *Mind* stopped and staggered, but the *Will* rolled forward still, like that Wheel on which Heaven and all the Stars revolve. Milton's conception of woman was Eastern, and was wholly without spirituality, tenderness, or chivalry. The highest thing about him was his conception of man, the being 'for contemplation and for valour formed.'

It appears to me that single poems of length lose even more by the 'superfluous,' than volumes of short pieces by want of weeding. Wordsworth's works would, I think, gain much by the omission of at least as many small poems as would make a volume; but far greater, as it strikes me, would be the gain to the 'Excursion' if most of the 'interstitial matter' were omitted. Indeed I believe it would be better still, if the exquisite 'Tales' and Philosophical Poems of which it chiefly consists were published in a form as separate as 'Michael' and 'Tintern Abbey.' Great and original poet as he is, even Wordsworth has much to fear from prolixity and repetition, as regards that idle prodigal Posterity, and he has already lost much. As for Coleridge, I used almost to quarrel with my dear friend Mrs. H. N. Coleridge, because she would not publish her father's volume of poems with the omission of the first hundred pages, the juvenile pieces. The statue is spoilt by the heap of rubbish at its base, and the building half hidden by the remains of what should have been regarded as mere scaffolding. Could Shelley's poems be reduced to half their collective bulk, their wonderfulness would be doubled. A Poet's less good things *betray him*: they show us how he worked. The Muse, if wise, no more admits us to her dressing-room than any other lady.

I once asked Mr. de Vere, who, among all the great souls he had known, had impressed him the most? He said instantly, 'Wordsworth and Newman; they are the two for whom my love has been most like idolatry.' There were precious pages about Newman in the 'Recollections,' but the great disappointment of that book was the comparative absence of any salient notes about Wordsworth. I think Mr. de Vere felt the subject almost too sacred for annotation, and yet in personal talk he was always ready to return to it. His loyalty to Wordsworth was a passion.

Notes

1 Aubrey de Vere's first cousin, Thomas Charles Spring Rice, married the daughter of William Marshall, an MP of Hallsteads, Cumberland. The sister of Thomas Rice married James Marshall.

2 Dora Wordsworth's marriage to Edward Quillinan (May 1841) took place after serious and sustained opposition from her father. The reasons for Wordsworth's reluctance to surrender his daughter to the man she deeply loved were complicated, and perhaps, even if disentangled one from another, did not reflect well on Wordsworth. Quillinan expressed anger several times. Only the intercession of Isabella Fenwick, Wordsworth's neighbor and a woman whom, he said, he loved and esteemed, managed to bring the engagement to its long-awaited concluding moment: a marriage in Bath, where Ms Fenwick had taken a house. Nevertheless, Wordsworth was so overcome by emotion that he chose not to attend the wedding ceremony.

Benjamin Robert Haydon (1786–1846)

A key document of the Romantic Movement is the diary kept by Benjamin Robert Haydon between 1808 and 1846. It may well have been intended to serve as a basis for a published book, but its existence was not even suspected by many of Haydon's friends during his lifetime. The *DNB* quietly notes that its 26 volumes, 'bulky, parchment-bound, ledger-like folios' form 'one of the most tragical records extant'.

Haydon's life was marked by a strong egotism that frequently ignored the limitations of his artistic capabilities; injudicious and often unnecessary quarrels with patrons and the press; mounting debts that he often did not plan to repay (including money owed to a financially strapped John Keats); a startlingly uneven history of successes and failures in art competitions and exhibitions; and an embarrassing series of domestic problems. His suicide on 22 June 1846 was not entirely unexpected to those who knew him.

Nevertheless, he kept afloat, and his determination to persevere doubtless contributes to a consensus that has held up for more than a century: he was an artist with unusually heroic aspirations; he earned and kept the friendship of an extraordinary cross-section of writers, artists, and theatrical people (Scott, Southey, Lamb, Keats, Mrs. Siddons, etc.); his conversations scintillated. He recognized and encouraged talent in others, and never saw a reason to differ strongly from Wordsworth, whom he consistently characterized as 'a Genius', over a surprisingly long period of years. (Wordsworth, who enjoyed his conversations with Haydon, addressed, as an unsolicited sign of friendship, two beautiful sonnets to him.)

The *Autobiography*, a rough and unfinished draft that Haydon would doubtless have revised had he been given the needed time, follows his life up to 1820. It was edited and published in 1853 by Tom Taylor, a man of letters as well as a barrister and a member of the faculty at London University. As in the case of the *Diary*, Taylor's editing is more Victorian than modern, and he freely omitted or adapted passages as he thought appropriate for his audience. The standard edition, prepared by Willard Bissell Pope, was published in five volumes by Harvard University Press (1960–63).

The quality of the writing is extraordinary even when the author is considered as a secret competitor with his contemporaries, who included many superb literary talents. One example of how Haydon reproduced the ambience of 28 December 1817, a notable evening of conversation and high spirits, is his description of an 'immortal dinner', an evening that brought together, among several other bon vivants, Wordsworth and Lamb in Haydon's studio, 'with Jerusalem towering up' behind them 'as a background'. Haydon's review of what happened there depicts Wordsworth in an unbuttoned mood. Elsewhere, in the excerpts that follow, we find Wordsworth candidly revealing his opinions on topics that interested him; the anecdotes, often recorded without Haydon's taking the opportunity to editorialize, are fresh, illuminating, first hand, and not easily equalled for their insight or almost uncanny rightness of phrasing. A reader of Haydon's journal will learn a great deal about all the great Romantic figures (even Byron, the only important poet whom Haydon never met personally, turns up in several telling entries). But Haydon's perspective on Wordsworth's character, when set against the strong reactions of many who took offence at his stiffness of manner, is both unique and welcome.

BRH, D, I, 446, 450–2

[1815] *May 23.* I Breakfasted with Wordsworth & spent delightful two hours. Speaking of Burke, Fox, & Pitt, he said, 'You always went from Burke with your mind filled, from Fox with your feelings excited, & from Pitt with wonder at his making you uneasy, at his having had the power to make the worse appear the better reason. Pitt preferred power to principle,' he said.

[1815] *June 13.* I had a cast made yesterday of Wordsworth's face. He bore it like a philosopher. Scott[1] was to meet him at Breakfast. Just as he came in the Plaister was covered over. Wordsworth was sitting in the other room in my dressing gown, with his hands folded, sedate, steady, & solemn. I stepped in to Scott, & told him as a curiosity to take a peep, that he might say the first sight he ever had of so great a poet was such a singular one as this.

I opened the door slowly, & there he sat innocent & unconscious of our plot against his dignity, unable to see or to speak, with all the mysterious silence of a spirit.

When he was relieved he came into breakfast with his usual cheerfulness, and delighted & awed us by his illustrations & bursts of inspiration. At one time he shook us both in explaining the principles of his system, his views of man, & his objects in writing.

Wordsworth's faculty is describing all these intense feelings & glimmerings & doubts & fears & hopes of Man, as referring to what he might be before he was born & to what he may be hereafter. He is a great Being, and will hereafter be ranked as one who had *a portion* of the spirit of Homer, Virgil, Dante, Tasso, Shakespeare, Chaucer & Milton, but as one who did not possess the power of wielding these feelings to any other purpose but as referring to himself and as wishing to make others feel by personal sympathy. This is, in my opinion, his great characteristic distinction.

We afterwards called on Hunt,[2] and as Hunt had previously attacked him & has now reformed in his opinions, the meeting was interesting. Hunt paid him the highest compliments, & told him that as he grew wiser & got older he found his respect for his powers & enthusiasm for his genius encrease. Hunt was ill or it would have been his place to call on Wordsworth. Here again he really burst forth with burning feelings & I never saw him so eloquent as today.

I afterwards sauntered along to Hampstead with him with great delight. Never did any Man so beguile the time as Wordsworth. His purity of heart, his kind affections, his soundness of principle, his information, his knowledge, his genius, & the intense & eager feelings with which he pours forth all he knows affect, enchant, interest & delight one. I don't know any man I should be so inclined to worship as a purified being.

Last night I was at an insipid rout and certainly the contrast was vivid. The beauty of the Women was the only attraction.

In speaking of Lucien Buonaparte's Poem,[3] I said the materials were without arrangement as referring to an end. 'Oh, I don't care for that,' said he, 'if there are *good things* in a Poem.' Now here he was decidedly wrong but he did not say this with reference to the Charlemagne because he thought little of it, but with reference to my idea.

Wordsworth is original surely on this principle — he has one part (& perhaps the finest) of the genius of the great but he has not all. He has not the lucidus ordo [clearness of order]; he does not curb, direct his inspirations for a positive moral, but leaves them to be felt only by those who have a capacity to feel with equal intensity. The moral is not obvious, only the feeling; but he that can feel the feeling will feel the moral too.

June 14. My feelings, my heart, yearn & are sick for a sweet woman on whose bosom I could lay my head & in whose heart I could confide. I would marry her from any class of life if she had elegant & tender feelings, but alas, I have seen so much of the weakness of women, or perhaps their vices, that I often sigh with agony that we can call these delicate creatures ours, but not *their appetites*. My love, my enthusiasm, my reverence for a woman of susceptibility & virtue is unbounded; to women I owe the change of my taste since Macbeth; their loveliness & softness & beauty have worked a reformation in my Soul, have expanded my sensations, & softened the fierceness of my Nature. Could I but meet with one! But even if I could, I must yet sacrifice my feelings till their gratification will not interrupt the great object of my being. How many feelings am I obliged to curb with iron grasp till that be accomplished.

At a house where I visited, a most elegant, lovely servant opened the door; an exchange of feeling took place in our eyes. When she came in nothing could be more graceful. The Mistress & family talked of her kindness of heart, elegance of manner, and said she had a mind above her situation. This affected me. I longed for her to be pure & virtuous, but alas, the next time I went a hang[?] of the head & smile of intelligent meaning gave indications of an easy conquest. I was melancholy, as I have often been, at such disappointments, to me at least when I had highest views, than corrupting their hearts [*the rest of the page is torn away*].

People find fault with Wordsworth for speaking of his own genius; to be sure they do! The World always find fault with a man of genius for speaking of his own genius [*the rest of the page is torn away*].

BRH, *D*, II, 147–8, 171–6, 182–3, 311–12, 469–70

[1817] *December 2*. Wordsworth is in Town again & looks better than ever. He sat to me today for his head & I made a drawing of him.[4] He read Milton & his Tintern Abbey & the happy Warrior, & some of his finest things. He is a most eloquent power. He looked like a spirit of Nature, pure & elementary. His head is like as if it was carved out of a mossy rock, created before the flood! It is grand & broad & persevering. That nose announces a wonder. He sees his road & his object vividly & clearly & intensely, and never turns aside. In moral grandeur of Soul and extension of scope, he is equal to Milton. He seems to me to be the organ of the Deity as to conduct & what ought to be cherished & what commended, to lead a Man to that immortal glory, endless & infinite!

[1817] *December 22*. Wordsworth sat to me today & I began to put his head into my Picture. He read all the book of 'Despondence Corrected'[5] in his Excursion in the finest manner.

Wordsworth's great power is an intense perception of human feelings regarding the mystery of things by analyzing his own, Shakespeare's an intense power of laying open the heart & mind of man by analyzing the feelings of others acting on themselves. The moral in

Shakespeare is inferred from the consequences of conduct, that of Wordsworth is enforced by a previous devellopement of Duty. Shakespeare is the organ of Nature; Wordsworth of Piety, Religion, & Virtue. Wordsworth lays down the duty of man, from which to swerve is to do wrong. Shakespeare has no moral code, and only leaves it at the option of all how to act by shewing the consequences of such & such conduct in acting. Wordsworth tries to render agreable all that hitherto has alarmed the World, by shewing that Death, the Grave, futurity are the penalties only to go to a happier existence. Shakespeare seems reckless of any principles of guidance. He takes futurity, Death, & the Grave as materials to act on his different characters, and tho' one may be horrified one moment in reading what Claudio says of Death, we may be reconciled the next by attending to what the Duke has said of Life,[6] and be uncertain which to believe, and leave off in intense and painful distraction.

In grief & the troubles of life Shakespeare solaces by our finding similar feelings displayed by others in similar situations; that is sympathy. In Grief & in misery the comfort & consolation Wordsworth affords is by consolidating the hopes & glimmerings man has from a higher power into a clear & perceptible reality. What we hope he assures us of. What we fear he exhibits without apprehension; of what we have a horror he reconciles us to, by setting it before us with other associations. Wordsworth is the Apostolic Poet of Piety & Pure thoughts, and Shakespeare, dear Shakespeare, the organ of nature herself, with all her follies & captivations & beauties & vices. Wordsworth's feelings are exclusive, because his intensity of purpose is so strong. His object is to reform the World, by pointing out to it how it *ought to be*; Shakespeare to delight it, by shewing Nature herself how she is. It would be the height of absurdity to say that the Power of dear Shakespeare, in its infinite variety,[7] does not entitle him to the highest place over all Poets, but in moral scope & height of purpose, Milton & Wordsworth have greater intention & nobler views than Shakespeare has shewn; take any one power separately & compare it with theirs. They have *but one*, but that one is the highest on Earth; it is to guide Man to deserving, endless happiness in futurity.

[1817] *December 26*. Got in Newton's head. Voltaire, Newton, & Wordsworth make a wonderful contrast.

[1817] *December 28*. Wordsworth dined with me; Keats & Lamb with a Friend made up the dinner party, and a very pleasant party we had. Wordsworth was in fine and powerful cue. We had a glorious set to on Homer, Shakespeare, Milton, & Virgil. Lamb got excessively merry and witty, and his fun in the intervals of Wordsworth's deep & solemn intonations of oratory was the fun & wit of the fool in the intervals of Lear's passion. Lamb soon gets tipsey, and tipsey he got very shortly, to our infinite amusement. 'Now, you rascally Lake Poet,' said Lamb, 'you call Voltaire a dull fellow.'[8] We all agreed there was a state of mind when he would appear so – and 'Well let us drink his health,' said Lamb. 'Here's Voltaire, the Messiah of the French nation, & a very fit one.'

He then attacked me for putting in Newton, 'a Fellow who believed nothing unless it was as clear as the three sides of a triangle.' And then he & Keats agreed he had destroyed all the Poetry of the rainbow, by reducing it to a prism. It was impossible to resist them, and we drank 'Newton's health, and confusion to mathematics!' It was delightful to see the good Humour of Wordsworth in giving in to all our frolics without affectation and laughing as heartily as the best of us.

By this time other visitors began to drop in, & a Mr. Ritchie,[9] who is going to penetrate into the interior of Africa. I introduced him to Wordsworth as such, & the conversation got into a new train. After some time Lamb, who had seemingly paid no attention to any one, suddenly opened his eyes and said, alluding to the dangers of penetrating into the interior of Africa, 'and pray, who is the Gentleman we are going *to lose?*' Here was a roar of laughter, the *victim* Ritchie joining with us.

We now retired to Tea, and among other Friends, a Gentleman who was *comptroller of the Stamp Office* came.[10] He had been peculiarly anxious to know & see Wordsworth. The moment he was introduced he let Wordsworth know *who* he officially was. This was an exquisite touch of human Nature. Tho' Wordsworth of course would not have suffered him to speak indecently or impiously without reproof, yet he had a visible effect on Wordsworth. I felt pain at the slavery of office. In command men are despotic, and those who are dependent on others who have despotic controul must & do feel affected by their presence. The Comptroller was a very mild & nice fellow but rather weak & very fond of talking. He got into conversation with Wordsworth on Poetry, and just after he had been putting forth some of his silly stuff, Lamb, who had been dozing as usual, suddenly opened his mouth and said, 'What did you say, Sir?' 'Why, Sir,' said the Comptroller, in his milk & water insipidity, 'I was saying &c., &c., &c.' 'Do you say so, Sir?' 'Yes, Sir,' was the reply. 'Why then, Sir, I say, hiccup, you are — you are a silly fellow.' This operated like thunder! The Comptroller knew nothing of his previous tipsiness & looked at him like a man bewildered. The venerable anxiety of Wordsworth to prevent the Comptroller being angry, and his expostulations with Lamb, who had sunk back again into his doze, as insensible to the confusion he had produced as a being above it; the astonishment of Landseer the Engraver, who was totally deaf, & with his hand to his ear & his eye was trying to catch the meaning of the gestures he saw; & the agonizing attempts of Keats, Ritchie, & I to suppress our laughter; and the smiling struggle of the Comptroller to take all in good part, without losing his dignity, made up a story of comic expressions totally unrivalled in Nature. I felt pain that such a Poet as Wordsworth should be under the supervisorship of such a being as this Comptroller. The People of England have a horror of Office, an instinct against it. They are right. A man's liberty is gone the moment he becomes official; he is the Slave of Superiors, and makes others slaves to him. The Comptroller went on making his profound remarks, and when any thing very *deep* came forth,* Lamb roared out,

> Diddle iddle don
> My son John
> Went to bed with his breeches on
> One stocking off & one stocking on,
> My son John

The Comptroller laughed as if he marked it, & went on; every remark Lamb chorused with

> Went to bed with his breeches on
> Diddle iddle on.

There is no describing this scene adequately. There was not the restraint of refined company, nor the vulgar freedom of low, but a frank, natural license, such as one sees in an act of Shakespeare, every man expressing his natural emotions without fear. Into this company, a little heated with wine, a Comptroller of the Stamp Office walked, frilled, dressed, & official, with a due awe of the powers above him and a due contempt for those beneath him. His astonishment at finding where he was come cannot be conceived, and in the midst of his mild

---

* Such as 'Pray, Sir, don't you think Milton a very *great genius?*' This I really recollect. 1823.

namby pamby opinions, Lamb's address deadened his views. When they separated, Wordsworth softened his feelings, but Lamb kept saying in the Painting [room], 'Who is that fellow? Let me go & hold the candle once more to his face—

   My son John
   Went to bed with his breeches on —

& these were the last words of C. Lamb. The door was closed upon him. There was something interesting in seeing Wordsworth sitting, & Keats & Lamb, & my Picture of Christ's entry towering up behind them, occasionally brightened by the gleams of flame that sparkled from the fire, & hearing the voice of Wordsworth repeating Milton with an intonation like the funeral bell of St. Paul's & the music of Handel mingled, & then Lamb's wit came sparkling in between, & Keats's rich fancy of Satyrs & Fauns & doves & white clouds, wound up the stream of conversation. I never passed a more delightful day, & I am convinced that nothing in Boswell is equal to what came out from these Poets. Indeed there were no such Poets in his time. It was an evening worthy of the Elizabethan age, and will long flash upon 'that inward eye which is the bliss of Solitude.'[11] Hail & farewell!

[1818] *January 15*. Wordsworth sat to me for a chalk sketch of his head. He sat like a Poet and Philosopher, calm, quiet, amiable. I succeeded in a capital likeness of him, and when it is framed shall send it to him as a mark of my affection — he was the first who wrote me a sonnet — when such a thing was indeed an elevation. It is quite impossible to convey by words the sensation I have when looking at Nature, so intense is her identity, so heavenly her beauty, so pure her simplicity, so divine her expression, that my soul becomes enamoured, I look till my nature akes with drinking her beauties. My own attempts look so wretched that after a model leaves me I walk about the room in a positive torture, & it is not till the impression of Nature wears off my own efforts are at all tolerable.

[1821] *March 7*. Wednesday. Sir Walter Scott breakfasted with me with Lamb, Procter,[12] & Wilkie, and a delightful morning we had. I never saw any man have such an effect on company as he; he operated on us like champagne & whisky mixed. He alluded to Waverley & there was a dead silence. Wilkie, who was talking to him, stopped & was agitated, you would have thought that *he* was the author. I was bursting to have a good round at them, but as this was the first visit, I did not venture yet, but I anticipate some fun bye & bye, for talk of those I will, & to

him. As he was in such request I feared he would not be able to keep his engagement, so went for him in a coach. When I got him in I could not conceal my pleasure. 'Well,' said I, 'I am delighted to have you,' at which his face seemed to wrinkle up with satisfaction, as if he saw through my character.

It is singular how success & the want of it operate on two extraordinary men, Wordsworth & Walter Scott. Scott enters a room & sits at table, with the coolness & self possession of conscious fame; Wordsworth with an air of mortified elevation of head, as if fearful he was not estimated as he deserved. Scott is always cool, & amusing; Wordsworth often egotistical and overbearing. Scott can afford to talk of trifles because he knows the World will think him a great man who condescends to trifle; Wordsworth must always be eloquent & profound, because he knows he is considered childish & puerile. Scott seems to wish to seem less than he is; Wordsworth struggles to be thought at the moment greater than he is suspected to be.

This is natural. Scott's disposition can be traced to the effect of Success operating on a genial temperament, while Wordsworth's takes its rise from the effect of unjust ridicule wounding a deep self estimation.

Yet I do think Scott's success would have made Wordsworth insufferable, while Wordsworth's failures would not have rendered Scott a bit less delightful. Scott is the companion of nature in all her feelings & freaks; Wordsworth follows her like an apostle, and shares her solemn meditations.

[1821] *March 29*. Met Moore at dinner, and spent a very pleasant three hours. He told his stories with a hit or miss air, as if accustomed to people of quick and refined sensibility. Rothschild at Paris (a Jew) asked who they would have as a God-Father for his child. 'Talleyrand,' said a French man. 'Pourquoi, Monsieur?' 'Parcequ'il est le moindre Chrétien possible,' replied he!

Moore is a delightful, gay, refined, voluptuous, natural creature, infinitely more unaffected than Wordsworth, not blunt & uncultivated as Chantrey, or bilious & shivering like Campbell — no affectation, but a true, refined, delicate, frank Poet, with sufficient air of the World to prove his fashion, sufficient honesty of manner to shew fashion had not corrupted his native taste; making allowance for prejudices instead of condemning them, by which he seemed to have none himself; never talking of his own works, from intense consciousness that every body else did, while Wordsworth is always talking of his own productions from apprehension that they are not matter enough of conversation.

[1824] One day Wordsworth in a large Party, at a moment of silence, leaned forward & said, '*Davy*, do you know the reason I published *my* White Doe in *Quarto*?' 'No,' said Davy, rather blushing. 'To express my own opinion of it,' he replied.

Once I was walking with Wordsworth in Pall Mall, & we ran in to Christie's, where there was a very good copy of the Transfiguration, which he abused through thick & thin. In the corner stood the group of Cupid & Psyche kissing. After looking some time, he turned round to me with an expression I shall never forget, & said, 'The *Dev-ils*.'

He was relating to me with great horror Hazlitt's licentious conduct to the girls of the Lake, & that no woman could walk after dark, for 'his Satyr & *beastly* appetites.' Some girl called him a black-faced rascal, when Hazlitt enraged pushed her down, '& because, Sir,' said Wordsworth, 'she refused to gratify his abominable & devilish propensities,' he lifted up her petticoats & *smote* her on *the bottom*.

BRH, D, IV, 565

[1839] *June 19.* Notwithstanding the seclusion & quiet of my little Room, I do not read with such Comfort as in my Painting Room, smelling of paint as it is. I have brought down my writing desk, & shall have about half [a] dozen favorites on the top — Milton, Shakespeare, Dante, Tasso, Homer, Vasari, &, above all, the Bible & Testament always to refer to — & Wordsworth.

BRH, D, V, 158–9, 168, 170, 441–2

[1842] *May 22.* Wordsworth called today, and we went to Church together. There was no seat to be got at the Chapel near us, belonging to the Rectory of Paddington, & we sat among publicans & sinners.[13] I was determined to try him, so advised to stay as we could hear more easily. He agreed like a Christian, and I was much interested in seeing his Venerable white head close to a Servant in livery, and on the same level.

The Servant in livery fell asleep, & so did Wordsworth. I jogged him at the Gospel, & he opened his eyes and read well. A Preacher preached when we expected another, so it was a disappointment. We afterwards walked to Rogers' across the Park.

[1842] As Wordsworth & I crossed the Park, we said, 'Scott, Wilkie, Keats, Hazlitt, Beaumont, Jackson, Charles Lamb are all gone — we only are left.' He said, 'How old are you?' '56,' I replied. 'How old are you?' '73,' he said; 'in my 73rd year. I was born [in] 1770.' '& I in 1786.' 'You have many years before you.' 'I trust I have — & you, too, I hope. Let us cut out Titian, who was 99.' 'Was he 99?' said Wordsworth. 'Yes,' said I, 'and his Death was a moral, for he was plundered as he lay dying of the plague, and could not help himself.'

We got on Wakely's abuse.[14] We laughed at him & quoted his own beautiful address to the Stock Dove.[15] He said, once in a Wood, Mrs. Wordsworth & a Lady were walking, when the Stock Dove was cooing. A Farmer's wife coming by said to herself, 'Oh, I do like Stock Doves.' Mrs. Wordsworth, with all the enthusiasm for Wordsworth's Poetry, took the old Woman to her heart; 'but,' continued the old woman, *'some like them in a pie; for my part there's nothing like them stewed in onions.'*

[1842] *June 14.* Out on business. Saw dear Wordsworth, who promised to sit at 3. Wordsworth sat & looked Venerable, but I was tired with the heat & very heavy, & he had an inflamed lid[16] & could only sit in one light, the light I detest, for it hurts my Eyes. I made a successful Sketch. He comes again tomorrow.

We talked of our merry dinner with C. Lamb & John Keats. He then feel asleep, & so did I nearly, it was so hot — but I suppose we are getting dozy.

June 16. Wordsworth breakfasted early with me, & we had a good sitting. He was remarkably well, & in better spirits, & we had a good set to.

I told him Canova said of Fuzeli, 'Ve ne sono [*sic* for *solo*] in Arte due cose, il fuoco & la fiamma.' 'He forgot the third,' said Wordsworth, 'that is il fumo, of which Fuzeli had plenty.'

His knowledge of Art is extraordinary in technical knowledge. He detects hands like a Connoiseur or Artist, & we spent a very pleasant morning. We talked again of our old Friends, and to ascertain his real height I measured him, & found him, to my wonder, 8 heads high, or 5 ft. 9 In. 7/8th — a very fine, heroic proportion. He made me write it down, in order, he said, to shew Mrs. Wordsworth my opinion of his *puportions.*

[1842] 'Pray,' said I to Wordsworth, 'what did you mean, many years ago, when I took you accidentally into Christie's (Pall Mall at that time) and we saw Cupid & Psyche kissing — what did you mean, after looking some time, by inwardly saying, *"the Devils." '* He laughed heartily & replied, *'I can't tell.'*

[May 1845] He [Henry Hallam][17] told me with great gusto Wordsworth at the Levee was passing by, when Lord Delawar[18] said, 'Kneel, kneel.' Wordsworth, totally ignorant of Court ways & Court etiquette, plumped down on both knees! — & when he was down, he was too feeble to get up again. Lord De la Warr & Lord Liverpool were obliged to help him up. The Queen was much touched. Oh, what a triumph for the Ultra Tory.

'Paint a Picture of it,' said Hallam, with a roguish look!

O Heavens, I hope I shall never be seized with a passion to go to Court!

O Wordsworth, how Sir George would have relished this offering to Royalty. Fancy the High Priest of Mountain & of Flood, on *both knees*, before a little, irritable King's Evil bit of In bred, half insane royalty!!! Good God!

I think these ceremonies constitutionally necessary. *I* never disdained them; *I* never was a Democrat; *I* never despised the Aristocracy, the Monarchy, or the law, but would shed my blood for the people & the Constitution with its estates.

To conclude after all this great Fuss, perhaps the whole thing will end in a failure, these Houses of Parliament.

May 16. Very anxious about the Future indeed. In going to the Exhibition & listening to the people, I don't think they are advanced one jot. Dined with my dear Friend Serjeant Talfourd. He said Wordsworth went to Court in Rogers' clothes![19] — buckles, stockings, & wore Davy's sword! Moxon had hard work to make the dress fit. It was a squeeze, but by pulling & hawling they got him in! Fancy the High Priest of Mountain & of Flood on his knees in a Court, the quiz of Courtiers, in a dress that did not belong to him, with a sword that was not his own & a coat which he borrowed.

Fit accompaniments for a Republican when he goes to Court & burks his early principles!

Notes

1   John Scott (1783–1821), editor of the *Champion* in 1815, when Haydon recorded this entry; later, editor of the *London Magazine*, an important Victorian periodical to which many distinguished authors contributed. Wordsworth held a high opinion of Scott's abilities and literary judgments.

2   Leigh Hunt (1784–1850), editor of the *Examiner* (a newspaper). At the time he was completing perhaps his most important literary work, *The Story of Rimini* (1816), an uneven narrative poem. Haydon's observation that Hunt,

after criticizing Wordsworth's poetry in several reviews, had revised his estimate upward, explains Wordsworth's willingness to call on him. Also to be taken into consideration was the fact that Hunt's illness prevented him from calling on Wordsworth.

3 Lucien, Napoleon's brother, wrote the epic *Charlemagne, ou l'Église deliverée* (2 vols, 1814).

4 *Christ's Entry into Jerusalem*, which took six years to complete, was Haydon's most ambitious and successful painting, attracting crowds of gallery visitors in exhibitions in London, Edinburgh, and Glasgow, and earned him a net profit of £1,200. Wordsworth's likeness accompanied other portraits, e.g., those of Voltaire and Sir Isaac Newton.

5 *The Excursion*, IV, 'Despondency Corrected'.

6 *Measure for Measure*, III, i, 118–19; III, i, 5–41.

7 *Antony and Cleopatra*, II, ii, 241.

8 *The Excursion*, II, 443, 484–6.

9 Joseph Ritchie (1788?–1819), a well-respected surgeon and a travel writer, set out to explore the Nigrition Soudan (1817). The expedition was badly managed and inadequately funded by the home authorities, and Ritchie died after a debilitating illness in Murzuk, Libya.

10 John Kingston, deputy comptroller. Two years later he rose to the position of Commissioner of Stamps. Lamb, writing to Wordsworth on 18 February 1818, claimed he detested all accountants and deputy accountants. Wordsworth's respect for Kingston's title did not keep him from enjoying Lamb's witticisms made at Kingston's expense.

11 Wordsworth's poem, 'I wandered lonely as a cloud', based on the entry for 15 April 1802, in Dorothy Wordsworth's *Journals*. In 2004 this lyric on the delight provided by daffodils was assigned, in readings closely synchronized throughout the United Kingdom, to more than 250,000 students.

12 Bryan Waller Procter (1787–1874), who wrote under the pseudonym 'Barry Cornwall'. A prolific writer of poems, songs, plays, literary essays, and biographies of Edward Kean and Charles Lamb, he was well liked and widely read, although his works are largely forgotten today.

13 Matthew 9:11.

14 Thomas Wakley, MP (1795–1862), a reformer who clearly laid down his position on various medical and social issues, such as the need for much closer supervision of the ways in which foodstuffs were grown and marketed. Haydon (who misspells his name) agreed with Wordsworth that Wakley's opposition to a copyright bill (1842) – delivered in a speech saying that writers deserved no more protection than scientists like Jenner, who worked more obviously in the public interest – had descended into 'Buffoonery'.

15 Wakley had singled out for censure Wordsworth's poems, 'Louisa', 'To a Butterfly', and his lines on the Stock-dove, ending with the peroration, 'Who could not string such lines together by the bushel?' But Wakley was the only dissenting voice when the Copyright Bill, extending what Wordsworth called 'postobit remuneration' in a letter sent to Viscount Mahon (11 April 1842), came up for a final vote.

16 Wordsworth in his final quarter-century suffered from recurring attacks of eye-inflammation; some spells were so painful that he had to give up both reading and writing for extended time periods.

17　Henry Hallam (1777–1859), whose three great works of Whig-slanted history provided generations of readers with their basic understanding of constitutional development in England: *The View of the State of Europe during the Middle Ages* (1818); *The Constitutional History of England* (1827); and *Introduction to the Literature of Europe in the 15th, 16th, and 17th Centuries* (1837–39). He championed several reform movements, such as abolition of the slave trade, and befriended many artists. The first of two sons who predeceased him, Arthur Henry Hallam, was the inspiration for the writing of Alfred, Lord Tennyson's *In Memoriam*.

18　The fifth Earl De La Warr (1791–1869), in his official capacity as Lord Chamberlain, extended an offer to Wordsworth to become the Poet Laureate (1843). Wordsworth, though impressed by the honor, wanted (and received) an assurance from the Prime Minister, Sir Robert Peel, that he would not be required to write poems on order; Sir Robert added that the Queen personally wished him to accept. Although Wordsworth declined to attend the Queen's Ball shortly after agreeing to the appointment, and cited as his reason the inconvenient lateness of the invitation, a second invitation to the Queen's Ball (May 1845) could not be so easily turned aside.

19　Samuel Rogers (1763–1855) was 82 years old when he and Edward Moxon (Wordsworth's publisher from 1835 on) joined forces to assist Wordsworth in his presentation at court. Rogers's clothes did not fit Wordsworth very well, but with Sir Humphrey Davy's sword at his side, conjoining 'science and art', the Poet Laureate (75 years old) enjoyed the 'most gracious' conversation of the young Queen. After his return to Mt. Rydal he remarked that, so far as he could tell, his years may have counted for more than his poetry: 'I daresay most likely she had not read many of my works.'

Henry Crabb Robinson (1775–1867)

Though remembered today as a great diarist, a man who kept copiously detailed records of how he mediated, with skill and tact, between warring parties, Henry Crabb Robinson contributed generously to the developing careers of major literary and political figures for a full seven decades. He helped Mme. de Stael understand better the writings of German philosophers; served as foreign editor of *The Times*, and wrote accurate, useful despatches from Spain during the Peninsular War; was a founding father of both the Athenaeum Club and University College, London; and assisted biographers of Goethe and Blake, among others, by contributing invaluable personal information. He was a good friend of Lamb, Coleridge, Southey, and any number of writers who, he believed, contributed to the cultural improvement of what, for want of a better phrase, may be called the English sense of good taste.

Robinson genuinely liked Wordsworth, and toured Scotland, Wales, Switzerland, and Italy with him on different occasions. He donated gossip to a storehouse of such stories kept by Wordsworth, who, as he aged, found it easier to accumulate well-wishers and would-be acolytes than long-term friends who could pleasantly but firmly disagree with some of his sweeping generalizations.

Robinson noted in his private jottings that Wordsworth's self-praise was sometimes hard to take. He did what he could to prevent (or at least minimize) Wordsworth's hostility to what he considered the presumptuous behavior and critical opinions of Jeffrey, Hazlitt, Southey, and Coleridge (among many others), though Robinson was fair enough to include the important observation that Wordsworth reacted most strongly against denigrations of his own poetry rather than his personality. Robinson could appreciate the syndrome too easily created by an excessive pride of authorship. He feared for Wordsworth's reputation after the 1815 edition of his poems included an intemperate *Essay, Supplementary to the Preface*. W. J. B. Owen and Jane Worthington Smyser, in their annotated edition of *The Prose Works of William Wordsworth* (Oxford: Clarendon Press, 1974), III, 60), characterize it as 'an exercise in restrained invective directed against the *Edinburgh*'. Some of Wordsworth's friends were skeptical about Robinson's belief that Wordsworth had restrained the major part of his anger at impercipient readers and reviewers. To them it looked undiluted.

In a letter written on 8 July 1819, Robinson praised the justness of an anonymous review of *Peter Bell* published in the *Eclectic Review* (July 1819): 'It is written by one who understands, as well as feels, the excellence of Wordsworth as well as his great faults.' He added that the reviewer (possibly Josiah Conder) had no business in imputing as vice what was, he believed, 'mere peculiarity of taste'.

Robinson's fair-mindedness inspires trust in his judgments. Our regret that he did not find the time to edit his journals – a promise he made to himself, and did not fulfill – is more than balanced by the richness of his observations. These humanize Wordsworth more than any other known record of his behavior.

The excerpts that follow are the relevant portions of letters written to (or by) members of the 'Wordsworth Circle'. Robinson wrote the majority of these letters, and many of them were addressed to his brother Thomas. However, he carefully tailored his remarks to the interests of each individual addressed.

A note of caution: the membership of the 'Wordsworth Circle' continually changed, as did that of all the 'circles' within which Wordsworth moved. For a tentative and befittingly qualified statement about the degrees of acquaintanceship enjoyed by those who met and conversed with Wordsworth, a reader should consult Stephen Gill's *Wordsworth and the Victorians* (Oxford: Clarendon Press, 1998), 12–14.

Modern readers have much to thank Edith J. Morley for; she not only edited these letters (1927), but her comments on earlier (much-abridged) texts clarify the reasons lying behind numerous erroneous assessments of Wordsworth's true opinions. In addition to *The Correspondence of Henry Crabb Robinson with the Wordsworth Circle (1808–1866)*, her three-volume edition of *Henry Crabb Robinson on Books and Their Writers* (1938) records much invaluable information about the entire Wordsworth family. These letters, taken as a whole, testify to Robinson's awareness that he enjoyed exceptional opportunities to watch, and pay respectful attention to, the changing moods of Wordsworth as he confronted public issues, arguments with his friends, visitors, and readers, and a wide range of domestic problems. Robinson, never a sycophant, understood the pressures converging on his aging Rydalite (a term sometimes employed by the Wordsworth family), and, more often successfully than not, sought to explain what they were.

These pressures became especially severe during Wordsworth's eighth (and last) decade, the 1840s, and the tone of these letters darkened as an inevitable response (both direct and indirect) to Wordsworth's unhappiness. The over-all record of this decade must be reckoned as increasingly bleak, and not only because of Wordsworth's failing health. His sorrows were not decreased much by any single event, such as his acceptance of the invitation to become Poet Laureate

(April 1843). He succumbed to a long period of severe grief when his beloved daughter Dora, suffering from a cold that severely aggravated her tubercular condition, finally succumbed (May 1847); members of the Wordsworth Circle had reason to despair at the probability that the poet would follow her to the grave. Though he rallied, his constitution and mental health suffered repeated blows. He outlived Joanna Hutchinson (Mary's sister), Edward Wordsworth (his grandson, 'one of the noblest creatures both in mind and body I ever saw'), Christopher Wordsworth (his brother), John Wordsworth (his nephew), Hartley Coleridge, and Tom Hutchinson.

As the death toll mounted, Robinson's loyalty to his beloved friend remained steadfast. After Wordsworth's death, he reaffirmed, in a letter to Isabella Fenwick, his certitude of 'the imperishability of such a mind'.

A generous tribute to the truly remarkable character and achievements of Robinson himself, written by Thomas Sadler, a close personal friend, is printed as the Preface to *Diary, Reminiscences, and Correspondence of Henry Crabb Robinson* (New York: Hurd and Houghton, 1877).

HCR, C, I, 52–4: letter from Henry Crabb Robinson to Thomas Robinson, March 1808

. . . I breakfasted with Wordsworth at Charles Lamb's on Tuesday And walked with him to Mrs Clarkson[1] afterwards who was at Hatcham house. W. begged me to come for him yesterday. I accordingly dined at Mr Hardcastles & W. & I returned together. We had therefore two long têtes a têtes. I feel obliged to Mrs C. for she must have spoken of me very kindly W. gave me his hand with cordiality on meeting he was confidential with me, has promised to call on me & made advances which were, from my high opinion of him, certainly very flattering. My Esteem for W's *mind* his philosophic & poetic view of things is confirmed & strengthened by these interviews. And I rejoice that you are so far initiated into a sense of his poetry that you can sympathise with my pleasure—Wordsworth is most opposite to Southey in his appearance. he is a sloven & his manners are not prepossing [*sic*] his features are large & course [*sic*]; his voice is not attractive his manners tho' not arrogant yet indicate a sense of his own worth he is not attentive to others and speaks with decision his own opinion. He does not spare those he opposes he has no respect for great names And avows his contempt for popular persons as well as favorite books which must often give offence. Yet with all this, I sho^d have a bad opinion of that person's discernm^t who sho^d be long in his company with^t contract^g an high respect, if not a love for him. Moral purity & dignity & elevation of Sentim^t are the characteristics of his mind & muse

As we were tête a tête I was gratified at being able to turn the conversation to *his* poetry He expatiated with warmth on them. And spoke of them with that unaffected zeal which pleased me, tho' the customs of life do not authorise it he explained some of the most exceptionable & I was flattered to find his own opinion of them so correspond^t with my own. The Sonnet which he is most anxious to have popular because he says, were it generally admired it would evince an elevation of mind an[d] a strength & purity which [*sic*] fancy which we have not yet witnessed. It is the admirable 'Two voices are there' you will recollect this was my favorite he explained the Beggars as I understood it; It is a poetical exhibition of the power of physical beauty & the charm of health & vigour in childhood even in a state of the greatest moral depravity

'Once in a lonely hamlet I sojourned' v. 2 p 109 displays, he says, more than other of his poems a profound knowledge of Womans heart —he could feel no respect for the Mother who could read it with^t emotion & admiration—Wordsworth quotes his own Verses with pleasure And seems to attach to the approbation of them a greater connection with moral worth which others may deem the effect of vanity— I think myself there is a danger of his not allowing enough for the influence of conventional & habitual taste in making those dislike his Poems as Poems whose sensibility is yet awake to the moral truths & sentiments they teach & exhibit He also speaks with a contempt of others which I think very censurable He asserts for instance that M^{rs} B[arbauld][2] has a bad heart; that her writings are absolutely insignificant, her poems are mere trash and specimens of every fault may be selected from them He quoted, to satirise, a Stanza you & I have certainly admired—

But thou o Nymph retired & coy!
In what brown hamlet dost thou joy
  To tell thy tender tale?
The lowliest children of the ground
  Moss-rose & Violet, blossom round
    And lily of the vale —

here, he says, there is no genuine feeling or truth. Why is the hamlet *brown*? Because Collins in a description of exquisite beauty describing the introduction of Evening says 'And hamlets brown & dim discovered Spires' Mrs B. therefore sets down brown hamlets with^t either propriety or feeling—And who are the lowliest children of the ground . . . ? Moss-rose—a Shrub !

Of Rogers, of course, he speaks with great contempt.[3]—

Wordsworth has thoughts of writing an Essay on the causes of the pleasure of bad poetry.—I wish he would do this I have no doubt he would illustrate your feelings very much to your satisfaction and make you well pleased with yourself for not loving some of these bad poems —Or explain very intelligibly why you had admired others of them— I must put an end to this immethodical narrativ[e].

I earnestly beg you to study W. I am convinced you would

[The letter ends here, in the middle of the sentence: dated March 1808 on reverse—in T. R.'s hand.]

HCR, *C*, I, 69–70: letter from Henry Crabb Robinson to Thomas Robinson, 20 May 1812

You have I suppose heard from Mrs Clarkson that Wordsworth is in town. His being here has contributed too much to distract my mind from what [ought] to be its' sole object of pursuit; but to shun such a man as W. or neglect to seize every occasion of being in his company is beyond my power. I have likewise had an occasion to see him in an interesting situation. I found that he & C.[4] had no common friend to interfere & by merely being the bearer of civil messages & explanatory letters heal the breach wh. has subsisted between them. And I therefore undertook the task And I rejoice to say with success. But do not speak of it I wrote an account of the negociation to Mrs Clarkson, because she was privy to the rupture, & was entitled to know the event, but I do not for obvious reasons mention my concern in the reconciliation. That two *such men* as W. & C. (One I believe the greatest man now living in this Country And the other a man of astonishing genius & talents tho' not harmoniously blended as in his happier friend to form a great & good man) sho^d have their relation towards each other affected by anything such a being as I could do seems strange and I do not wish to have the thought excited certainly not by my own uncalled for mention of the transaction There is no affected humility in this remark W. without saying a complimentary thing to me has done what has really flattered me, has offered to go & visit any one of my friends to whom I wish to introduce him. . . .

HCR, C, I, 243–4: letter from Henry Crabb Robinson to Thomas Robinson, 4 July 1833

I sent off my portmanteau by the coach on the 14th And walked to *Ambleside* over the Troutbeck heath, & having stationed myself there I went on in the Evening to *Rydal Mount*—I continued between Ambleside and Rydal to the 26th—During about half the time Wordsworths' house was full and during that time I was permitted to sleep & breakfast at the Salutation—The rest of the time I was the inmate of Wordsworth—Miss W. is wonderfully recovered from a state of such debility that her death was looked for from day to day. Still I co^{d} only see her for an hour at a time—She was able to be drawn in a carriage in the garden And co^{d} partake of conversation, but was too nervous to bear disputation—I found Wordsworth very agreeable— he is an alarmist. And the great difference between him & me is that he is a *despairing* and I am a *hoping* alarmist He thinks that nothing can save this country from perdition but an interposition of providence He believes that the national church will be annihilated—that the funds will be attacked All aristocratical distinctions & privileges as well as the rights of property invaded—And then . . . 'Not must, but may' is my reply to all this—And then we discuss the means of averting the evil—I have found *Southey* pretty much in the same mood as Wordsworth—With only that difference which flows from their personal peculiarities—There is a solemnity & an earnestness about W: which inspire respect; A more chearful & dashingly polemical tone in Southey, which provokes hostility But I know on the other side, no individuals so perfectly candid and essentially liberal as they are—

HCR, C, II, 377: letter from Henry Crabb Robinson to Thomas Robinson, 19 January 1839

Then I am slowly reading Carlyle's French Revolution which should be called Rhapsodies—not a history—Some one said—a history in flashes of lightening—And provided I take only small doses and not too frequently—it is not merely agreeable but fascinating. It is just the book one should buy—to muse over and spell rather than read through. For it is not English, but a sort of Original Compound from that Indo-Teutonic primitive tongue which philologists now speculate about— mixed up by Carlyle more suo. Now he who will give himself the trouble to learn this language will be rewarded by admirable matter—

Wordsw: is intolerant of such innovations And cannot & will not read C. Southey both reads him and extols him And this tho' C. characterises the French noblesse at the Etats Generaux as changed from their old position, drifted far down from their native latitude like arctic Ice-bergs got into the Equatorial Sea & fast thawing there'—And the French clergy as an Anomalous class of men of whom the whole world has a dim understanding that it can understand nothing . . . . .

HCR, C, I, 479: letter from Henry Crabb Robinson to Mary Wordsworth, 16 February 1843

[After congratulations on W. W. junior receiving an appointment]
But I cannot suffer a post to elapse without congratulating you on the news which Mʳ Quillinan has just written about—This must have filled your hearts with joy—I have not for a long time heard of any thing so fairly a subject for congratulation Coming after the Pension and the office change, it reminds one (against one's will) of the envious remark of one whose name shall not stain this paper—a remark that was made in the spirit of malice & envy—Viz That Mʳ Wordsworth is 'a prosperous man'—I believe *fortunate* was the word—as if the faculty of composing the Lyrical ballads & the Excursion was a gift of fortune!!! . . .

HCR, C, I, 479: letter from Henry Crabb Robinson to Thomas Robinson, 29 March 1843

I heard from Wordsworth yesterday. He will attend Southey's body to the grave, invited or not—he writes with feeling as might be expected from him . . .

HCR, C, I, 491: letter from Henry Crabb Robinson to Mary Wordsworth, 10 April 1843

I have just written one of the very necessary but at the same [time] by no means sentimental letters which it seems profanation to address to a head crowned with laurel—It is hardly decorous to inclose this under the same cover, but let that pass—You may if you think it expedient shake this letter well before you read any further
So then the poet of Rydal Mount is also the poet of St. James's Court —Has he weighed all the consequences of this step?—Tho' he will not be forced like the rhapsodists of old to sing his own odes, or hear them

set to musick, yet I suppose he must attend to kiss hands—The Queen
will never be content until she has seen her poet in proper person bend
his knee before her—And he who never before worshipped any king
but king Apollo must now pay his devotions to Queen Victoria—There
is no help for this you may depend upon it.

HCR, C, II, 620–2: letter from Harriet Martineau to Henry Crabb Robinson, 8 February 1846 [extract copied by HCR]

8th Feb. 1846

The Ws are in affliction just now—His only brother died a few days ago
And a nephew here is dyeing And they have bad accounts from their
sick daughter in law in Italy—But as yo can well conceive *he* can lose
himself completely in any interestg subject of thought, so as to forget
his griefs His mind is always completely full of the thing that is in it
And there he was on Wednesday his face all gloom & tears at two
O'Clock from the tidings of his brother's death reced an hour before
And lo! at three he was all animation discussing the rationale of my
extraordinary discourses (in the Mesmeric state)—his mind so wholly
occupied that he was quite happy for the time He is very interestg
merely as an old poet without any W—ism to those who have seen
him oftener than once or twice—His mind must always have been
essentially liberal, but now it is more obviously & charmingly so than
I understand it used to appear—The mildness of age has succeeded to
what used to be thought a rather harsh particularity of opinion &
manners. His conversation can never be anticipated Sometimes he
flows on in the utmost grandeur, that even yo can imagine, leavg a
strong impression of inspiration At other times we blush & are
annoyed at the extremity of bad taste with wch he pertinaciously
dwells on the most vexatious & vulgar trifles—The first mood is all
informed & actuated by knowle of man; the other, a strange & ludi-
crous proof of his want of knowle of men. I, deaf, can hardly conceive
how he with eyes & ears & a heart which leads him to converse with
the poor in his incessant walks can be so unaware of their social state.
I dare say yo need not be told how sensual vice abounds in rural dis-
tricts. Here, it is flagrant beyond any thing I ever cod have looked for
& here while every justice of the peace is filled with disgust & every
clergyman with almost despair at the drunkenness quarrells & extreme
licentiousness with women—here is dear good old W. for ever talkg of

rural innocence & deprecat[g] any intercourse with towns lest the purity of his neighbours sho[d] be corrupted. He little knows what elevation self denial & refinem[t] accrue in towns from the superior cultiv[n] of the people . . .[†] [See end of extract. The dagger & insertion are H. C. R.'s.]

. . . You know Ws worldly affairs are most comfortable in his old age. His wife is perfectly charm[g] & the very angel he sho[d] have to tend him. his life is a most serene & happy one on the whole & while all goes on methodically he is happy & cheery & courteous & benevolent; so that one co[d] almost worship him. But to secure this everybody must be punctual, the fire must be bright & all go orderly as his angel takes care that every thing shall as far as depends on her—he goes every day to Miss Fenwick (he always needs some such daily object) she is the worthiest possible, gives her a smacking kiss, & sits down before her fire to open his mind—Think what she could tell if she survives him—He does me the honour (to my amazement & *his* honour) to be fond of me: but I see less of them than I shall do when I get to the Knoll—I do not ask him to come so far as my lodgings & so only meet him in company or when I call at the Mount & then only *hear* him when he talks expressly to me—So I miss a good deal—I feel a growing love & tenderness for him but cannot yet thoroughly connect—compact incorporate him with his works. Cannot yet feel him to be so great as they—But I shall ere long if we live & he talks of coming to my cottage —I have not 1/2 done but I must stop for this Time '—[†] The virtues of the people here are also of a sort differ[t] we think from what he supposes. The people are very industrious thrifty prudent & so well off as to be liberal in their dealings. They pride themselves on doing their work capitally: & in this point of honour they are exemplary.

HCR, *C*, II, 625–6: letter from Harriet Martineau to Henry Crabb Robinson, 21 May [1846]

The Wordsworths are quite well;—and he very amiable except (entre nous) when the Archb[p] of Dublin is present,—whom he despises. It is a pity they sh[d] ever meet. Their minds have no point of contact. Wordsworth's is not always accessible, either, & Whateley's apparently never so. How *bewitching* Wordsworth is *when* he is so! And he very often— usually—appears happy & gay.—Whateley is excessively merry,—very clever in his mirth,—& quite simple, but he does not now, & never did, interest me much, except in print. . . .

HCR, C, II, 639–40: letter from Henry Crabb Robinson to Thomas Robinson, 5 February 1847

The fact is that during my late visit I had much less than I used to have of conversation with him [Wordsworth]—He spoke very little to any one And said on one occasion when it was remarked that he was silent —'Yes, the Silence of old age'. It was not that his judgement or sense was in any respect impaired, but his activity—He was quite happy quite cordial quite amiable; but not so animated or energetic as he used to be.

He allowed me uncontradicted to state heresies which would not have been tolerated a few years ago—This is the full extent of what I consider as the inroad of age— . . .

HCR, C, II, 641: letter from Henry Crabb Robinson to Thomas Robinson [26/27 March 1847]

You ask also which of Wordsworth's poems refers to W. S. Landor— Answer—No one—Landor's reproach of W. is that he did *not* acknowledge where he ought his obligations to him Landor—It is a long story which I could amuse a party for a quarter of an hour in narrating, but it would fill too large a space of this paper were it written down. And probably my pen would drop in the writing And your eyes in the reading— . . .

HCR, C, II, 642–3: letter from Sara Coleridge to Henry Crabb Robinson, 28 March 1847

Miss Hughes has placed in my hands the Dawson lectures on C. & W. The latter I have read; they seem to me quite in the right as far as they go; but they view M^r W's productions morally & philosophically rather than peculiarly in their poetical aspect. The lecturer is of the Carlyle school,—which is partly the product of the times, partly produced by the individual—*genius* I think—spite of the great Poet's verdict to the contrary, of the man Carlyle himself. One great characteristic of that genius is *humour*, & M^r W never in his life appreciated any genius in which that is a large element. Hence his disregard for Jane Austen's novels, which my Father & Uncle so admired. I shall have great pleasure in talking with you about our dear old venerated friend and entering more *into him* and his present state than I can now. Upon the whole I find him better in mind than I expected to do, & in body he is

as vigorous as almost any man at 77. Dear Mrs Wordsworth is a wonderful person of her years—so active and so independent. Her face is
aged since I saw her last & her voice is fainter than it used to be,
though it was always low.

HCR, C, II, 652: letter from Isabella Fenwick to Henry Crabb Robinson, 12 August 1847

I know that a few lines from Rydal Mount will be acceptable to you &
ever since I have been here I have been intending to write them—our
dear Friends finding such efforts too painful just yet—I trust the time
will come when they may be able to resume their usual habits and fill
each day with the little duties which belong to it—now it is enough for
them to bear the burthen which it has pleased the Almighty to lay
upon them and to seek those consolations which can come alone from
Him. Should we meet again My dear Mr Robinson, I will speak to you
of the blessed death of beloved Dora—but now—I will only say a few
words of her afflicted Parents—in health so far they have suffered less
than one might have expected—dear Mrs Wordsworth looks more aged
& feeble—but she is still able to move about with her accustomed
activity—& she has fallen into her usual rest—which is more than
might be looked for after her long watching upon her child.—
Mr Wordsworth says he never was better in his life in his mind there
seems no room now for the fancies he used to have in regard to his
health—and he has forgotten he ever had any—his poor Sister now is
his chief employment—attending on her both indoors & out of doors –
in these sad offices he seems to find relief from a heavy burthen—both
he and Mrs Wordsworth are aware how truly they have your sympathy
and request me to say so with their affectionate regards—requesting
you to accept the same from myself, believe me

My dear Mr Robinson
Very kindly & truly yours
Isabella Fenwick

HCR, C, II, 654: letter from Henry Crabb Robinson to Thomas Robinson, 23 December 1847

24th a. m. What I anticipated I have found confirmed. Both M^r & M^rs
Wordsworth have received a blow, the effects of which I fear they will
never be able to counteract—Neither of them has yet ventured to pro-
nounce the name of their beloved daughter—And very few & slight

have been the allusions to their loss—Who feels the most intensely—
who shall say?—But at least Mrs W. is able to mix more with her
friends And discharge as she has been accustomed the ordinary func-
tions of her domestic life

Mr W. keeps very much alone And whichever room I may happen to
be in, he goes into the other—All the ordinary occupations in which
his daughter took a part are become painful to him—I brought as usual
a pack of cards and proposed a hand of Whist to M^{rs} W: in his absence,
but even she rejected it with a shudder—I have been able to draw him
out of the house but for a short time—And when I this morning proposed a call on old Mrs Cookson at Grasmere, this produced a flood of
tears—This renders it difficult on my part to avoid giving pain—
Neither of them go anywhere. And very few of their friends even
call....

HCR, C, II, 655–6: letter from Henry Crabb Robinson to Isabella Fenwick, 24 December 1847

You would probably interpret my continued silence into an intimation
that I found our friends here in too sad a state to be written about—
This would be an erroneous inference I have found them quite as well
as I expected. In bodily health Mrs W. has nothing to complain of And
Mr W. suffers only from a slight cold, which is rather an excuse than a
reason for not going out—M^{rs} W is able to go about her ordinary concerns—And seems therefore to be more recovered from the shock—
M^r W does nothing & seems indisposed to every thing he used to do.

I brought down cards as usual And asked M^{rs} W: whether I might
propose a game—She replied Oh no! with a shudder—Mr W. sits generally alone And whichever room I may be in, he goes into the other—
He speaks little And I have not seen him take up newspaper or book—

This morning I proposed a walk to Grasmere, to call on Mrs Cookson.
This produced a flood of tears The only active expression of his suffering that I have yet witnessed—One of the consequences of this sad
state of his mind is that he has never once ventured to go into M^r Q's
house—And I am sorry indeed to perceive that this is resented by M^r Q:
as if it were an insult to his wife's memory—I do not mean that he
openly resents it, for he comes to the Mount frequently—dined with me
here on my arrival And is invited to dine here tomorrow, tho' I have
been *considerately* invited to Mrs Davys—'Anniversarys being most
melancholy under such circumstances'

But Q: expresses himself so strongly that I fear the foundation is laid
for a lasting estrangement which might widen and lead to an entire
alienation

HCR, *C*, II, 659: letter from Henry Crabb Robinson to Thomas Robinson, 14–15 January 1848

I left Rydal Mount on Saturday. Poor Wordsworth took leave of me in silence weeping.—Your apprehension is too correct There has been no great improvement yet But he has a strong nature in body as well as mind And he may yet rally. . . .

HCR, *C*, II, 665: letter from Henry Crabb Robinson to Mary Wordsworth, 7 March 1848

I recollect once hearing Mr W. say, half in joke, half in earnest—' I have no respect whatever for Whigs, but I have a great deal of the Chartist in me'. To be sure he has. His earlier poems are full of that intense love of the people, as such, which becomes Chartism when the attempt is formally made to make their interests the especial object of legislation as of deeper importance than the positive rights hitherto accorded to the privileged orders. . . .

HCR, *C*, II, 673–4: letter from Edward Quillinan to Henry Crabb Robinson, 23 July 1848

I have just brought your note of yesterday home with me from Rydal Mount that I might thank you for it, for Mrs Wordsworth who received it this morning, and who begs me to tell you, with kindest regards from herself & her husband, that she hopes to be able to make amends soon by a long letter for the fault of holding two of your's, though short ones, as yet unanswered. But you understand all about that and you know moreover that no one's letters are more valued than your's are at Rydal Mount.—At this time of year, leisure hours, & indeed all hours of the day, are *there* necessarily divided among strangers who coming from a distance with introductions must be received, or strangers who happen to be visitors of ' friends who live within an easy walk'—and I think such perpetual interruptions, which would drive some men mad, are rarely disagreeable to Mr Wordsworth ; and in my opinion all these callers do him good, by taking him out of himself— though they leave his Wife but little time for the indulgence of a more quiet intercourse with such friends as you some 300 miles off.—You are not to infer from what I have said that there is any unusual bustle of pilgrims to the Poet's house this year, as compared with former years, except the last ; but as hardly any one was admitted, and few sought to be admitted, last year, and as a good many of the strangers now in the lake-country do find their way up to him, he and M^{rs} W.

have perhaps in reality just now more demands upon their energies than they ever had formerly when they were some years younger & the world was brighter, and they had a daughter.—This evening however they have none with them but persons who are in some sort of their own family. I just now left them at tea with 'quite a family party' –

HCR, *C*, II, 684–5: letter from Henry Crabb Robinson to Isabella Fenwick, 15 January [1849]

The account I have to give of our friends is so much better than that of last year that I should certainly have sent it, tho' I had not received a friendly intimation of your wish to hear from me. I found Mr Wordsworth more calm & composed than I expected—Whatever his feelings may be, the outward expression of them he can repress—I heard no sighs, no moaning—And he never refused to join in any conversation on the topics of the day. I feared that the visit to the Churchyard last Tuesday with Mr Coleridge to fix on the spot where Hartley might be interred would overset him, but, on the contrary, I returned with him alone, And he talked on a literary subject on our return with perfect self-possession and full of the subject. But his mind is not as active as it was—and M^rs W s[ays] he has not composed a line during the year and scarcely *written* one. I can therefore account for the report concerning the supposed loss of his faculties [which] was a gross exaggera[tion] if not a malicious misrepresentation of his actual condition

The most agreeable circumstance is that he goes occasionally to Mr Quillinan's And that they stand in a friendly relation towards each other—Every unpleasant impression on the mind of M^r Qu: is quite removed—

HCR, *C*, II, 692–3: letter from Mary Wordsworth to Henry Crabb Robinson, 28 March 1849

We left Willie & his Wife on Monday morn^g—she remarkably well—he poor fellow, neither quite well in health or spirits. He is more cast down by the prospects before him than a less anxious temper would be —but truly his case is a hard one—& I think he feels the '*indignity*', as he calls it, with which the higher powers are treating their faithful Sv^t than the loss of income which if the change is to take place must entirely alter his arrangements—The notion of the Office to be placed under the supervision of the 'Ganger' galls him. Without any official notice the head Office has already *advertised* in the newspapers some part of what has been the Stamp-distributors duty to be removed to the Excise department.—After 20 years devotion to the Service—& that the prime of his life W^m feels this to be unjust—If no remunerating plan lurks behind of which he has no hope. But why should I write this to you—merely because I feel you are interested in what concerns him.

HCR, C, II, 698: letter from Henry Crabb Robinson to Thomas Robinson, 27 June 1849

Wordsworth was in good *health*, but the *strength* of his mind has declined—There is no want of intelligence, but of vigour—No delusions but little power—happy but not active Is not this a comfortable old age? He is four months younger than you—he is able to walk still & on Sunday crossed the Malvern Hill *twice* without suffering any inconvenience— . . .

HCR, C, II, 725: Edward Quillinan to Henry Crabb Robinson, 23 April 1850

M^r W's mind is, when it is brought out, *perfectly clear*, & has been so throughout; but tranquil & reserved; he has for the most part been so quiet as almost to seem asleep when he was not so; except when aroused by those about him, or by his *doctors*. *All* of the latter he has dreaded; he felt that they disturbed him, or caused him to be disturbed, by ordering him 'to be *got up*' (of all things what he most shrinks from) or by suggesting other expedients that did him no good; & perhaps he thought, perhaps knew, that they *could* do no good.

It seems doubtful whether he may not yet survive many days, & have much suffering to go through; or whether he may pass away very soon & almost insensibly.—

HCR, C, II, 726: letter from Harriet Martineau to Henry Crabb Robinson [23 April] 1850

I don't know whether you will hear today from any other quarter of the death of our old friend Wordsworth. Yesterday it was thought—& *feared*—that he might linger for some days—suffering sadly from long lying in one posture. He sank much during the night, & died at noon today.

I have just time to say this much to you & to Mr Moxon (to whom I send a line) before post time. Believe me ever, with much sympathy in the emotions this event will call forth,

Yours most truly
H. Martineau

HCR, C, II, 736: Henry Crabb Robinson to Isabella Fenwick, 20 May [18]50

There is a sad imperfection in language after all that men of genius & thought have done. We want a distinct set of words by which we may express our feelings at an incident by which pain is assuaged and suffering relieved and an approach made to enjoyment. I felt this when I sat down just now to address a few lines to you. For I felt the impropriety of saying that I was *glad* or *rejoiced* to hear of your arrival at Rydal Mount—A considerable time must elapse before joy or gladness can be associated with Rydal Mount—Yet I have at the same time felt that the grief which must be felt at the departure of the husband the brother the father & friend is, if not overpowered, yet modified by a sense of his greatness—And of the imperishability of such a mind—!

HCR, C, II, 768–9: letter from Edward Quillinan to Henry Crabb Robinson, 16 January 1851

I have not seen Mr Landor's letter to C. S. [Cuthbert Southey] in Fraser: I am told it is as disparaging to Wordsworth as it is eulogistic of R. S.— But censure or affected under-valuation of Wordsworth, coming from Mr Landor, will make little or no impression. The motive is too transparent. L. was ever *yearning* after the praise of distinguished writers; Southey praised him & he puffed Southey; Cuth^t reproduced those praises all through his 6 vol Life, and Landor gratefully does his best to give Cuth^t S^y a lift. The thing is as plain as a pikestaff—L. also praised Wordsworth, excessively praised him for years, and I believe the praise was sincere; but he looked to be praised by W. in return; he looked in vain; W. 'slow to admire', as he tells us himself, and perhaps not sufficiently liberal of commendation to contemporary writers,—especially to fellow-poets,—disappointed him by his silence. Hope deferred made his heart sick; hopelessness at last embittered his liver.— In short I consider Landor a perfect humbug so far as relates to his unworthy conduct to Wordsworth alive and to Wordsworth dead. But he kicks against the pricks and only wounds his own shins.

Notes

1 Catherine Clarkson, a good friend who attempted on more than one occasion to lighten the stress created by Coleridge's feelings of being misunderstood by Wordsworth, introduced the Wordsworths to the Hardcastles. (Mr. Hardcastle, at whose home Robinson dined when he met Wordsworth for the first time, was Catherine Clarkson's uncle.)
2 Anna Letitia Barbauld, a minor poet whose work was scorned by Wordsworth. Her more important work may have been in the preparation of several editions of other writers: *The Correspondence of Samuel Richardson* (1797), as well as the writings of Mark Akenside (1795), William Collins (1797), several English essayists, and a 50-volume edition of *British Novelists* (1810). Her longest poem, *Eighteen Hundred and Eleven* (1811), was a gloomy assessment of Britain's future prospects.
3 Samuel Rogers (1763–1855), author of *The Pleasures of Memory* (1792), successfully pushed Wordsworth forward as a worthy candidate for the position of a stamp distributor. The modest salary accompanying this government post (Distributor of Stamps for Westmorland and the Penrith district of Cumberland) proved to be considerably less than the £400 per annum that Wordsworth had anticipated (closer to £100 when necessary expenses were deducted). Nevertheless, it provided an important fraction of the income that enabled the Wordsworths, from March 1813 on, to live at a reasonably comfortable level. (Three decades later, in 1842, Sir Robert Peel granted Wordsworth £300 per annum out of the civil list.)

  In 1850, after the death of Wordsworth, Rogers respectfully declined the offer of the Poet Laureateship because of his advanced age. He lived his last five years as an invalid, the consequence of a fall in the street.
4 Robinson's efforts in 1812 to act as a mediator between Wordsworth and Coleridge, though appreciated by both poets, had mixed results; the breach that had opened between the two poets, the end-result of years of friction, was too large for any diplomacy to succeed.

Matthew Arnold (1822–88)

The publishing firm of Macmillan invited Matthew Arnold (January 1877) to serve as editor of an anthology of selected poems by Wordsworth, largely because Arnold's admiration of the poet was both well established and well known to his friends. Arnold responded wholeheartedly to the challenge, and immediately set to work. After a momentary period of inactivity (1878) he returned to the double task of winnowing Wordsworth's better poems from an oeuvre containing much that he believed to be inferior creative work, and writing a Preface that would make a convincing case for the continuing importance of Wordsworth's contribution to English literature.

The Preface appeared first in an issue of *Macmillan's Magazine* (July 1879),[1] and the book itself, *The Poems of Wordsworth*, a few months later (September). Arnold's conviction that Wordsworth's poetry occupied, and deserved to occupy, a niche well above that occupied by any other of his contemporaries was, for him, an easy case to make. The modest price of the volume, 4s. 6d., attracted 4,000 buyers within five months, and a second edition was printed in November. Arnold's interest in getting Wordsworth right led to his rigorous corrections of a new edition that appeared in 1886, and it is that edition which has been reprinted more than forty times. Indeed, it is still in print.

The significance of Arnold's contribution to the popularizing of Wordsworth as the century's greatest poet can hardly be overstated, inasmuch as enthusiasm for Wordsworth's achievement had largely died down by the late 1870s. In English literature only Shakespeare and Milton, Arnold argued, deserved to be classed as superior to Wordsworth, and he added – in a letter to his sister (14 April 1879) – that Milton's work, though greater than Wordsworth's, was not 'so interesting'. (Arnold's habit of ranking the quality of poets in England, France, and Germany nettled many who disagreed with his choices and his air of certitude.)

Arnold changed the thinking of many readers on the question of how to read and better appreciate Wordsworth. He dismissed as confusing and even self-destructive Wordsworth's system of classifying his own poems (a system that was first printed in the two-volume edition of 1815). He singled out the decade between 1798 and 1808 as the one in which 'almost all his really first-rate work was produced'. (A counterargument that Wordsworth's poems written after 1808 deserve equal admiration or affection does not seem to have convinced a majority of readers.) Arnold implied, in other words, that Wordsworth could not, and did not, judge his own output discriminatingly.

He conceded that Wordsworth lacked 'humour, felicity, passion', qualities present in the poetry of Burns, Keats, Heine, and others; but Wordsworth dealt with '*life*, as a whole, more powerfully'. His formal philosophy, Arnold argued, had to be dismissed because even at its best it was 'doctrine such as we hear in church . . .'

For Arnold 'poetry is at bottom a criticism of life', and 'the greatness of a poet lies in his powerful and beautiful application of ideas to life, — to the question: How to live'. And despite his limitations, Wordsworth 'feels the joy offered to us in nature', and communicates it to those who need it most: 'Wordsworth tells of what all seek, and tells of it at its truest and best source, and yet a source where all may go and draw for it.'

Arnold's interest in Wordsworth derived partly from his father, who had enjoyed conversations with the Rydal poet so much that he decided to rent living quarters at Allan Bank in Grasmere Valley, an action taken because he wanted to further and deepen the acquaintance. Shortly afterward Arnold's father built a home at Fox How, near Ambleside. His mother also thought of Wordsworth as a great man, once she got past her surprise that he was 'mild and gentlemanly, with considerable dignity in his appearance and manner',[2] and her respect counted for much with the observant Matthew. He listened attentively to Wordsworth's declaiming his own verse; he knew, and reveled in the knowledge, that Wordsworth liked him; and, late in the 1840s, he was a charmed listener to Wordsworth's unburdening himself of opinions on the unpoetical nature of the age, the 'undue influence' of towns and trades, and the urgent need for developing a 'disinterested imagination' to cope with such pressures on daily living.[3] He was therefore to write of Wordsworth with a special tenderness, in his famous Preface, and to recast in his own language Wordsworth's conception of the true aims of poetry.

Jane Martha Arnold, his sister, felt uneasy about Matthew's absorbing so much of Wordsworth's teaching. Her objection may have arisen from the conviction that her brother's poetry would not suit the mood of the country: 'Matt's philosophy holds out no help in the deep questions which are stirring in every heart in the life & death struggle in which the world is every year engaged more deeply, and poetry which does not do this may charm the taste, excite & gratify the intellect but not, I think take lasting possession of the heart.' Wordsworth had been successful in leading men back to nature, but now, she went on, 'we seem to want something more direct still, surrounded by tumults & perplexities without & within, we want to know the spell which shall evoke a righteous and peaceful order from this chaos, and what but our Christian Faith can give us this?'[4]

Nevertheless, her dismay at her brother's stance as an 'Eastern Philosopher' whose poems did 'not suit the European mind' did not deflect the direction of his developing career. Quite apart from Arnold's prose writings that cite Wordsworth as a model and authority for younger generations, the list of poems which directly trace back to Wordsworth's inspirational influence, as enumerated in Stephen Gill's important study, *Wordsworth and the Victorians*, includes not only 'Memorial Verses' (an elegy composed shortly after Wordsworth's death), but the following: 'The Scholar-Gipsy', 'The Youth of Nature', 'The Terrace at Berne', 'Resignation', 'To a Gipsy Child by the Sea-shore', and 'The Buried Life'. Several additional poems are cited by Gill to demonstrate a less direct influence,[5] but one conclusion on perusing this list is inescapable, namely, that Arnold, partly on the basis of personal knowledge and memory, and partly in an effort to define more sharply the reasons for welcoming Wordsworth's looming presence in the second half of the century, was more directly responsive to Wordsworth than to any other writer of the age.

MEMORIAL VERSES
APRIL, 1850[6]

GOETHE in Weimar sleeps, and Greece,
Long since, saw Byron's struggle cease.
But one such death remain'd to come;
The last poetic voice is dumb —[7]
We stand to-day by Wordsworth's tomb.

When Byron's eyes were shut in death,
We bow'd our head and held our breath.
He taught us little; but our soul
Had *felt* him like the thunder's roll.
With shivering heart the strife we saw
Of passion with eternal law;
And yet with reverential awe
We watch'd the fount of fiery life
Which served for that Titanic strife.

When Goethe's death was told, we said:
Sunk, then, is Europe's sagest head.
Physician of the iron age,[8]
Goethe has done his pilgrimage.
He took the suffering human race,
He read each wound, each weakness clear;
And struck his finger on the place,
And said: *Thou ailest here, and here!*
He look'd on Europe's dying hour[9]
Of fitful dream and feverish power;
His eye plunged down the weltering strife,
The turmoil of expiring life —
He said: *The end is everywhere,*
Art still has truth, take refuge there!
And he was happy, if to know
Causes of things, and far below
His feet to see the lurid flow
Of terror, and insane distress,
And headlong fate, be happiness.[10]

And Wordsworth! — Ah, pale ghosts, rejoice!
For never has such soothing voice
Been to your shadowy world convey'd,
Since erst, at morn, some wandering shade
Heard the clear song of Orpheus come
Through Hades, and the mournful gloom.[11]
Wordsworth has gone from us — and ye,[12]
Ah, may ye feel his voice as we!
He too upon a wintry clime
Had fallen — on this iron time
Of doubts, disputes, distractions, fears,
He found us when the age had bound
Our souls in its benumbing round;
He spoke, and loosed our heart in tears.
He laid us as we lay at birth
On the cool flowery lap of earth,
Smiles broke from us and we had ease;
The hills were round us, and the breeze
Went o'er the sun-lit fields again;
Our foreheads felt the wind and rain.

Our youth return'd; for there was shed
On spirits that had long been dead,
Spirits dried up and closely furl'd,
The freshness of the early world.[13]

Ah! since dark days still bring to light
Man's prudence and man's fiery might,
Time may restore us in his course
Goethe's sage mind and Byron's force;
But where will Europe's latter hour
Again find Wordsworth's healing power?
Others will teach us how to dare,
And against fear our breast to steel:
Others will strengthen us to bear —
But who, ah! who, will make us feel?
The cloud of mortal destiny,
Others will front it fearlessly —
But who, like him, will put it by?

Keep fresh the grass upon his grave
O Rotha, with thy living wave![14]
Sing him thy best! for few or none
Hears thy voice right, now he is gone.

Notes

1 Full annotations accompany the reprinting of Arnold's Preface in Vol. IX
   (*English Literature and Irish Politics*) of the definitive edition of Matthew
   Arnold's prose works, edited by R. H. Super (Ann Arbor: University of
   Michigan Press, 1973), 36–55.
2 Quoted by Park Honan in *Matthew Arnold: a Life* (New York: McGraw-Hill
   Book Company, 1981), 10.
3 Ibid., 196–7.
4 Letter from Jane Martha Arnold to Thomas Arnold, 26 October 1848, in *The
   Letters of Matthew Arnold: I (1829–1859)*, edited by Cecil Y. Lang (Charlottes-
   ville, Va.: The University Press of Virginia, 1996), 123–4.
5 Stephen Gill, *Wordsworth and the Victorians* (Oxford: Clarendon Press,
   1998), 177–88. Gill reviews fairly the arguments made by Algernon Charles
   Swinburne and Dante Gabriel Rossetti against an uncritical acceptance of
   Arnold's strong championing of Wordsworth's poetry. His following
   chapter, 'The Wordsworth Renaissance', makes the point that by the mid-
   1880s 'the most energetic phase of critical activity was closing' (220). Even
   taking into account other eulogistic contributions made during the 1870s
   and early 1880s – by Leslie Stephen, Richard Holt Hutton, Walter Pater,

Aubrey de Vere, William Knight, and John Ruskin – Gill believes that Arnold's essay, written in the late 1870s, had done the most for Wordsworth's posthumous reputation. (A lengthy chapter on George Eliot's life-long fascination with Wordsworth points out that, after the publication of *Silas Marner* in 1861, 'Wordsworth's role in George Eliot's creative life diminished' [164], though she continued to write until her death in 1880.)

6 Wordsworth's death on 23 April 1850 preceded the writing of 'Memorial Verses' by only a few days; a MS. at Yale bears the date 'April 27th 1850'. The poem was published in *Fraser's Magazine* in June 1850.

Edward Quillinan, immediately after Wordsworth's death, urged Arnold to write a suitable elegy. Several months later he wrote to Henry Crabb Robinson (16 January 1851) praising the linkage of Goethe and Wordsworth in Arnold's 'Epicede' (i.e., a funeral elegy), but he was not happy that Arnold had included Byron: 'I think, leaving other objections out of the question, [Byron] is not tall enough for the other two . . .' *The Correspondence of Henry Crabb Robinson with the Wordsworth Circle: 1844–1866*, edited by Edith J. Morley (Oxford: Clarendon Press, 1927), II, 769.

7 A slighting comment, inasmuch as Tennyson and Browning were already prominent poets.

8 A traditional way of implying that the times were uncongenial, and that historic and social values were eroding.

9 Probably an allusion to the end of the Enlightenment.

10 Lines 29–33 paraphrase Virgil's *Georgics*, II, 480–2.

11 Wordsworth's arrival in Hades suggests that Arnold was not thinking of his death in Christian terms. Orpheus descended to the Underworld in an effort (unsuccessful) to rescue his wife Eurydice.

12 A direct address to those who dwell in Hades.

13 A set of images designed to remind readers of Wordsworth's 'Ode: Intimations of Immortality from Recollections of Early Childhood'.

14 'Rotha' [Rothay]: a stream that flows by Grasmere churchyard.

Ralph Waldo Emerson (1803–82)

After a deeply disappointing meeting with Coleridge ('the visit was rather a spectacle than a conversation, of no use beyond the satisfaction of my curiosity'), followed by a more bracing and satisfactory exchange of views with Carlyle, Emerson continued his shorter version of the Grand Tour with a visit to Rydal Mount (28 August 1833). By then Wordsworth, in his sixty-third year, had perfected the pattern of his behavior in a casual encounter with any visitor who had come to pay his respects. He would deliver firm opinions on writers and political issues, recite his own poems, and walk his visitor around the gravel path in his garden (sometimes going further, for an additional mile, pointing out local sights, but only if he wanted to prolong the conversation). Emerson deferred to Wordsworth on social issues. He also reconsidered his initial – and unspoken – objection to a recitation ('so unlooked for and surprising'), deciding that he had come 'thus far to see a poet'. Wordsworth, he told himself, was entitled to the privilege of soliloquizing. But he did not care for the hardness of Wordsworth's opinions, and concluded that Wordsworth, however committed he was to his narrow definition of 'truth', was an authority only in his own realm of poetry: 'Off his own beat, his opinions were of no value.'

Emerson's second visit took place while he was on a wildly successful lecture tour in England and Scotland. He accepted an invitation from Harriet Martineau, who was living at the Knoll in Ambleside, and took the opportunity, on his first full day at her home, to walk over to Rydal Mount (28 February 1848). Now 77, bereaved by the recent death of his daughter Dora, and perhaps unappreciative of the much increased fame of his guest (it is possible that he may not have associated Emerson with the younger man who had visited him some fifteen years earlier), Wordsworth dismayed Emerson with a long list of bitter opinions 'on Scotchmen' (e.g. Wordsworth detested Carlyle for both his style and his 'inhumanity'), the French, and the Irish. Emerson recorded the opinions of 'different literary men' in London that Wordsworth had no personal friends, was parsimonious, and 'never praised any body'. He himself disliked aspects of Wordsworth's poetry that he had forgiven or ignored in 1833; but, generously, he thought of Wordsworth as a writer who had formed a poetic creed on the basis of 'real inspirations', and he named the 'Ode: Intimations of Immortality' as 'the high-water mark which the intellect has reached in this age'.

RWE, CW, V, 9–12, 165–8: *English Traits,* **edited by Douglas Emory Wilson (Cambridge, Mass.: Harvard University Press, 1994)**

On the 28th August, I went to Rydal Mount, to pay my respects to Mr. Wordsworth. His daughters called in their father, a plain, elderly, white-haired man, not prepossessing, and disfigured by green goggles.[1] He sat down, and talked with great simplicity. He had just returned from a journey. His health was good, but he had broken a tooth by a fall, when walking with two lawyers, and had said, that he was glad it did not happen forty years ago; whereupon they had praised his philosophy.

He had much to say of America, the more that it gave occasion for his favorite topic,—that society is being enlightened by a superficial tuition, out of all proportion to its being restrained by moral culture. Schools do no good. Tuition is not education. He thinks more of the education of circumstances than of tuition. 'Tis not question whether there are offences of which the law takes cognizance, but whether there are offences of which the law does not take cognizance. Sin is what he fears, and how society is to escape without gravest mischiefs from this source—? He has even said, what seemed a paradox, that they needed a civil war in America, to teach the necessity of knitting the social ties stronger. 'There may be,' he said, 'in America some vulgarity in manner, but that's not important. That comes of the pioneer state of things. But I fear they are too much given to the making of money; and secondly, to politics; that they make political distinction the end, and not the means. And I fear they lack a class of men of leisure,—in short, of gentlemen,—to give a tone of honor to the community. I am told that things are boasted of in the second class of society there, which, in England,—God knows, are done in England every day,—but would never be spoken of. In America I wish to know not how many churches or schools, but what newspapers? My friend, Colonel Hamilton, at the foot of the hill, who was a year in America, assures me that the newspapers are atrocious, and accuse members of Congress of stealing spoons!' He was against taking off the tax on newspapers in England, which the reformers represent as a tax upon knowledge, for this reason, that they would be inundated with base prints. He said, he talked on political aspects, for he wished to impress on me and all good Americans to cultivate the moral, the conservative, &c., &c., and never to call into action the physical strength of the people, as had just now been done in England in the Reform Bill,—a thing prophesied by Delolme. He alluded once or twice to his conversation with Dr. Channing, who had recently visited him, (laying his hand on a particular chair in which the Doctor had sat.)[2]

The conversation turned on books. Lucretius he esteems a far higher poet than Virgil: not in his system, which is nothing, but in his power of illustration. Faith is necessary to explain any thing, and to reconcile the foreknowledge of God with human evil. Of Cousin, (whose lectures we had all been reading in Boston,) he knew only the name.

I inquired if he had read Carlyle's critical articles and translations. He said, he thought him sometimes insane. He proceeded to abuse Goethe's Wilhelm Meister heartily. It was full of all manner of fornication. It was like the crossing of flies in the air. He had never gone farther than the first part; so disgusted was he that he threw the book across the room. I deprecated this wrath, and said what I could for the better parts of the book; and he courteously promised to look at it again. Carlyle, he said, wrote most obscurely. He was clever and deep, but he defied the sympathies of everybody. Even Mr. Coleridge wrote more clearly, though he had always wished Coleridge would write more to be understood. He led me out into his garden, and showed me the gravel walk in which thousands of his lines were composed. His eyes are much inflamed. This is no loss, except for reading, because he never writes prose, and of poetry he carries even hundreds of lines in his head before writing them. He had just returned from a visit to Staffa, and within three days had made three sonnets on Fingal's Cave, and was composing a fourth, when he was called in to see me. He said, 'If you are interested in my verses, perhaps you will like to hear these lines.' I gladly assented; and he recollected himself for a few moments, and then stood forth and repeated, one after the other, the three entire sonnets with great animation. I fancied the second and third more beautiful than his poems are wont to be. The third is addressed to the flowers, which, he said, especially the oxeye daisy, are very abundant on the top of the rock. The second alludes to the name of the cave, which is 'Cave of Music;' the first to the circumstance of its being visited by the promiscuous company of the steamboat.

This recitation was so unlooked for and surprising,—he, the old Wordsworth, standing apart, and reciting to me in a garden-walk, like a schoolboy declaiming,—that I at first was near to laugh; but recollecting myself, that I had come thus far to see a poet, and he was chanting poems to me, I saw that he was right and I was wrong, and gladly gave myself up to hear. I told him how much the few printed extracts had quickened the desire to possess his unpublished poems. He replied, he never was in haste to publish; partly, because he corrected a good deal, and every alteration is ungraciously received after printing; but what he had written would be printed, whether he lived or died. I said, 'Tintern Abbey' appeared to be the favorite poem with the public, but more contemplative readers preferred the first books of the 'Excursion,' and the Sonnets. He said, 'Yes, they are better.' He preferred such of his poems as touched the affections, to any others; for whatever is didactic,—what theories of society, and so on,—might perish quickly; but whatever combined a truth with an affection was κτῆα ἐς ἀεί, good today and good forever. He cited the sonnet 'On the feelings of a high-minded Spaniard,' which he preferred to any other, (I so understood him,) and the 'Two Voices;' and quoted, with evident pleasure, the verses addressed. 'To the Skylark.' In this connection, he said of the Newtonian theory, that it might yet be superseded and forgotten; and Dalton's atomic theory.

When I prepared to depart, he said he wished to show me what a common person in England could do, and he led me into the enclosure of his clerk, a young man, to whom he had given this slip of ground, which was laid out, or its natural capabilities shown, with much taste. He then said he would show me a better way towards the inn; and he walked a good part of a mile, talking, and ever and anon stopping short to impress the word or the verse, and finally parted from me with great kindness, and returned across the fields.

Wordsworth honored himself by his simple adherence to truth, and was very willing not to shine; but he surprised by the hard limits of his thought. To judge from a single conversation, he made the impression of a narrow and very English mind; of one who paid for his rare elevation by general tameness and conformity. Off his own beat, his opinions were of no value. It is not very rare to find persons loving sympathy and ease, who expiate their departure from the common, in one direction, by their conformity in every other.

At Ambleside in March, 1848, I was for a couple of days the guest of Miss Martineau, then newly returned from her Egyptian tour. On Sunday afternoon, I accompanied her to Rydal Mount. And as I have recorded a visit to Wordsworth, many years before, I must not forget this second interview. We found Mr. Wordsworth asleep on the sofa. He was at first silent and indisposed, as an old man suddenly waked, before he had ended his nap; but soon became full of talk on the French news. He was nationally bitter on the French: bitter on Scotchmen, too. No Scotchman, he said, can write English. He detailed the two models, on one or the other of which all the sentences of the historian Robertson are framed. Nor could Jeffrey, nor the Edinburgh Reviewers write English, nor can ***,[3] who is a pest to the English tongue. Incidentally he added, Gibbon cannot write English. The Edinburgh Review wrote what would tell and what would sell. It had however changed the tone of its literary criticism from the time when a certain letter was written to the editor by Coleridge. Mrs. W. had the Editor's answer in her possession.[4] Tennyson he thinks a right poetic genius, though with some affectation. He had thought an elder brother of Tennyson at first the better poet, but must now reckon Alfred the true one. . . . In speaking of I know not what style, he said, 'to be sure, it was the manner, but then you know the matter always comes out of the manner.' . . . He thought Rio Janeiro the best place in the world for a great capital city. . . . We talked of English national character. I told him, it was not creditable that no one in all the country knew any-thing of Thomas Taylor, the Platonist, whilst in every American library his translations are found. I said, if Plato's Republic were published in England as a new book to-day, do you think it would find any readers? —he confessed, it would not: 'and yet,' he added after a pause, with that complacency which never deserts a true-born Englishman, 'and yet we have embodied it all.'

His opinions of French, English, Irish, and Scotch, seemed rashly for-mulized from little anecdotes of what had befallen himself and members of his family, in a diligence or stage-coach. His face some-times lighted up, but his conversation was not marked by special force or elevation. Yet perhaps it is a high compliment to the cultivation of the English generally, when we find such a man not distinguished. He had a healthy look, with a weather-beaten face, his face corrugated, especially the large nose.

Miss Martineau, who lived near him, praised him to me not for his poetry, but for thrift and economy; for having afforded to his country-neighbors an example of a modest household, where comfort and culture were secured without any display. She said, that, in his early housekeeping at the cottage where he first lived, he was accustomed to offer his friends bread and plainest fare: if they wanted any thing more, they must pay him for their board. It was the rule of the house. I replied, that it evinced English pluck more than any anecdote I knew. A gentleman in the neighborhood told the story of Walter Scott's staying once for a week with Wordsworth, and slipping out every day under pretence of a walk, to the Swan Inn, for a cold cut and porter; and one day passing with Wordsworth the inn, he was betrayed by the landlord's asking him if he had come for his porter. Of course, this trait would have another look in London, and there you will hear from different literary men, that Wordsworth had no personal friend, that he was not amiable, that he was parsimonious, &c.[5] Landor, always generous, says, that he never praised any body. A gentleman in London showed me a watch that once belonged to Milton, whose initials are engraved on its face. He said, he once showed this to Wordsworth, who took it in one hand, then drew out his own watch, and held it up with the other, before the company, but no one making the expected remark, he put back his own in silence. I do not attach much importance to the disparagement of Wordsworth among London scholars. Who reads him well will know, that in following the strong bent of his genius, he was careless of the many, careless also of the few, self-assured that he should 'create the taste by which he is to be enjoyed.' He lived long enough to witness the revolution he had wrought, and 'to see what he foresaw.' There are torpid places in his mind, there is something hard and sterile in his poetry, want of grace and variety, want of due catholicity and cosmopolitan scope: he had conformities to English politics and traditions; he had egotistic puerilities in the choice and treatment of his subjects; but let us say of him, that, alone in his time he treated the human mind well, and with an absolute trust. His adherence to his poetic creed rested on real inspirations. The Ode on Immortality is the high-water-mark which the intellect has reached in this age. New means were employed, and new realms added to the empire of the muse, by his courage.

Notes

1   Wordsworth's eye-inflammation was a recurring health problem, often noted in his letters. Four days before Emerson's visit, he wrote to George Huntly Gordon, apologizing for this condition, which required his employment of an 'Amanuensis'.
2   William Ellery Channing (1780–1842), a Boston pastor who preached for forty years from a pulpit at the Federal Street Congregational Church in Boston, eloquently defended Unitarianism, a creed which Wordsworth detested. Greatly impressed by the spiritual message of Wordsworth and Coleridge, whom he visited in 1822, Channing was well liked personally by both Lake poets. Wordsworth's recollection, more than a decade later, of the very chair in which Channing sat signifies something of the pleasure he took in their conversation.
3   Thomas Carlyle. The name, recorded in Emerson's notes of his conversation with Wordsworth, was diplomatically omitted from *English Traits*.
4   This correspondence is not in the *Collected Letters* of Coleridge. The editors suggest that Coleridge may have reserved an expression of his dislike of Jeffrey and the reviewers for the final chapter of *Biographia Literaria*.

5 *Notebook ED*, in *The Journals and Miscellaneous Notebooks of Ralph Waldo Emerson*, Vol. VII, edited by A. W. Plumstead and Harrison Hayford (Cambridge, Mass.: The Belknap Press of Harvard University Press, 1969), 263–484. Emerson's *Notebook ED* identifies the 'different literary men' in London as basically one person, Bryan Waller Procter (Barry Cornwall). Procter toned down his criticism when he published *The Literary Recollections of Barry Cornwall*, ed. Richard Willard Armour (Boston, Mass.: Meador, 1936).

More Opinions

A reader who wants to know more about Wordsworth's relations with several of his more important contemporaries will encounter fewer difficulties in determining what Wordsworth thought of them than in learning what they thought of Wordsworth. We know a great deal about Wordsworth's opinions, which can almost be charted on a daily basis throughout his adult years. But there is less in the way of interviews and reminiscences for at least four major figures (not to mention scores of less-prominent men and women who met him on various occasions) than both scholars and general readers would like to have.

It seems desirable in an anthology of opinions held by those who knew Wordsworth well that there be some discussion, however limited by the paucity of needed documentation, of William Godwin, Sir Humphry Davy, Percy Bysshe Shelley, and Lord Byron.

William Godwin (1756–1836)

Around 1800 Wordsworth urged his audience – most likely Basil Montagu, who was then a student at Lincoln's Inn – to 'throw aside' books of chemistry, and to read Godwin on Necessity. (William Hazlitt recorded this anecdote.) The high valuation he placed on Godwin's teaching did not last beyond the mid-1790s. It should not be taken as a reliable index to Wordsworth's fast-waning interest in the truly committed radicalism of William Godwin; at best it represented a passing moment of veneration.

The relationship began even before the two men met in February 1795, at the London residence of William Frend, a former tutor at Jesus College, Cambridge, who had been expelled from Cambridge in 1793 for publishing a pamphlet attacking the war on France. Godwin's writings influenced Wordsworth's thinking (mostly in 1794) about the motivations of human behavior. A moral freedom could, and did, develop from the kind of reason that Godwin promulgated in *Political Justice*. Within a year, however, Wordsworth would turn away from mathematics as a discipline; it could not settle moral questions despite its alluring emphasis on logic and step-by-step rationalism. He would find in Nature the true source (for him) of restorative health. His liberation from any sense of indebtedness may be traced, at least partially, in his judgment of the second edition of *Political Justice* (1796): 'Such a piece of barbarous writing I have not often seen. It contains scarce one sentence decently written. I am surprized to find such gross faults in a writer who has had so much practise' (letter to William Mathews, 21 March 1798). By late December 1799, Wordsworth, writing to Coleridge, felt free to ridicule Godwin as a philosopher, attacking not merely his ideas but his very character.

Godwin claimed more than once that Wordsworth, in conversations with him, became a convert from self-love to the doctrine of benevolence; but Wordsworth, who had read *Political Justice* in 1794, a year prior to his meeting Godwin, would have rejected the claim. The enlargement of his understanding came about primarily because of a convergence of other influences: Rousseau, for example, one of many other authors who confirmed his evolving anger at the limitations of the ruling class, showing up as an excessive attachment to property. Wordsworth resented, for strong reasons pertaining to his family situation, the injustice of laws inflicted upon the poor and downtrodden. (Although he would agree, in February 1803, to the legal settlement of Viscount Lowther's financial obligations to the Wordsworth family, he felt cheated out of more than two thousand pounds of accumulated interest on the debt owed.) He had traveled in France during a period of rising revolutionary enthusiasm, and well understood the bitter causes of riots in the streets. And the major part of his strongly radical *Letter to the Bishop of Llandaff* was written in 1793. (Wordsworth did not attempt to publish it; it was among his papers after he died.)

Yet Wordsworth lived for a short period on Chalfont Street, Somers Town, and was thus a close neighbor of Godwin, who resided on the same street; he dined frequently with Godwin, one on one and sometimes in a larger company; he associated with a large circle of radicals and dissenters, with Godwin ever at its center; and echoes of Godwin's teachings in both *Political Justice* and *Caleb Williams* may be heard in Wordsworth's planning of his proposed magazine, *The Philanthropist*, his revisions of *Guilt and Sorrow*, his devising ideas and speeches for suitable declamation by the characters in his tragedy, *The Borderers*, and poems such as 'The Old Cumberland Beggar'.

The biographer Stephen Gill considers 'Adventures on Salisbury Plain' to be Wordsworth's most Godwinian poem. *The Prelude* has some remarkable passages lauding the doctrine of benevolence that Wordsworth, in preparing the revised edition of 1850, retained; they remind readers of ideas promulgated by Godwin in various contexts.

Some critics insist on seeing Godwinian doctrine in several of the *Lyrical Ballads*, though it is not necessary to overstate what surely amounted to a thrilling and welcome stimulus to Wordsworth's creative endeavors in the middle 1790s.

Godwin, in his preface to *The Poetical Class Book* (1810), maintained, stoutly and perhaps unexpectedly, that poetry, representing to readers 'the passions and feelings of the soul', is 'in this sense a school of morality'. (Godwin included a few poems by Wordsworth; the intention of his anthology was to provide reading lessons. It is worth remembering that Godwin, who never mentioned Wordsworth in his *Autobiography* or other autobiographical fragments collected in Mark Phillips's edition of *Collected Novels and Memoirs of William Godwin*, I (London: William Pickering, 1992), admitted that he did not know what poetry was, and added for good measure that he liked 'a story told with animation, or an operation of the mind happily delineated, and that in verse'. He neither sought for 'imagery' nor rejected it.

It would not be accurate to describe the two men as having been close friends even when they saw a good deal of each other. In a more modest way they benefitted by having the chance to discuss a wide variety of topics (not all political) for more than a decade. Wordsworth, according to Godwin's *Diary* (in manuscript), visited Godwin in London on nine occasions between 1806 and 1835, a fact which indicates primarily a desire to maintain friendly relations.

Sir Humphry Davy (1778–1829)

Sir Humphry Davy, the foremost experimental chemist of his era, did not commit to paper an extended description of his impressions of Wordsworth. In his voluminous writings, though he mentions time and again his generalized respect for literature and his specific love of the great poetry of the past, he quietly bypasses several opportunities to characterize Wordsworth, whom he knew well, and for whom he entertained a genuine affection.

Many readers know Davy principally for his invention of a safety lamp (1815). Within a year, it won wide adoption as an invaluable means of improving working conditions in mines. In his own time, however, Davy earned a major part of his fame for the destruction of Lavoisier's excessive emphasis on theory; he also seriously damaged the validity of Lavoisier's faith in the overarching significance of oxygen in chemistry.

As a popular lecturer, he defined a whole class of supporters of combustion, established innumerable 'facts on the ground', assigned a credible function to potassium (the newly discovered element of the alkali metal group), and consistently urged the public to agree with him that the true function of science was to improve the conditions under which men and women lived. He succeeded Sir Joseph Banks as the President of the Royal Society, and helped to found, among the institutions created during the Age of Enlightenment, the Geological Society, the Zoological Gardens, and the Athenaeum.

He was a good friend of Sir Walter Scott and Coleridge. In 1799, Coleridge called on Heaven to bless Davy; more strikingly, he confessed that whatever passion for science he possessed might be termed 'Davyism'. Davy, he wrote, 'would have established himself in the first rank of England's living poets, if the Genius of our country had not decreed that he should rather be the first in the first rank of its philosophers and scientific benefactors'.

Davy valued the friendship of Robert Southey, and Southey in turn was eager to enroll him as one of the five founders of a new colony that might navigate round the treacherous shoals of human behavior; this scheme became known as 'the Pantisocratic adventure'. Southey also asked Davy to collaborate with him on more than one poetic undertaking. Davy's lament for the death of Lord Byron, written in 1824, is reprinted in *Memoirs of the Life of Sir Humphry Davy*, edited by his brother John Davy, and published in 1839.

Many of Sir Humphrey Davy's poems are under the spell of a Wordsworthian influence, perhaps most strongly in the several drafts of a work that he later titled 'On the Immortality of the Mind'. He projected a 'philosophic epic' on the deliverance of the Israelites from Egypt, titled it 'Moses', planned it in six 'books', and tried his hand at sample passages.

Many of the poems Davy wrote (also included in the *Memoirs*) echo the kind of poetry Wordsworth was working on from the late 1790s on until 1805: 'The Sons of Genius', 'Written after Recovery from a Dangerous Illness', 'To a Young Lady on her Birthday', 'Vaucluse', 'To the Fire-flies', and several untitled fragments written after a visit to Ulswater (4 August 1825).

The Wordsworth connection is worth considering in even greater detail, since it involved Coleridge at the time of his highest regard for Wordsworth's talent. Davy had come to Bristol in 1798 to work with Dr. Thomas Beddoes, a close friend of Coleridge, at the Pneumatic Institution. Wordsworth, trading on mutual friendships, wrote to Davy in July 1800, even before he had been formally introduced, requesting Davy to be kind enough to look over several enclosed poems ('Hart-Leap Well', 'There was a Boy', 'Ellen Irwin', and 'The Brothers') and correct 'any thing' he might find amiss in the punctuation ('a business at which I am ashamed to say I am no adept'). He begged an additional favor: 'I write to request that you would have the goodness' to look over the proofsheets of the second volume of a revised, two-volume edition of *Lyrical Ballads* 'before they are finally struck off'. Davy cheerfully obliged.

On subsequent occasions Wordsworth enjoyed talking to Davy, at great and even exhausting length, and taking long walks with him. What he saw of Davy pleased him 'highly'. Though Wordsworth found fault with the looks and fidgets of Davy's wife, he never demeaned his friend. Dorothy Wordsworth spoke for her brother in a remark written at the end of a letter to Lady Beaumont (27 October 1805): 'Such a man as Mr Davy is a treasure any where.'

More than once Wordsworth looked forward to 'angling' with Davy, who, in his own right, was a notable fisherman; Davy's book, *Salmonia* or *Days of Fly-fishing*, written toward the end of his life, is a discursive text intended to be a parallel to Izaak Walton's famous study of *The Compleat Angler*. It enjoyed a wide readership for well over a century.

John Davy's interpretation of his brother's character, which bracketed selections from Sir Humphry's journals, lectures, and miscellaneous writings, used, on its opening page, two epigraphs: one from Cicero's *Philippics*, and the other from Wordsworth's first *Essay upon Principles*: 'The affections are their own justification. The Light of Love in our Hearts is a satisfactory evidence that there is a body of worth in the minds of our friends or kindred, whence that Light has proceeded.' Further confirmation of Wordsworth's capture of Davy's imagination may be seen in the fact that Davy visited Tintern Abbey by moonlight.

Perhaps the most important service whereby Davy stimulated Wordsworth's thinking about the craft of poetry took place when he defined the differences between a Poet and a Scientist, on the occasion of a lecture he gave while Wordsworth was in the audience. This fine line was drawn in his *Introductory Discourse* to a series of lectures on chemistry (beginning on 21 January 1802) at the Royal Institution. The similarities to Wordsworth's line of argument may be traced in several passages of his *Preface* to the second edition of *Lyrical Ballads*; these passages were revised in the weeks immediately following Davy's presentation.

For fuller information, see Roger Sharrock's 'The Chemist and the Poet: Sir Humphry Davy and the *Preface* to *Lyrical Ballads*', in *Notes and Records of the Royal Society of London*, xvii (1962), 57–76; and the notes in *The Prose Works of William Wordsworth*, edited by W. J. B. Owen and Jane Worthington Smyser (Oxford: Clarendon Press, 1974), I, 181–2. A thoughtful article by Alice Jenkins, 'Humphry Davy: Poetry, Science and the Love of Light', in *1798: the Year of the Lyrical Ballads*, edited by Richard Cronin (London: Macmillan, 1998), 133–50, should also be consulted.

Percy Bysshe Shelley (1792–1822)

Shelley never met Wordsworth, or (for that matter) attempted to meet him. Nor is there any discernible Wordsworthian influence, either in subject matter or in manner, in Shelley's poetry. Yet Thomas Medwin, who chronicled Byron's conversations, notes that Shelley more than once – 'even to nausea' – praised Wordsworth to him; read excerpts from Wordsworth's poetry to him (Byron conceded that a stanza from *Peter Bell* was 'inimitably good'); and drew from Byron an admission that Wordsworth's 'feeling of Nature' justified, at least in his early years, Shelley's commendation. (Southey was skeptical of some statements in Medwin's chronicle, and blamed their unreliability on Shelley's Boswell rather than on Shelley himself.)

The evidence that Shelley paid close attention to Wordsworth's publications lies partly in these casual comments; partly in his reading and rereading *The Excursion* in 1814 and 1815; and in the fact that he hastened to buy a copy of the two-volume edition of Wordsworth's poems (published in 1815). Proof of his continuing interest in Wordsworth lies in his authorship of *Peter Bell the Third* (a 'party squib', he later called it). He wanted to publish it anonymously in 1819, a fact which suggests that he was uneasy about being publicly identified as a parodist of a poet he genuinely respected. At any rate, he had not read the full text of Wordsworth's *Peter Bell* before he wrote his parody, and the quality of his burlesque falls below that of John Hamilton Reynolds's comparable exercise.

Living in Florence in 1819, he found sufficient reason to write it because of John Keats's remarks and Leigh Hunt's slighting references to it, both of which were published in *The Examiner*; he shared with Keats, Hunt, and Reynolds a deepening distrust of Wordsworth's political opinions. Yet he more than once spoke of his admiration of 'Tintern Abbey' and 'Laodamia'.

Shelley's sonnet to Wordsworth (published in 1816) strongly approves of Wordsworth's ability to inspire his readers:

> Thou wert as a lone star, whose light did shine
> On some frail bark in winter's midnight roar . . .

But it also condemns Wordsworth's desertion of liberal causes, and his endorsement of Government policies that Shelley detested. Its concluding lines are remarkably similar in tone to Browning's 'The Lost Leader':

In honoured poverty thy voice did weave
Songs consecrate to truth and liberty, —
Deserting these, thou leavest me to grieve,
Thus having been, that thou shouldst cease to be.

George Gordon Byron, 6th Baron Byron (1788–1824)

Lord Byron's attitude toward Wordsworth began amiably, and was
marked by a willingness to be impressed by an authentic poetic talent.
At the age of 22, Byron met Wordsworth at a party given by Samuel
Rogers (11 May 1812); this was the occasion when Byron told Rogers
and Wordsworth about the assassination of the Prime Minister, Spencer
Perceval. In the words of Stephen Gill, writing in *William Wordsworth:
a Life* (293): 'To hear such news, so quickly, in such a way and at such a
place – Wordsworth knew that he was at the quick of national life.'

Both men's attitudes changed before the second meeting (their last),
which took place on 18 June 1815.

In July 1807, Byron published in *Monthly Literary Recreations* an
unsigned endorsement of a few of the poems that Wordsworth had
published after *Lyrical Ballads*. Because Byron's praise even for the
poems he liked was hedged round with qualifications (he seemed to
single out 'Ode: Intimations of Immortality' as worth a closer look),
most of the other poems struck him as the effusions of 'a genius
worthy of higher pursuits'. The subject matter, he added, was 'trifling'.

Wordsworth may never have learned that Byron had written this
brief notice, but he immediately knew that he was a major target in
'English Bards and Scotch Reviewers' (published in March 1809). He
vehemently denied that he had bothered to read the entire poem, but
if he had read only lines which singled him out (175–94), he recognized the fact that Byron was attacking both style and content, and did
not choose to give quarter to his victim:

Next comes the dull disciple of thy school,
That mild apostate from poetic rule,
The simple WORDSWORTH, framer of a lay
As soft as evening in his favourite May,
Who warns his friend 'to shake off toil and trouble,
And quit his books, for fear of growing double,'
Who, both by precept and example, shows
That prose is verse, and verse is merely prose,
Convincing all by demonstration plain,

Poetic souls delight in prose insane,
And Christmas stories tortured into rhyme,
Contain the essence of the true sublime.
Thus when he tells the story of Betty Foy,
The idiot mother of 'an idiot Boy,'
A moon-struck silly lad who lost his way,
And, like his Bard, confounded night with day,
So close on each pathetic part he dwells,
And each adventure so sublimely tells,
That all who view the 'idiot in his glory,'
Conceive the Bard the hero of the story.

Byron went on to say (l. 1633) that Wordsworth was 'crazed beyond all hope'. Wordsworth's hurt feelings were made all the more sharp because Byron's poem on *Childe Harold* had made its author the popular 'rage' of London, while his own poetry, often dealing with similar scenes and sentiments, attracted a much smaller audience. From late 1815 on, moreover, Byron made no secret of his intense dislike of Wordsworth's personality and poetry.

Wordsworth believed that Byron's attitude toward the beauties of Nature, particularly in Canto III of *Childe Harold's Pilgrimage*, was not only insincere but his adoption of the attitude constituted an act of plagiarism. (He resented the success of the poem as well, and told many people interested in his opinions how inferior to his own poetry *Childe Harold's Pilgrimage* was. See, for example, *WW, L*, II, 212, and *WW, L*, IV, 237.)

Though willing to cite his indebtedness to various classic authors, Byron refused to acknowledge that he had stolen anything from Wordsworth's poetry, or, indeed, from any other contemporary.

Byron lacked feeling (Wordsworth's emphasis). Blake's poems, Wordsworth said to Henry Crabb Robinson (24 May 1812), exhibited 'the elements of poetry a thousand times more than either Byron or Scott'. When he wrote to Samuel Rogers (5 May 1814), he argued that 'no honest Poet' could thrive while 'Lord B. was flourishing at such a rate', and was sufficiently pleased with this comment that he repeated it in a letter written in Scotland to Dorothy Wordsworth (19 or 20 August 1814).

As the bitterness intensified, Wordsworth added new charges: Byron wrote doggerel; he was licentious; he was contemptuous of religious decorum; there was insanity in Byron's family; and Byron would 'probably end his career in a madhouse'. A decade later, immediately after the publication of an intense attack on himself in *Don Juan* (Byron characterized Wordsworth's poetry as 'trash'; see *DJ*, III, 93–5, and

98–100), Wordsworth wrote, in a letter to an unknown correspondent (1 May 1820), that Byron's works afforded 'abundant proofs of sensual, corrupt, and malignant propensities'. The charge was prefaced by an unconvincing disclaimer, 'With Lord B's private life I have nothing to do—I know nothing of it . . .'

There were several reasons for Byron's disenchantment, more so than Wordsworth realized. The latter thought that the chill in their relationship originated when Byron learned of a letter that he had written, most likely to a Mary Ryan of Bristol, a poetaster whom he was encouraging. In the letter she received a warning about Byron's 'perverted' poetic feeling. (Samuel Rogers, noted for his untactful and sometimes malicious remarks, shared this story with Tom Moore who, not long after, told Byron about it.)

Yet, although Wordsworth repeated this story more than once (without denying that he had in fact said what Rogers and Moore had accused him of saying in the letter), Byron entertained more serious objections to Wordsworth's 'self approbation as a Poet, and holding other Poets as beneath Him'; to the notion that Wordsworth thought himself the leader of a school of poets (one of whom, Byron believed, might be considered by the public to be himself); what Byron believed was his general deterioration as a poet after the publication of *Lyrical Ballads*; his ungrateful dismissal of Southey's work (Wordsworth owed more to Southey than he cared to acknowledge) and others who had helped him in his career; and his acceptance from the government of a salaried position. 'It is satisfactory to reflect', Byron said to Thomas Medwin in the early 1820s, 'that where a man becomes a hireling and loses his mental independence, he loses also the faculty of writing well'.

Byron was incensed that 'Poet Turdsworth' (a term that he enjoyed circulating), like several of his friends, denigrated Dryden, Gray, and Pope, all of whom wrote more clearly and logically than any of the Lake Poets. Byron pledged to take up the cudgels against the 'renegado rascals', as he wrote to Francis Hodgson (22 December 1820), especially so on behalf of Pope, 'the Swan of Thames'. Pope knew what needed to be known about Windsor Forest, while the Lakers whined about Nature ('because they live in Cumberland') and their imitators, who, knowing even less about 'earth, and sea, and Nature', waxed 'enthusiastical for the country because they live in London'.

Byron, who believed he had ample cause to react splenetically against a long list of Wordsworth's failings as a human being, concentrated primarily on Wordsworth's failings as a poet. Understandably, and regrettably from almost anybody else's point of view, Wordsworth never forgave his tormentor.

Index

'Cave of Music', 178
Centlivre, Isabella, *Bold Stroke for a Wife*, 99
Chalfont Street (Somers Town), 184
Champion, The, 95
Channing, William Ellery, 177–8
Chantrey, Sir Francis Legatt, 57, 147
Charles I, 130
Charles II, 34
Chatham, Lord, 53
Chatterton, Thomas, 88
Chaucer, Geoffrey, 98, 141; WORKS: *Canterbury Tales*, 60; 'The Mauncipal's Tale', 65
'Chevy Chase', 127
Childe Harold, 87
Christian Faith, 172
Christie's, 148–9
Cicero, 122; WORKS: *Philippics*, 187
Clarke, Charles, *Recollections of Writers*, 85
Clone, Mr., 5
Coleridge, Hartley, 11, 15, 155, 166
Coleridge, Henry Nelson, 4, 15, 135
Coleridge, Mrs. Henry Nelson, 138
Coleridge, Samuel Taylor (1772–1834), 1–17; 3, 5, 6, 8, 24–5, 29–30, 45, 49, 51, 55, 57–8, 65, 67, 78, 80–2, 103, 112, 136, 153, 157, 162, 166, 176, 178, 180, 186; WORKS: 'The Ancient Mariner', 2, 18, 21; *Biographia Literaria*, 2; 'Christabel', 4; 'Dejection', 109–10; *The Friend*, 10–11, 29; 'Love', 2; 'The Nightingale', 2; *Osorio*, 2, 5, 79; *Remorse*, 79; 'Thalaba', 80; 'To William Wordsworth', 14
Coleridge, Mrs. Sara, 80, 162–3
Collins, William, 60, 67, 88, 156
Conder, Josiah, 154
Congress (US), 177
Cookson, Canon William, 164
Cottle, Joseph, 6
Covent Garden, 22
Cowper, William, 103, 126
Crabbe, George, 103, 119
Critical Review, 79, 125
Cronin, Richard, ed., *1798: the Year of the Lyrical Ballads*, 187

Crosthwaite, Miss, 15
Crowe, William, *Lewesdon Hill*, 103
Crusoe, Robinson, 20, 61
Cupid and Psyche (statue), 148

Dalton, John, 179
Dante Alighieri, 60, 137, 141, 148
Davy, Mrs. (Apreece), 187
Davy, Sir Humphry (1778–1829), viii, 148, 185–7; WORKS: *Introductory Discourse*, 187; *Memoirs*, 186; 'Moses', 186; 'On the Immortality of the Mind', 186; *Salmorica*, 187; 'The Sons of Genius', 186; 'To a Young Lady on her Birthday', 186; 'To the Fire-flies', 186; 'Vancluse', 186; 'Written after Recovery ...', 186
Davy, John, 186, 187
Dawson lectures, 162
De La Warr, Earle, 150
De Lolune, John Louis, 177
De Quincey, Thomas (1785–1859), 29–50, 51, 95; WORKS: 'Autobiographic Sketches', 42; 'Lake Reminiscences', 43; 'On Wordsworth's Poetry', 31; *Reminiscences*, 43; *Works*, 42
De Stael, Mme, 153
De Vere, Aubrey Thomas (1814–1902), 79, 91, 101, 105, 133–8; WORKS: *Legends of St. Patrick*, 133
De Vere, Ellen 133
De Vere, Sir Vere Hunt of Curragh, 134
Dilke, Sir Charles, 87
Don Quixote, 57, 59
Donne, John, 48
Dove Cottage, 29
Drawcansir, 61
Dromore, Bishop of, 127
Dryden, John, 60, 191; WORKS: 'Alexander's Feast', 50, 59
Dyce, Alexander, 18

Eclectic Review, 153
Edinburgh, 30
Edinburgh Review, 51, 75, 153, 180
Elizabeth I, 34

years she grew', 67; 'Tintern Abbey', 18, 21, 23, 79, 81, 84, 138, 179, 188; 'To a Sexton', 20; 'To a Skylark', 179; 'To Joanna', 20, 22; 'Two Voices', 156, 179; *The Waggoner*, 19; 'We are Seven', 72; 'Westminster Bridge', 67; 'The White Doe of Rylstone', 19, 148; 'Willy', 159; 'The world is too much with us', 67; 'Written in London, September, 1802', 46

Wordsworth Circle, 2, 154
Wordsworth Society, 131
Wray, Sir Cecil, 48

Yellow Dwarf, The, 95
Young, Edward, 88